STRATEGIES FOR TEACHING STRINGS

STRATEGIES FOR TEACHING STRINGS

Building a Successful String and Orchestra Program

DONALD L. HAMANN

ROBERT GILLESPIE

New York   Oxford
OXFORD UNIVERSITY PRESS
2004

Oxford University Press

Oxford   New York
Auckland   Bangkok   Buenos Aires   Cape Town   Chennai
Dar es Salaam   Delhi   Hong Kong   Istanbul   Karachi   Kolkata
Kuala Lumpur   Madrid   Melbourne   Mexico City   Mumbai
Nairobi   São Paulo   Shanghai   Taipei   Tokyo   Toronto

Published by Oxford University Press, Inc.
198 Madison Avenue, New York, New York, 10016
http://www.oup-usa.org

Oxford is a registered trademark of Oxford University Press

Library of Congress Cataloging-in-Publication Data
Hamann, Donald L.
    Strategies for teaching strings : building a successful string and orchestra program / by
    Donald L. Hamann and Robert Gillespie.
        p. cm.
    Includes bibliographical references (p.) and index.
    ISBN 0-19-514887-8 (cloth : alk. paper)
    1. Orchestra—Instruction and study—United States. 2. Bowed stringed
instruments—Instruction and study—United States. 3. School music—Instruction and
study—United States. I. Gillespie, Robert, 1951– II. Title.
MT730.H36 2003
787'.193'071—dc21   2003041935

Printing number: 9 8 7 6 5 4 3 2 1

Printed in the United States of America
on acid-free paper

CONTENTS

Preface   xi

Chapter 1   **THE STRING INSTRUMENT FAMILY**   **1**

Instruments   1
Bows   4
Accessories and Supplies   5
Selecting String Instruments   7
Care and Maintenance of String Instruments
and Bows   9
Summary   12
Resources   12

Chapter 2   **THE SCHOOL ORCHESTRA PROGRAM**   **14**

A Brief History of Orchestra Programs
in the Schools   14
Values of Orchestra Programs in the School
Music Curriculum   16
Strategies for Defending the School
Orchestra Program   18
Developing Community Support for the
Orchestra Program   21
The School Orchestra Curriculum   22
Enhancing the Orchestra Curriculum   24
References   27
Additional Resources   27

Chapter 3   **BEGINNING STRING CLASS INSTRUCTION**   **29**

Guiding Principles for Teaching Beginning
String Classes   29
Performance Goals and Objectives of First-
and Second-Year String Classes   30
Strategies for Determining Proper
Instrument Sizes   31

Pedagogy for Teaching Instrument Position   33

Additional Instrument Position Teaching
Strategies   39

Left-Hand Shape: General Guidelines   40

Pedagogy for Teaching the Left-Hand Shape   42

Pedagogy for Teaching Pizzicato   45

Pedagogy for Teaching Beginning
Finger Placement   45

Bowing Instruction: General Guidelines   47

Bow Hand Shape: General Guidelines   47

Pedagogy for Teaching Bow Hand Shape   49

Détaché Bowing: General Guideline   52

Pedagogy for Teaching Détaché Bowing   52

Beginning String Crossings: General Guidelines   56

Pedagogy for Teaching String Crossings   56

Staccato and Hooked Bowings:
General Guidelines   58

Pedagogy for Teaching Staccato and
Hooked Bowings   58

Pedagogy for Teaching Slurs   59

Aural Skill Development in Beginning Classes:
General Guidelines   59

Pedagogy for Teaching Beginning Aural Skills   59

Strategies for Teaching Instrument Tuning in
Beginning String Classes   60

Problem Solving: Beginning Students' Common
Playing Problems and Solutions   60

Chapter 4 INTERMEDIATE STRING CLASS
INSTRUCTION   63

Performance Goals and Objectives of Third- and
Fourth-Year String Classes   63

Pedagogy for Teaching Parallel Bowing   64

Pedagogy for Teaching Smooth Direction Changes   65

Pedagogy for Teaching Tone Production at
Different Dynamic Levels   65

Pedagogy for Teaching Moderate-to-Faster Tempo
String Crossings   66

Pedagogy for Teaching Slurring More than
Four Notes   66

Pedagogy for Teaching Martelé Bowing   66

Pedagogy for Teaching Basic Spiccato   67

Pedagogy for Teaching Consistent Lengthened and
Balanced Body Posture   68

Pedagogy for Refining Instrument Position   68

Intermediate Left-Hand Skills: General Guidelines   70

Pedagogy for Refining Left-Hand Shapes   82

Pedagogy for Teaching Cello Extensions   82
Shifting: General Principles   83
Pedagogy for Teaching Shifting   84
Vibrato: General Principles   85
Pedagogy for Teaching Vibrato   86
Double Bass Pivoting: General Guidelines   92
Pedagogy for Developing Intermediate Aural Skills
in the School Orchestra   92
Intermediate Instrument Tuning   94
Problem Solving: Intermediate Students' Common
Playing Problems and Solutions   95

Chapter 5   ADVANCED STRING CLASS INSTRUCTION   **97**

Goals and Objectives of Advanced Playing Skills   97
Pedagogy for Teaching Expressive Détaché Bowing   98
Pedagogy for Teaching Louré (Portato) Bowing   98
Pedagogy for Teaching Sul Tasto Bowing   99
Pedagogy for Teaching Ponticello Bowing   99
Pedagogy for Teaching Controlled Tremolo Bowing   101
Pedagogy for Teaching Collé Bowing   102
Pedagogy for Teaching Fast String Crossings   102
Pedagogy for Teaching Expressive Spiccato   103
Two-Octave Scales through Four Sharps and Four Flats:
General Guidelines   104
Introducing Three-Octave Scales: General Guidelines   112
Pedagogy for Refining Shifting   122
Pedagogy for Refining Vibrato   123
Pedagogy for Developing Advanced Aural Skills in the
School Orchestra   124
Advanced Instrument Tuning   126
Problem Solving: Advanced Students' Common Playing
Problems and Solutions   127

Chapter 6   PLANNING THE SCHOOL ORCHESTRA
REHEARSAL   **128**

Your Goals and Objectives   128
Guidelines for Organizing the Rehearsal   131
Differences and Commonalities in Teaching Wind,
Brass, and String Instruments   133
Keys to Efficient and Effective Development of Playing
Technique in the String Class   139
Guidelines for Choosing Music   141
Preparing a Score   144
Lesson Plans   151
Evaluation of Teaching   154

The National Standards   160
References   168
Additional Resources for Teaching the National
Standards in the School Orchestra   169
Additional Sample Repertoire for Use in Teaching the
National Standards in the School Orchestra   169

Chapter 7   REHEARSAL TECHNIQUES   **171**

Planning for the Year   171
Your Rehearsal Room and Equipment   171
Tryouts   172
The Rehearsal   178
Tuning   178
Warm-Ups   181
Review of Old and Introduction of New Materials   182
Sight Reading   184
End of the Rehearsal   184
Rehearsal Format   185
Other Considerations   186
The First Rehearsal   187
Troubleshooting during Rehearsals   189
References   193

Chapter 8   PRACTICAL APPROACHES TO TEACHING
IMPROVISATION IN THE SCHOOL
ORCHESTRA   **195**

A Creative Drone Approach   196
A Riff Approach   196
A Call-and-Response or Question-and-Answer
Approach   197
A Chordal Approach   198
A Rhythmic Ostinato Approach   199
Summary   199
References   199

Chapter 9   STRING STUDENT RECRUITMENT
AND RETENTION   **200**

Philosophy   200
Preparation for Recruitment   200
Recruitment Procedures   203
Retention   208
References   212

Chapter 10 METHOD BOOKS AND MUSIC FOR THE
              SCHOOL ORCHESTRA PROGRAM   **213**

              Printed Method Books   214
              Recommended Publishers   215
              String Orchestra Literature   216
              Full Orchestra Literature   219
              References   220
              Additional Resources   220

              APPENDIX: ADDITIONAL
              PEDAGOGICAL RESOURCES   **222**

              Special Pedagogical Approaches   222
              Professional String Associations   225

Index   227

PREFACE

Welcome to the world of string teaching! We hope that you have this book in hand because you are interested in becoming a string teacher or in improving your skills. If this is the case then the information provided in our book will certainly help guide you to this goal.

AUDIENCE

We wrote this book primarily for university students preparing to become string and instrument teachers in the schools, but we are hopeful that experienced teachers may also find it useful to further develop their string teaching skills and their school orchestra programs. We've assumed that readers will have a basic understanding of music fundamentals, but beyond that we hope only that readers come to the book with an interest in learning more about strings and string teaching.

APPROACH

Our goal in this book is twofold: to provide teaching strategies that foster individual skill development on all the bowed string instruments and to offer rehearsal strategies that will help students advance their large group ensemble techniques. Our book offers numerous creative and useful suggestions and procedures to help students with both.

FEATURES

The content of *Strategies for Teaching Strings* is based on the recognized standards. National content standards for teaching music in the schools were established by the Music Educators National Conference (MENC) in 1994. Incorporating MENC's standards, the American String Teachers Association (ASTA) established national standards in 1998 for preparing people to teach strings and orchestra in the schools.

The preparation standards represent the skills and knowledge necessary for successfully teaching strings and orchestra in the schools. Developed to guide universities in determining the content of their string teacher training curricula, the standards also serve as benchmarks that certified teachers may use to evaluate their success in string teaching. This text presents the related string pedagogy, materials, skills, and program information specified in the standards that need to be mastered to teach strings successfully in the schools.

The book also features a section on the historical development of the orchestra, strategies for developing community support, procedures for the development of successful school orchestra rehearsals, suggestions for music selection, approaches to improvisation, recruitment and retention ideas, and analyses for teaching and performing string literature. While we have not included printed music to play, since there are many excellent string methods series and materials that can be used to develop playing skills, we do include music selection information and an appendix that serves as a ready reference of resources for both new and seasoned string teachers.

CONTENT

The content is divided into ten chapters. Chapter 1 describes string instruments, bows, and accessories. It also includes important instrument care and maintenance information, as well as rental and purchase guidelines for use in helping students obtain their instruments and bows.

Chapter 2 describes the school orchestra program. The first part of the chapter offers a background for school orchestra programs. A brief history of orchestra programs in the schools is given, followed by a rationale for the existence of string programs in the schools, strategies for defending their values, and methods for developing community support for them. The second part of the chapter presents a model school orchestra curriculum and musical activities to enhance the curriculum.

Chapters 3, 4, and 5 present the pedagogical principles and related teaching activities for developing beginning, intermediate, and advanced string instrument playing skills. At the end of each chapter is a checklist of common playing problems that students experience and suggested solutions for use in remedying the problems.

Chapters 6 and 7 are devoted to the school orchestra rehearsal. Chapter 6 discusses how to organize, plan, and select music for the rehearsal. Chapter 7 includes music rehearsal strategies, along with sample performing problems common to school orchestras and possible rehearsal solutions for them.

Chapter 8 describes practical ways to teach fundamental aural skills and beginning improvisation in the young, intermediate, and advanced school orchestra rehearsal. Teaching improvisation and music creativity appears in the national standards, and Chapter 8 offers some "how tos" for doing that.

Chapter 9 presents vital information for recruiting and retaining students in the school orchestra program. Sample strategies are offered for recruiting new students to the program, in addition to descriptions of effective string recruitment demonstrations and methods to use to keep students committed to playing their string instruments.

Chapter 10 offers information about string and full orchestra composers and arrangers. While no list is ever complete and fully up-to-date, Chapter 10 presents foundational repertoire upon which to build a successful school orchestra music library.

Following Chapter 10 is the Appendix. It provides additional resources on teaching strings and developing school orchestra programs.

The string teaching profession continues to make great strides. String pedagogues are ever searching for better ways to teach, new materials and repertoire are continually being created, and orchestra programs keep spreading and expanding in the schools. *Strategies for Teaching Strings* is for those who are currently in the "trenches" teaching strings and those who are preparing to join us there. Nothing is better than helping young people in the schools play, create, and live string music. We wish you success in your teaching.

ACKNOWLEDGMENTS

We would like to thank a number of individuals who have made this book possible. We wish to thank Herman Knoll, vice president of Hal Leonard Corporation, who granted permission to use graphics from the *Essential Elements for Strings* series in our book, as well as Michael Allen and Pamela Tellejohn Hayes, who helped create those graphics. We would like to thank the reviewers who spent countless hours reading and reviewing our manuscript and offering insightful and helpful suggestions: Gail Barnes, University of South Carolina; Joanne Erwin, Oberlin Conservatory; Marion Etzel, Georgia State University; Janet Jensen, University of Wisconsin—Madison; Judy Palac, Michigan State University; and Phyllis Young, University of Texas at Austin.

We would also like to thank the outstanding staff at Oxford University Press, whose guidance and advice have been priceless. To Jan Beatty, whose confidence in this project and invaluable support made this book possible; to Talia Krohn, for her ability to keep us updated and informed; and to Brian Kinsey and his colleagues in the production department, who have offered numerous and critical editorial suggestions and have contributed countless hours to the production of this book.

Special Thanks from Don

Books are shaped by and reflect the life experiences of their authors. In turn, authors are shaped by and reflect those who have touched their lives. I would like to thank those who have given me the wonderful life experiences that have enabled me to write this book:

To all of the students with whom I have had the opportunity to study—they have been my teachers.

To my parents, Walter and Dorothy Hamann, who provided me with the life foundation upon which I have so easily been able to build.

To Mr. Lovell Ives, who encouraged me to pursue music as a career.

To William Joe Dick, who encouraged me to advance my study of strings and string teaching.

To Phyllis Young, who opened my life to the world of string teaching and cello playing.

To James Sherbon, who showed me the intricacies of writing and conducting research.

To Sheila, my loving, supportive wife and life mate, who shared her expertise of the English language by proofreading and editing my manuscript.

Special Thanks from Bob

This book is a tribute to all who have touched my life professionally and personally. I am indebted to those who never gave up on me, including my parents, who took me to all those violin lessons! I especially thank my mentors who gave me the best possible teaching and encouragement: Wallace Graham, Marvin Mutchnik, Kelly Farris, Stephen Clapp, Phyllis Young, Bob Culver, and Barbara Eads.

I thank all my students who have allowed me to touch their lives, challenging me to grow, explore, think, and create. I particularly thank Brandy Strawser, a wonderful future string teacher, who spent countless hours scanning figures and proofreading the text.

I especially acknowledge the support of my wife, Jan. She has put up with way too much. (We type A's die early and have to move fast to get everything done before the end comes!) Jan has loved me through it all, including giving us five wonderful children: Pete "the Poot," Anne "the Snugs," Maria "the Special One," Christine "the Character," and Natalie "the Peach."

Above all, I thank the Lord for His constant love, direction, and grace to live and pursue.

STRATEGIES FOR
TEACHING STRINGS

THE STRING
INSTRUMENT FAMILY

INSTRUMENTS

Instruments in the modern string family include bowed, plucked, and hammered strings. The bowed string family instruments include violin, viola, cello, and double bass. The plucked string family instruments include the guitar, harp, and harpsichord, while the piano belongs to the hammered string family. There are also folk instruments such as the dulcimer and banjo that are plucked and, in the case of the dulcimer, are also hammered.

The focus of this chapter will be on the bowed string instruments. While there exists another body of bowed instruments that includes viols and gambas, the focus will be placed only on the modern bowed string instruments. Those instruments are the violin, viola, cello, and double bass.

The best modern bowed string instruments are made of wood; however, other types of materials, such as carbon fiber or fiberglass, are being used to produce student-grade instruments. Laminated wood is also used in the production of student-grade cellos and double basses. High-grade, evenly narrow-grained resonant pieces of spruce are used to make the tops of stringed instruments. Generally, a single piece of wood is split in half to make a top for any given string instrument. The back and sides of most instruments are constructed of maple, while the fingerboard, nut, saddle, inlaid purfling, pegs, tailpiece, and end button are usually constructed of ebony.

Parts of the Instruments

The terms used to label the various parts of the stringed instruments are universal for the violin, viola, cello, and double bass. Cellos and double basses do not have chin rests, but because they rest on the floor, they have endpins with adjusting screws, which the violin and viola do not have. The various parts of the stringed instruments are shown in Figure 1.1 and Figure 1.2.

One of the major elements of a bowed string instrument is the strings. The strings are supported by an integral system of parts. On the bottom of the instrument is the button or end button. The end button is generally made of

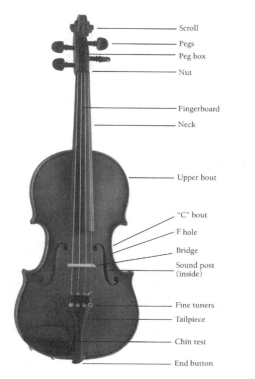

Figure 1.1 Parts of the violin.   **Figure 1.2** Parts of the cello.

ebony and is inserted into the bottom of the instrument and then into the end block. The function of the button is to secure the tailpiece gut to the tailpiece.

The tailpiece gut is flexible and wraps around the end button. The tailpiece gut attaches directly to the tailpiece. At one time, most tailpiece guts were made out of gut. Today, tailpiece guts are generally made out of high-grade plastics.

The saddle helps guide the tailpiece gut over the top of the instrument to the end button. It adds additional support to the instrument and is generally made of ebony.

The tailpiece holds one end of the strings. It is often made of ebony. Often one or more fine tuners are attached to the tailpiece. The function of fine tuners is to help adjust string tension, which changes the pitch of the string. Double basses do not use fine tuners.

The bridge supports the strings and is often made of a hardwood such as spruce. Vibrations travel through the bridge to the sound post, which helps produce the characteristic bowed string sound. The sound post sits directly behind the right foot of the bridge (the higher-pitched string side). The sound post is basically a high quality wooden dowel. Sound is also enhanced by the bass bar located under the top of the left side of the bridge (the lower-pitched string side).

The nut, made of ebony, supports the strings at the top of the instrument. The nut helps guide the strings to the pegs, which are located in the peg box. The ebony pegs rest in holes that are drilled in the peg box. Small holes are drilled into the pegs, through which the strings are attached. The peg box is ornately finished with a carved scroll.

The body of the instrument consists of the top, sides or ribs, and the back. The top and back of higher-quality bowed string instruments have an inlay referred to as purfling. Purfling helps prevent cracks from beginning at the edge of the top or back and traveling farther than the purfling. Purfling is also considered to be ornamental. F holes are cut into the top of the instrument. F holes allow the sound to travel from the instrument. The "C" bout is formed at either side of the instrument and is sometimes referred to as the waist.

The neck block supports the neck. The neck supports the fingerboard. Fingerboards are generally made of ebony or rosewood. The fingerboard allows the player to shorten the length of a string by holding it down with a finger. When the string length is changed, the string vibrates at a different rate, producing a different pitch.

Violins and violas have a chin rest. The chin rest can be made of wood or plastics. The chin rest is used to help support and hold the instrument. Cellos and basses have an endpin that is used to help support the instrument.

Instrument Ranges

When discussing instrument ranges, one can talk of possible playing ranges and practical playing ranges. The practical playing ranges of the bowed string instruments are more germane to our purposes. Therefore, each of the bowed string instruments has a practical, playable range, defined as a range in which players, such as moderately advanced high school students, would be able to perform with some degree of ease and ability. On the stringed instruments, this playable range is usually from three to four octaves, beginning on any open string. The open string pitches on the instruments are g^0, d^1, a^1, e^2 for the violin, c^0, g^0, d^1, a^1 for the viola, C_0, G_0, d^0, a^0 for the cello, and E_1, A_1, D_0, G_0 for the double bass. Thus, a moderately skilled cellist should be able to play a three-octave C-major scale easily beginning on C_0, and could also play a four-octave scale without great difficulty. Similar instrument range possibilities are also evident on the other bowed string instruments. Within the context of an orchestral selection, the practical playing range should be a smaller consideration, as elements of pitch accuracy and technical skill need to be considered. It should be noted, however, that string players who do not have difficulty performing in the upper ranges of their instruments when playing by themselves often find it difficult to play in the upper ranges of their instruments when they play with a group.

Instrument Sizes

Bowed string instruments are made in various sizes to accommodate various-sized people. As the orchestra director, you may be working with students as young as six years (first grade students) to high school students. Since many string programs begin in the fourth, fifth, or sixth grades, the smallest instruments you may encounter in your orchestra program are half-sized instruments. However, smaller-sized instruments are made, especially for the violin and cello, and are often referred to as Suzuki instruments. Note that 4/4 or 7/8 size basses are generally used only by professional players and are not normally suitable for school use. The standard double bass size at the high school level is the 3/4 size bass. The following chart, from *The Complete String Guide: Standards, Programs, Purchase, and Maintenance* (MENC 1988), provides the approximate lengths for the various-sized instruments. Measurements are provided in inches.

Instruments	Size	Overall Length	Body Length	Vibrating String Length
Violins	$4/4$	23 $1/8$	14	12 $13/16$
	$3/4$	21 $5/8$	13 $1/4$	12
	$1/2$	20 $3/8$	12 $3/8$	11 $5/16$
	$1/4$	18 $3/5$	11 $1/4$	10 $3/8$
	$1/8$	17	10	9 $1/4$
	$1/10$	15 $1/2$	9 $1/4$	8 $3/8$
	$1/16$	14 $1/4$	8 $1/4$	7 $5/8$
Violas	16 $1/2$	27 $3/8$	16 $1/2$	14 $7/8$
	16	26 $1/2$	16	14 $3/8$
	15 $1/2$	26 $1/16$	15 $1/2$	14 $5/16$
	15	25 $1/4$	15	13 $5/8$
	Intermediate	23 $1/8$	14	12 $13/16$
	Junior	21 $5/8$	13 $1/4$	12
Cellos	$4/4$	48 $1/4$	29 $5/8$	27 $1/8$
	$3/4$	44 $3/8$	27 $3/8$	24 $1/2$
	$1/2$	41 $1/2$	25 $1/2$	22 $15/16$
	$1/4$	33 $1/2$	21	18 $7/8$
	$1/8$	29	17 $7/8$	16 $1/2$
	$1/10$	26 $1/4$	16	14 $5/8$

BOWS

It is important for your students to have as good a bow as possible. The bow is one of the most important components in sound production. In general, students who have higher-quality bows have a better chance to produce a higher-quality tone and execute various bowing styles. The highest-quality bows are made of pernambuco wood; however, many carbon-fiber bows perform very well compared with pernambuco wood bows. The highest-quality bows are generally equipped with ebony frogs with nickel silver, silver, or gold trim and are strung with horsehair. Other types of wood are also used for lower-quality bows. Brazilwood has been considered to be of sufficient quality for

Figure 1.3   Parts of the bow.

use in these student-line bows. Fiberglass has also been used in student bow construction. Bows, made from brazilwood or fiberglass, are strung with synthetic hair or horsehair and may have plastic frogs instead of ebony frogs.

Parts of the Bow

The main part of the bow is referred to as the stick. See Figure 1.3. The head of the bow is called the tip. The frog is located at the other end of the stick. The adjusting screw tightens or loosens the bow hair and is directly behind the frog on the stick. In front of the frog, on the stick, is the winding or finger grip. The ferrule is usually made of nickel or silver and is located on the bottom portion of the frog.

The German Bow

The double bass is the only instrument that uses two styles of bows: French and German. The French bow, the same style of bow used on the violin, viola, and cello, is more commonly used in school programs. Many teachers believe that the French bow is easier for string crossings and short articulations, while the German bow is easier for legato passages. Some teachers believe that the German bow hold is easier for beginning double bass players to learn unless they are switching from cello, viola, or violin. Nevertheless, both the German and French bows tend to complement each other.

ACCESSORIES AND SUPPLIES

Bowed string players should consider owning or should have several accessories and supplies. General accessories and supplies include the following:

1. A clean cloth for removing rosin from the strings.
2. A tuning device such as a tuning fork or pitch pipe.
3. A metronome.
4. Some type of humidifier to protect the wood from cracking. The Dampit is a brand of humidifier used to increase humidity in stringed instruments.
5. Peg compound. This is a product that helps pegs move easily.
6. Powered graphite is an excellent lubricant and can be used on fine tuners, the adjusting screw on the bow, and other instrument parts that require ease of movement.

powdered

7. Mutes. Some mutes slide onto the bridge, and others clip on or are placed onto the bridge. Mutes are made of wood, rubber, or a combination of materials. Practice mutes made of metal, rubber, and plastic are sometimes used for practicing, especially when sound production needs to be reduced to a minimum.

8. Rosin. Violin and viola rosin are less coarse and harder than cello or bass rosin, with bass rosin being the softest and most coarse of the rosins.

9. Fine tuners are essential when metal-core strings are used. Fine tuners enable your students to make slight adjustments to string tension. Such slight adjustments are needed when metal-core strings are being tuned, as small adjustments to metal-core strings create rapid pitch change.

10. Endpin holders are needed to help hold and stabilize the endpin in cellos and basses. Endpin holders come in a variety of styles. Some require an anchor to a chair leg, and some do not require such an anchor. Endpin holders not only help hold the instrument but also prevent damage to floors.

11. Chin rests are made of ebony, boxwood, rosewood, and plastic and are used to help support the violin and viola. Because it is important that the chin rest be comfortable, chin rests come in a variety of shapes and sizes. Finding the correct size and height of a chin rest is an individual matter, and each student should try out various chin rests until the appropriate one has been found. Chin rest pads, available commercially, and covers (a soft cloth, for example) can also be used to make the player more comfortable.

12. Shoulder rests or shoulder pads are used by violin and viola players to help support their instruments. The shoulder rest or pad is placed between the shoulder and the back of the instrument. Shoulder pads can be as simple as a folded handkerchief or sponge placed underneath the instrument, to a crafted, commercially produced device that attaches to the back of the instrument. The use of shoulder rests or pads should be encouraged, especially if students are raising their left shoulders to help secure the instrument. Shoulder rests or pads help reduce this tension and thus promote better playing habits.

13. An adjustable bridge can be an important accessory, especially for double bass players. Bowed string instruments are made of wood. Wood tends to contract and expand with climatic changes, causing the bridge height to change. Adjustments to bridges to maintain appropriate string height distances from the fingerboard are often necessary. An adjustable bridge has a metal turn-screw device built into the feet of the bridge that enables the bridge height to be varied. Because some tone quality may be lost because of this device, it is generally not recommended for all bowed string instruments. However, it is widely used on the double bass.

14. A bridge jack enables the strings of the instrument to be raised and a bridge to be removed for repair or replacement without the fear of losing tension on the top of the instrument, which could result in the sound post falling. In climates where bridges must be changed frequently to maintain appropriate string height, the purchase of a bridge jack is important.

15. A variety of strings are on the market, but the three basic types are metal (steel, aluminum, etc.), gut-core, and synthetic core—often known as perlon-core. Because each type of string produces a different sound, and because individual instruments respond differently to the various string types, many players experiment with the various types and brands of strings. Most student instruments, especially beginning instruments, are strung with metal strings. Metal strings tend to maintain their pitch better and generally are more durable than nonmetal strings. Perlon-core and gut-core strings tend to be less brilliant and produce a softer tone than metal strings and thus are preferred by some players. The choice of strings is as much a matter of personal taste as it is an issue of matching the most appropriate string to the instrument. Whatever strings are chosen, it is important that the string end conforms to the fine tuner. Additionally, it is important that the player have an extra set of strings available should a string need to be replaced immediately, as in a concert situation.

SELECTING STRING INSTRUMENTS

Good-quality string instruments for student use are essential to the success of a string program. The instruments must be in good playing condition and their tone pleasing to attract and keep students in the school orchestra. Less expensive, lower-quality instruments may be initially more attractive to school systems when purchasing string instruments, but their tone will be inferior. Also, cheaper instruments are harder to play, wear out faster, and require more maintenance over the life of the instrument.

School systems need to provide cello and bass instruments for the orchestra program. Some violas and violins may need to be purchased by the schools if local rental fees are too expensive for families in lower economic areas.

Guidelines for Purchasing String Instruments

School System Instrument Purchases

1. Determine the number and type of instruments needed.
2. Consult local dealers and national mail-order companies for prices and available instruments. Some national instrument manufacturing companies also offer school system lease-purchase plans.
3. Compare the price of purchasing an instrument outfit that includes a bow and case to the price of purchasing those items separately.

4. Prepare a bid and present it to those vendors that have the highest-quality instruments for the price. Close the sale once the price is negotiated and after you have inspected and approved the instruments upon their arrival.

Parent Instrument Purchases

1. Encourage parents to purchase the best quality they can afford. More expensive instruments sound better and are easier to play. Point out to parents that string instruments are a good investment because their financial value remains the same or increases over time if an instrument is well cared for. Also, educate parents that a higher-quality instrument sounds better when played with a better bow. The quality of the bow has much to do with the quality of sound produced on an instrument. Perhaps the parents should consider purchasing a better quality bow along with the instrument.

2. Suggest more than one string instrument shop for the buyers to visit. Comparison shopping helps parents find the best instrument for the price.

3. Suggest they have an independent repair technician inspect the playing condition of the instrument if they are considering purchasing an older instrument.

4. Suggest that they narrow their selections to two or three possible instruments and that they request a loan of the instruments for at least one week. This gives the player time to play and evaluate the instruments outside of the dealer's shop.

5. Once an instrument is selected for purchase, advise parents to negotiate the price of the instrument with the dealer. Much like car dealers, string instrument dealers expect buyers to negotiate prices.

Guidelines for String Instrument Rental Programs

If students are renting their string instruments to play, we recommend that they rent from a local dealer. A local business can be easily contacted if necessary, and service may be obtained more readily. Local companies must provide good-quality instruments for rent that are in excellent playing condition. An instrument that produces a pleasing tone and is easy to tune is critical for students' success. Rental violins, violas, and cellos should have fine tuners for each string that turn easily. Violin and viola shoulder rests and cello and bass end pin rests should be available.

String instrument rental programs should include rental purchase and step-up provisions. In a rental-purchase agreement, rental money for an instrument should be applied toward the purchase of the instrument, less maintenance and insurance, if any. In effect the renter is purchasing the instrument over time.

A step-up provision specifies that (1) the rental money toward an instrument applies to the purchase of a larger size instrument of similar quality as the players' arms lengthen as they grow, and (2) the rental money may apply toward the purchase of a better-quality instrument.

CARE AND MAINTENANCE OF STRING INSTRUMENTS AND BOWS

Instruct students to carefully follow these guidelines for caring and maintaining their instruments and bows:

1. Only the player should be allowed to touch the instrument and bow. String instruments and bows are very fragile. Well-meaning parents and curious siblings can easily damage an instrument or a bow without intending to do so.

2. Keep the instrument and bow in the case when not in use, with the case latched or completely zipped.

3. Keep the instrument and bow out of direct sunlight.

4. Keep the instrument and bow in moderate temperatures only. String instruments and bows warp and crack in extreme temperatures and high humidity.

5. Clean the instrument and bow after every use. Use a cotton cloth to wipe perspiration and rosin off the instrument and bow stick. Students should keep a cloth for cleaning in the instrument case.

6. Have all cracks repaired and open seams glued immediately.

7. Every time after playing, loosen the bow hair. Loosen until just before individual bow hairs begin to touch the stick.

8. Never touch the bow hair. Do not attempt to clean it.

9. Hold the instrument only by the neck. Touching the body of the instrument will eventually damage the varnish.

10. Store music away from the violin or viola case unless there is a specific zippered compartment designed to hold music.

11. Rubbing alcohol or an alcohol-based product such as cologne or perfume may be applied to a soft cloth or cotton ball and used to clean the strings, fingerboard, and chin rest. The alcohol must not touch any varnish on the instrument, as it will damage it.

12. Periodically clean the instrument and bow stick with professional string instrument cleaner applied to facial tissue. Only cleaner manufactured for cleaning string instruments should be used, not wood furniture cleaners.

13. Replace strings when they break, fray, or become false.

14. Replace the bow hair annually.

String Instrument Repair Checklist

Use the following stringed instrument and equipment checklist when evaluating instruments for repair.*

	Needs
OK	**Attention**

Instrument:
____ Cleaned ____ Polished ____   ____
____ Pegs: Stick ____ Slip ____   ____
____ Tension pegs: Loose ____   ____
               Need tightening ____
____ Strings: Wound straight on all pegs ____   ____
               Frayed ____ False ____ Replace ____
____ Fingerboard: Clean ____ Grooved ____   ____
               Needs dressing ____
____ Bridge: Off-center ____ Leans ____   ____
               Warped ____ Grooves to deep ____
               Curvature too flat ____ Replace ____
____ Sound post: In wrong place ____ Missing ____   ____
____ Tuners: Too low ____ Need to turn up ____   ____
               Bent ____ Replace ____
____ Tail loop: Too long ____   ____
____ End button (violin and viola): Poor fit ____   ____
____ Endpin (cello and bass): Too short ____   ____
               Bent ____
____ Opening in seams: Upper bout ____   ____
               Lower bout ____ Sides ____
____ Open cracks: In top ____   ____
               At bottom saddle ____
               In rib ____ Other ____

Bow:
____ Tightened too tightly ____   ____
____ Bow grip: Loose ____ Missing ____   ____
               Needs replacement ____
____ Bow stick: Needs cleaning ____ Warped ____   ____
               Too straight ____
____ Bow facing: Cracked ____ Chipped ____   ____
               Missing tip ____ Replace ____
____ Frog: Cracked ____ Ferrule loose ____   ____
               Slide cracked ____ Screw worn ____

*From *The Complete String Guide: Standards, Programs, Purchases, and Maintenance.* Copyright © 1998 by Music Educators National Conference. Used by Permission.

					Needs
OK					**Attention**

____ Bow hair: Twisted ____ Dirty ____   ____
               Needs rosin ____
               Repair ____ Replace ____

Case:
____ Fasteners: Loose ____   ____
               Lock doesn't close tightly ____
____ Handles: Worn ____ Loose ____ Replace ____   ____
____ Bow clips: Bent ____ Worn ____ Broken ____   ____
____ Recommend instrument be covered in case ____   ____

Miscellaneous:
____ Shoulder pad ____   ____
____ Endpin stop (cellos and basses)   ____
____ Cleaning cloth ____   ____

Guidelines for Replacing Strings

Replace strings when they break, fray, or become false. When they are false, they do not ring and cannot be tuned accurately. Metal E strings become false quickly and need to be replaced frequently, especially before special concerts or contest performances. Students can successfully change their strings by following seven steps.

Step 1

Remove only one string at a time so that the bridge and sound post do not move.

Step 2

Check to see if the peg turns smoothly. If not, apply a small amount of peg compound to the peg. Apply graphite from a pencil to the groove on the top of the bridge where the string rests and the string's groove on the nut. This will help the string slide on top of the bridge.

Step 3

Insert and pull the end of the string through the hole in the peg. The string should rest on top of the peg, not underneath.

Step 4

Turn the peg so that the string wraps around the peg. Be sure to bind the end under the string as you are turning the peg. This helps prevent the string from moving in the peg and changing pitch frequently. Tweezers may be used to pull the string through the peg hole.

Step 5

The highest- and lowest-pitched strings should be positioned next to the sides of the peg box. As you are turning the peg, guide the direction of the wrapping so that the string will end up next to the peg box. The other two strings should be positioned closer to the middle of the peg box. If wrapped properly, the length of the string should end up positioned straight, or at a ninety-degree angle across the nut.

Step 6

Place the other end of the string through its corresponding hole at the end of the tailpiece. Sometimes the end will need to be knotted to remain secure in the hole. The ball at the end of a metal string is designed to fit in a metal tuner.

Step 7

Slowly tighten the string until it is in tune. Push in on the peg as you are turning so it will stay secure in the peg box. Once it is in tune, you may slightly pull up on the string to stretch it. Retune. You may repeat this process a few times. This helps adjust the string to its tension. As a result, it will shorten the length of time it takes for a new string to adjust and stay in tune.

SUMMARY

The purpose of the chapter was to help familiarize you with the bowed string family and its accessories. Many articles, books, and manuals are available that can provide you with purchase decision criteria. Some of these sources are listed in the resources section of this chapter. In addition to the basic maintenance suggestions provided in this chapter, you may wish to know many other instrument care and repair procedures. Excellent sources on this topic are available and are listed in the resources section of this chapter.

RESOURCES

General

Dillon, Jacquelyn A., and Casimer Kriechbaum. 1978. *How to design and teach a successful school string and orchestra program.* San Diego: Kjos West.

Goodrich, Katherine, and Mary Wagner, eds. 2003. *Getting it right from the start: A guide to beginning and enriching a successful string orchestra program.* 2d ed. Washington, D.C.: American String Teachers Association.

Green, Elizabeth A. 1999. *Teaching stringed instruments in classes.* Bloomington, Ind.: American String Teachers Association with National School Orchestra Association c/o Tichenor Publishing.

Klotman, Robert H. 1996. *Teaching strings: Learning through playing.* 2d ed. New York: Schirmer Books.

Littrell, David, and Laura Reed Racin, eds. 2001. *Teaching music through performance in orchestra.* Chicago: GIA Publications.

Music Educators National Conference (MENC). 1988. *The complete string guide: Standards, programs, purchase, and maintenance.* Reston, Va.: Music Educators National Conference.

———. 1991. *Teaching stringed instruments: A course of study.* Reston, Va.: Music Educators National Conference.

Tellejohn-Hayes, Pamela, ed. 2003. *The school symphony orchestra experience: A guide to establishing a full orchestra in the schools.* Washington, D.C.: American String Teachers Association.

Selecting and Repairing String Instruments

Bearden, Larry, and David Bearden. 1972. *Emergency string repair manual.* 2d ed. Tuscaloosa: University of Alabama Press.

Klotman, Robert, Charles Avsharian, et al. 1988. *The complete string guide.* Reston, Va.: Music Educators National Conference.

Sibert, Polly. 2001. Stringed instrument maintenance and repair in the studio or classroom. *American String Teacher* 51 (1):80–87.

Zurfluh, John D. 1978. *String instrument repair and maintenance manual.* Reston, Va.: American String Teachers Association.

2

THE SCHOOL
ORCHESTRA PROGRAM

A BRIEF HISTORY OF ORCHESTRA PROGRAMS IN THE SCHOOLS

The history of vocal music in America's schools is long and rich, beginning as far back as the first half of the 1800s. However, band and orchestral instruction existed rarely as a part of school music instruction in the nineteenth century (Humphrey 1989). Society preferred vocal sacred music, and not many performances were given of high-quality instrumental music in local communities. Also, few qualified instrumental teachers were available, and there was little class instrumental instruction in Europe to serve as a model (Mark and Gary 1999).

Interest in orchestras began to appear by the mid-1800s (Humphrey 1989). European orchestras began to tour America frequently. Orchestral musicians began to immigrate to America, and larger cities such as New York, Cincinnati, and Philadelphia established orchestras. Orchestras began to appear in the schools toward the end of the nineteenth century and the beginning of the twentieth century (Humphrey 1989). These ensembles were first established in high schools and were made up of students studying privately outside of school. They were similar to theater or salon orchestras. The role of the teacher was to gather the students and try to create a performing ensemble from the instrumentation of the students. Among the first were high school orchestras in Chelsea, Massachusetts; Hartford, Connecticut; New Albany, Indiana; Sullivan, Indiana; Richmond, Indiana; and Oakland, California.

By the turn of the century, the violin was very popular in America. In 1908 Charles Farnsworth, a professor from Columbia University, observed class violin instruction in a school in Maidstone, England. Farnsworth was inspired with the concept of young students learning to play the violin in groups (Mark and Gary 1999). In 1910, Albert Mitchell, a teacher in the Boston schools, went to England to study the violin classes in Maidstone. Upon his return, he organized classes in the schools in Boston modeled after those he had observed (Mark and Gary 1999). Word of his success traveled quickly, and Mitchell began giving summer workshops to teachers so that others could establish similar classes. In 1924 his *Violin Class Method* was published (Mitchell 1924).

By the end of the 1920s, orchestra programs appeared frequently in the schools. The results of a 1919–1920 study reported that of 359 cities surveyed, 278 had orchestras in the schools (Humphrey 1989). In addition, teachers began to experiment with teaching beginning heterogeneous instrumental classes. One of the most widely used heterogeneous methods series of the time was *The Universal Teacher* by Joseph E. Maddy and Thaddeus P. Giddings (Giddings and Maddy 1923).

The rapid growth of orchestras and bands was fueled in part by the prevailing philosophy of progressive education and the contest movement (Humphrey 1989). In the late 1910s and early 1920s, school systems began to provide orchestra programs with instruments, rehearsal time, and academic credit. In 1928 the first statewide orchestra contests were held and occurred in fifteen states; the first national orchestra contest was held in 1929 in Mason City, Iowa (Humphrey 1989). The first national high school orchestra performed at the 1926 Music Supervisors National Conference (MSNC)—the predecessor of the Music Educators National Conference (MENC)—and at the 1927 conference of the National Association for School Superintendents (Mark and Gary 1999).

Following World War I, orchestras were firmly established in the school music curriculums of the larger cities in America (Mark and Gary 1999). The number and quality of orchestra programs continued to increase. In the 1930s, the number of school orchestra programs stabilized as the number of school bands began to increase and dominate (Turner 2001). Instrument manufacturers began offering band contests to attract interest in wind instruments and increase sales. A large number of potential band teachers became available for the first time. Performers who had played in the World War I military bands returned to America and became school band teachers. With the advent of talking films, the decline of theater orchestras put more musicians in the teaching market. Because of the Great Depression of 1929, many performing musicians who played wind and percussion instruments were thrown out of work and turned to teaching.

By the end of the 1930s, the number of bands in the schools outnumbered the orchestras (Turner 2001). School bands were continually in the forefront of the public, marching and performing for civic and sports events. Band directors effectively promoted their ensembles, often better than orchestra directors did. Orchestra programs struggled to survive in the 1940s and 1950s. The development of methods for teaching large groups of string students was slow. String teachers were not as effective in recruiting students as band directors. Some string teachers developed an elitist attitude by allowing only the brightest and most gifted students to enroll in their classes. Often a school had just one instrumental teacher. Frequently that teacher was a musician who felt more prepared to teach band and therefore favored the school band over the orchestra. Also, very little string teacher training was offered to college students who were studying to become music teachers (Turner 2001).

In the late 1940s and 1950s, professional associations such as the American String Teachers Association (ASTA) and the National School Orchestra Association (NSOA) were formed to respond to the decline in the number of string teachers. However, the very existence of orchestra programs in the schools was threatened by the 1960s. There was a severe shortage of qualified string teachers for those programs that did exist (Turner 2001). In 1963 and 1964, symposia were held in Tanglewood to address the lack of preparation of string teachers and performers in America (Mark and Gary 1999). The symposia and the premier performance of Suzuki students in 1964 in Philadelphia brought recognition and renewed interest in strings.

By the 1970s, orchestra programs begin to build again in the schools. Between the 1980s and today, surveys of instrumental programs across the country indicate that the number of school orchestras and students studying string instruments has continually increased (Gillespie and Hamann 1997).

VALUES OF ORCHESTRA PROGRAMS IN THE SCHOOL MUSIC CURRICULUM

Why is it important for students to have the opportunity to play string instruments in the schools? What do children gain from playing stringed instruments? Answers to these questions are found in the ways school orchestra programs benefit children, enhance school music programs, and increase the value of the school district.

The Music Curriculum Is Not Complete without the Orchestra

Hands-on learning is one of the most effective ways children master new skills and knowledge. Educators have known this for years. School music classes offer hands-on learning every day. A wide array of music classes is necessary to meet the varied interests of students. Not all students are attracted to the sounds of band instruments, marching, or singing. The large number of students who play piano or guitar points to this. Also, some children simply prefer the sound of string instruments. Therefore, an arts or music curriculum designed to reach the largest number of students is not complete without offering string instrument instruction. It is like a school district offering math without including algebra or science without including chemistry.

In a music curriculum, the orchestra offers students a hands-on opportunity of recreating some of the masterworks by those composers considered the greatest in music, such as Bach, Beethoven, and Mozart. More of the world's greatest composers have written original compositions for orchestra than for any other type of instrumental ensemble. School orchestras can play many of these compositions. Through performing this literature, students have the opportunity to experience firsthand what the great composers intended, unlike transcriptions or arrangements that have been created for other school ensembles.

Further, orchestras should be a part of the school music curriculum to help meet the national standards. The *National Standards for Arts Education* describe the knowledge and skills that every child should have in the arts, as specified by the Music Educators National Conference (MENC 1994). To meet those standards, the Music Educators National Conference states that schools should offer a varied music curriculum, including band, chorus, and orchestra.

The school orchestra also enhances school choral programs. By combining strings, choral programs may perform some of the great choral literature composed for chorus and orchestra, such as Handel's *Messiah* and Vivaldi's *Gloria*. Without an orchestra, such masterpieces cannot be experienced as the composer originally intended. A pit orchestra to accompany school drama productions may be formed from a school orchestra. This allows Broadway musical productions, such as *Fiddler on the Roof* and *South Pacific*, to be performed without the expense of hiring an orchestra of professionals or just using a keyboard for accompaniment.

A school orchestra also may raise the performance standard of the band program. Wind players who play in the symphonic orchestra develop additional solo and expressive skills because there are fewer players per part than required in band literature. More playing opportunities for the woodwinds, such as oboe and bassoon, are available as they are used throughout orchestral literature. These experiences increase the wind students' musicianship and can be taken back to the band to raise its performance standard.

The School Orchestra Increases the Value of a School District

Not all school systems have orchestra programs. One that does shows the serious commitment toward excellence in education. Schools with orchestra programs have a unique opportunity to touch their communities through performance. School orchestra performances in the community offer one way for the community to be reminded of the results of their support of their school system. The orchestra program brings recognition to the school system before the public. In addition, families often are attracted to particular communities because string instruction is available in the schools.

Large orchestra programs can increase the cost-effectiveness of school districts, according to the theory of reverse economics. Large music classes taught by a small number of music teachers enable a school system to hire fewer classroom teachers (Benham 1992).

School Orchestra Programs Benefit Students

School orchestra programs offer many personal benefits to students. More children may experience the arts and discover their unique talents—talents that may not be discovered if string instruction is not available, as not all children are attracted to playing other instruments or singing.

Wind players from the band who also participate in the orchestra develop additional solo and expressive performing skills. These same wind students learn to play in keys such as A major that do not frequently appear in band literature and have the opportunity to play firsthand some of the original masterpieces by symphonic composers such as Beethoven and Brahms. Choral students may experience performing the great choral masterworks with orchestra as composers intended. The experience of a choral student performing the *Messiah* with orchestra as Handel intended rather than with a keyboard is a much different artistic experience.

Learning to play a string instrument helps develop a student's personal character and creative expression. String instruments are uniquely complex to play. A highly refined level of physical and aural skill is required. This degree of effort and concentration required to play a string instrument successfully fosters a child's commitment to a task, as well as responsibility, perseverance, and self-discipline. Playing in an orchestra fosters the development of teamwork and social skills as the student learns to collaborate with fellow students with different opinions, cultures, personalities, and styles. Performing also allows children to experience the rewards and successes of their efforts, which contributes to the development of students' self-concept and self-esteem.

Playing a string instrument enhances a child's quality of life. In an increasingly technological society with the worth of the individual defined by job and income, playing a string instrument helps relieve stress and offers relaxation and comfort. Some of our country's greatest leaders, such as Thomas Jefferson, Benjamin Franklin, and Albert Einstein, not only made outstanding contributions but also played string instruments for personal fulfillment throughout their lives.

The study of string instruments also may assist students in attending college. Many string scholarships are available as colleges and universities attempt to staff their student orchestras. College scholarships to play in the university orchestra are sometimes available to qualified students who are not majoring in music but agree to play in the college orchestra.

Career opportunities are also available to those string students who pursue degrees in music. String teaching positions both in the schools and privately are frequently available in communities throughout the country. According to the American Symphony Orchestra League, lifelong leisure is offered to string students by playing in one of approximately eighteen hundred adult orchestras in the country.

STRATEGIES FOR DEFENDING THE SCHOOL ORCHESTRA PROGRAM

Though there are many important reasons for establishing orchestra programs in the schools, string teachers frequently must defend the continued existence of their programs. Those questioning school orchestras cite factors such as poor administrative support for strings, declining funding for schools, small size of the student body or community, conflicts in scheduling, overly popular band or choral programs, lack of student or community interest, or an increase in graduation requirements. The best strategies to defend school orchestras as important to the music curriculum are built on a strong offense based on five pillars.

Pillar One: Inform and Educate Those in Power about the Values of Orchestra Programs

Those in power to eliminate school orchestra programs include school boards and administrators. If they do not understand the intrinsic value of orchestral instruction to the music curriculum, they will use the wrong criteria when evaluating its importance during times of budget cutting. Those who make decisions regarding programs often are professionals who have not participated in orchestra programs. The job of the string teacher and those that support the orchestra program is to inform and educate regarding the values of school orchestras. Effective strategies to do so include the following:

1. Provide administrators and the school board with a well-developed orchestral curriculum that includes the values of orchestra programs, goals and objectives of playing skills taught by grade level with related methods of evaluation, suggested teaching strategies and materials, and a listing of all orchestra activities, including concerts, trips, student handbooks, and community outreach activities.

2. Perform at school board and administrator meetings.

3. Invite and inform school board members and administrators to all orchestra activities.

4. Invite school board members and administrators to visit the string classes and rehearsals to see the orchestra teaching and learning activity in process.

5. Dedicate concerts to the board members and administrators. Ask them to participate in some way, such as by speaking or performing.

6. Inform teachers and administrators of the results of classroom pullout research. Studies suggest that first- and second-year string students score significantly higher on standardized math and reading tests despite being pulled out of their regular classroom for string instruction (Gillespie 1992).

7. Develop support for the orchestra program by performing frequently throughout the community. Perform in churches, at local civic service groups (e.g., Lions Club and Kiwanis meetings), for the chamber of commerce, at PTA meetings, and in shopping malls.

8. Design a public relations campaign. Involve elected officials in concerts; apply for civic proclamations that focus on the orchestra; use local cable television, radio, and newspapers to advertise upcoming orchestra events; and distribute free concert tickets and advertising posters to local businesses

9. Study printed resources that suggest strategies for developing support for music, such as those published by MENC, music manufacturers, and ASTA with NSOA.

10. Appoint parents as local media coordinators to assist in getting the word out about the school orchestra. Listen to suggestions from ad-

ministrators, teaching colleagues, and parents for effective ways to get the orchestra program before the community.

Pillar Two: Be a Good String Teacher

Being a good teacher develops support for the orchestra program among administrators, students, and parents. Administrators highly value positive feedback about instruction. Understand the pedagogy for teaching string instruments. Be able to demonstrate the playing fundamentals of string performance. Relate well to students. Plan your teaching activities. Be an effective recruiter. Keep up-to-date with the string teaching profession by attending teaching workshops and seminars. Participate in professional music teaching associations and read professional publications. Teach effectively so that the students play well and the concerts sound good.

Pillar Three: Identify and Emulate Model Orchestra Programs

Ask professional colleagues to identify the best orchestra programs in your state. Ask the teachers of those programs how they developed their programs to be successful. Ask them for suggestions for how best to develop your program. Many better programs have common characteristics that may serve as benchmarks: competent teachers, well-organized curriculum, adequate teaching time, effective recruiting process, adequate funding, and a high standard of musical performance. Compare your program with the models. Determine strategies for developing yours into a model program.

Pillar Four: Gather Data and Use It Effectively

Two guiding principles can help develop a strong offense to defend the orchestra program: (1) facts and figures often go further than emotional arguments and (2) numbers speak louder than words. Those in power over orchestra programs value data when making decisions. Emotional arguments may be effective in the short run, but the impact of data lasts.

Be aware of research that supports the benefits of music study. The results of studies are reported frequently by the Music Educators National Conference, companies in the music industry, and in research journals such as the *Journal of Research in Music Education* and the *Journal of String Research*. Also gather data about your program that is important to administrators. Figures to determine include the number of students in the orchestra program, the number of students taught per hour by the orchestra teachers, the rate of string student retention and dropout, the number of people in attendance at orchestra events, the equity of teaching loads across the entire instrumental curriculum, and the overall cost of the program, considering salaries, inventory, and materials, to determine the cost per student hour of instruction. Knowing such figures helps plan strategies to defend the program when budget-cutting time comes. Determine how best to use the data when promoting the values of the orchestra program.

Pillar Five: Organize Support

Organize those in support of the orchestra program to lead the defense. Booster organizations, individual parents, and supporters who are leaders in the community are great resources. Administrators listen to parents. Mobilize them to write and defend the program. With their leadership you will be free to focus more on teaching students rather than defending the life of the program. Your best defense is a large orchestra program with organized support. Back up the defense with quality teaching, and your orchestra program will be able to touch the lives of students for years to come.

DEVELOPING COMMUNITY SUPPORT FOR
THE ORCHESTRA PROGRAM

School orchestra programs must be a vital, active part of the local community. Voters and administrators who are not exposed to the school orchestra are more likely not to fund it. Orchestra concerts and activities must be before the public frequently, just as the marching band and show choir. If not, those in power—voters, school boards, the public—will not understand the value of orchestra programs.

Draw up a marketing plan so that every segment of the community will be exposed regularly to the orchestra program. Based on the plan, make the program visible throughout the school system and community. Intentionally design events that include senior citizens—the segment of the population that frequently votes down school funding.

The following is a sample list of places in the community for performances:

- local service organizations (e.g., Rotary Club, Lions Club, Elks Club)
- churches
- chamber of commerce meetings
- city council meetings
- school board meetings
- PTA meetings
- shopping malls, with handouts about the orchestra program
- special theme concerts performed in the community (e.g., Halloween, patriotic, pops)
- community parks and neighborhoods
- lunchtime concerts at local businesses and government buildings
- nursing homes, senior citizen centers, rest homes
- hospitals

Organize a public relations campaign so that the community leaders and the general public are regularly informed of the activities of the school orchestra. Some ideas are the following:

- Invite the political leaders of the community to orchestra concerts. Dedicate performances to them. Ask them to emcee.
- Request civic proclamations to publicize the orchestra program (e.g., School Orchestra Day).
- Broadcast performances and special orchestra events on local cable television, the Internet, and local radio.
- Distribute free tickets for concerts to community businesses and community leaders. Ask them to display posters advertising upcoming orchestra events.
- Send special invitations to senior citizens for orchestra events. Organize transportation for seniors to orchestra concerts.
- Ask local real estate, bank, or fast-food restaurants to advertise orchestra events.
- Provide a constant stream of information about the orchestra program to local newspapers, including descriptions of upcoming events with pictures.
- Appoint a parent to become the public relations coordinator to organize publicity for the orchestra program.

School boards and administrators make the final decision regarding funding for programs. Keep them regularly informed of orchestra events. Organize parents to communicate to them the values of the school system offering an orchestra program. Be an excellent teacher that brings recognition to the school system and its supporters.

Organize parent booster support for the orchestra program. Lead and coordinate the parents' efforts. Request them to suggest ideas for developing community awareness and support for the orchestra program. Ask principals, colleagues, and local salespeople for suggestions. Allow parents to organize and carry out orchestra activities to build support for the orchestra program.

Orchestra directors need to show the community and administrators how an orchestra program benefits students, the school system, and the community. The orchestra program should be a vital part of the community and a source of pride. Then orchestras in the schools will flourish to everyone's advantage.

THE SCHOOL ORCHESTRA CURRICULUM

The school orchestra curriculum specifies the sequential learning outcomes of students in the orchestra program. These outcomes include the fundamental skills and concepts necessary for playing string instruments with musical understanding. The following table* describes the general skills and concepts, listed in sequential level, that make up the content of the model school orchestra curriculum. Specific goals and objectives for beginning string classes

*From *Teaching Stringed Instruments: A Course of Study.* Copyright © 1991 by Music Educators National Conference. Used with permission.

appear in Chapter 3, intermediate string class goals and objectives in Chapter 4, and those for the high school orchestra in Chapter 5.

	Tone Quality	Rhythm and Bowing	Finger Patterns and Scales
I	Demonstrates: correct bow hair tension bow adequately rosined ability to draw straight bow proper contact point between bridge and fingerboard even bow speed	Demonstrates: détaché (legato) two-note slur and tie bow lifts (') right-hand pizzicato rhythms using these note values: ♩, ♩, ♩., o, ♫ and corresponding rests Imitates bowing exercises	Plays scales: violin—G, D, A viola/cello—C, G, D bass—G, D Plays finger patterns: violin/viola—0 1 23 4 0 12 3 4 cello—0 1 34 0 12 4 bass—0 1 4 0 12 second and third positions
II	Plays forte and piano dynamic levels with good tone Experiments with preliminary vibrato motions Demonstrates proper tone production on all four strings	Demonstrates: staccato three- and four-note slurs left-hand pizzicato (+) hooked bow rhythms using these patterns: ♩ ♪, ♬ and corresponding rests double open strings	Plays G, D, C scales Plays finger patterns: violin/viola—0 1 2 34 cello—0 1 234 (forward extension) 01 234 (backward extension) bass—1/2 position Plays octave harmonics on each string
III	Demonstrates basic vibrato motion Performs crescendo, diminuendo, and other dynamic markings Broadens dynamic range to include *pp* to *ff*	Demonstrates: detached slurs spiccato (near frog) accent/martelé rhythms using ♫(3) , ♪♩(3) and corresponding rests $\frac{6}{8}$ meter and rhythms	Plays scales: violin/viola/cello— two two-octave scales bass—one two- octave scale Plays finger patterns: violin/viola— 01 2 3 4 01 2 34 cello—reinforce extensions bass—reinforce third position Plays one one-octave minor scale Plays familiar basic melodies in higher positions

(continued)

Tone Quality	Rhythm and Bowing	Finger Patterns and Scales
IV Demonstrates increased use of vibrato Refines tone production with greater control of bow speed and distribution Demonstrates the relationships between bow weight, bow speed, and bow placement, and their individual effects on tone	Demonstrates: rapid string crossings with separate bows tremolo trills double stops spiccato (at middle) Understands appliations of basic bow strokes to various musical styles	Plays scales: one-octave chromatic violin/viola—one three-octave major three two-octave major cello/bass—two two-octave major Plays in positions: violin/viola—third, fifth cello—second, third, fourth bass—fourth, fifth
V Varies vibrato speed and width Maintains given dynamic levels with varied bow speeds Changes tone quality and dynamic levels by varying bow speed, weight, and placement	Demonstrates: rapid string crossings with slurs sul tasto ponticello triple stops (chords) Selects appropriate bowings	Plays scales: three two-octave minor violin/viola—three three-octave major cello—four two-octave major bass—three two-octave major Plays in positions: violin/viola—second, fourth cello/bass—thumb
VI Demonstrates refined bow control and vibrato, resulting in a high degree of musicality	Demonstrates: sautillé ricochet Plays appropriate bowing styles for different periods	Plays scales—all major and minor, four shares to four flats Plays in positions: violin/viola—sixth, seventh, and higher cello/bass—fifth and higher Selects appropriate fingerings

ENHANCING THE ORCHESTRA CURRICULUM

Many valuable activities can enhance the basic orchestra curriculum. These opportunities broaden and deepen students' musical experiences and understanding, expand the orchestra curriculum, and enrich the community. Included among these expanded curricular offerings is chamber music; special interest performing groups such as strolling strings, fiddle groups, and mariachi bands; and involving guitar or harp in the string class.

Chamber Music

Incorporating chamber music in the school orchestra program is extremely valuable. Playing in a chamber group helps develop students' listening skills; musical expression and independence; rehearsal skills; sensitivity to balance, blend, and intonation; and musical leadership. Studying chamber music exposes students to music composed by master composers. A wealth of string chamber music literature has been composed by Beethoven, Mozart, Haydn, and other great outstanding composers.

Chamber music in the school orchestra program may be practically incorporated in many ways. One approach is to have chamber music study be the focus of one part of the school year's schedule. Another approach is to devote one day per week of orchestra class throughout the year to chamber music rehearsals so that everyone in the orchestra has an opportunity to play in a chamber group. Rehearsals before or after school may also be held. Featuring student chamber groups on a chamber music concert or including chamber performances on orchestra concerts helps reward students for their chamber music study.

Scheduling coaches to guide each chamber group in their rehearsals is necessary. In addition to the orchestra director, older, more experienced players may coach younger chamber groups. Local private teachers or performers may serve as coaches. Also, other school music teachers such as band directors, general music teachers, or choir directors can coach.

Resources for organizing, coaching, and selecting literature for chamber music groups is available through organizations such as Chamber Music America and ASTA with NSOA. Texts such as *Establishing School Programs in Chamber Music* (Doan 1994), published by Chamber Music America, and *String Syllabus*, vol. 1 (Littrell 1997), published by ASTA with NSOA, are valuable resources. Articles about chamber music appear frequently in the *American String Teacher* journal published by ASTA with NSOA.

Strolling Strings

Strolling strings involves groups of students performing light classical and popular music while walking among an audience. The experience gives students the opportunity to study music that complements their standard orchestral repertoire. Playing in a strolling group helps motivate students to practice because of the increased number of performances and helps develop their sight-reading and aural discrimination skills. Strolling also helps develop students' poise and self-confidence.

Strolling groups may serve as public relations tool for both the orchestra program and a school system. Strolling groups typically perform for local civic associations, school administrator meetings, parties, and businesses in the community. Performances by young students entertaining with popular music while strolling have wide audience appeal.

One of the best resources for information about strolling strings is *Getting Started with Strolling Strings* (Gillespie, Gilbert, and Jones 1995), published by the Music Educators National Conference. It gives practical information on how to form a group and prepare a concert, in addition to performance tips and repertoire.

Mariachi Bands

Mariachi folk ensembles continue to develop in schools across the country. Because mariachi groups include violins, they are yet another way to expand the traditional school orchestra curricula. Mariachi ensembles typically consist of guitars, trumpets, violins, percussion instruments, and vihuela (a type of guitar), and the six-stringed guitarrón. Performances of mariachi music involve both singing and playing. Melodies are either sung or played by the violins or trumpets while the other instruments accompany. Mariachi literature consists of Mexican folk songs such as "Las Mananitas Tapatias," "La Valentia," "La Negra," "Guadalahara," "Las Altenitas," and "La Cumparsita."

Two articles published in the *American String Teacher* are excellent resources about starting mariachi groups in the schools: "The Estudiantian of East Los Angeles" (Ensley 1991a) and "Engaging Interest in Strings through Mariachi" (Fogelquist 2001).

Hispanic culture is rapidly spreading across America. Establishing mariachi ensembles in the schools is one way to honor Latin American and Mexican students, expose others to the music of different cultures, and enhance the orchestra curriculum.

Fiddle Groups

Fiddle tunes such as "Cripple Creek" and "Bile 'em Cabbage Down" are part of our rich American folk tune culture. Organizing students to form a group that exclusively performs fiddle tunes gives orchestra students an additional experience within the school orchestra curriculum.

The size of a fiddle group can vary greatly. Membership can range from two to the entire orchestra string section. In addition to violins, violas, cellos, and double basses, instrumentation may include guitars, mandolins, banjos, autoharps, and keyboard. Fiddle groups need instruments to play the tune, a bass line, and harmony.

Many resources include fiddle tunes. Printed tune books and orchestral arrangements are available from most of the major string publishers. Videos that feature prominent bluegrass, Celtic, and old-time and folk music are accessible. Websites and fiddle journals can be used to find fiddle literature and to learn about the art of fiddling.

Fiddle groups may perform on a traditional school orchestra concert and as a separate organization performing throughout the community, much like a marching band or show choir. Diverse audiences are attracted to fiddle music. Fiddle group performances attract interest to the school orchestra program, enrich students' experiences of playing string instruments, and help develop administrative and community support for the program.

REFERENCES

American String Teachers Association. 1998. *Standards for the preparation of school string and orchestra teachers.* Bloomington, Ind.: American String Teachers Association.

Benham, John. 1992. Forestalling budget problems. *Instrumentalist* 47:12–17.

Fogelquist, Mark. 2001. Engaging interest in strings through mariachi. *American String Teacher* 51 (2):50–58.

Giddings, Thaddeus, and Joseph Maddy. 1923. *The universal teacher.* Elkhart, Ind.: Conn Limited.

Gillespie, Robert. 1992. The elementary pull-out crisis: Using research effectively. *American String Teacher* 42 (2):79–81.

Gillespie, Robert, Beth Gilbert, and Mary L. Jones. 1995. *Getting started with strolling strings.* Reston, Va.: Music Educators National Conference.

Gillespie, Robert, and Don Hamann. 1997. The results are in! A survey on the status of orchestra instruction in the public schools. *American String Teacher* 47 (4):45–49.

Humphrey, Jere. 1989. An overview of American public school bands and orchestras before WWII. *Bulletin for the Council for Research in Music Education* 101:50–60.

Klotman, Robert, Charles Avsharian, et al. 1988. *The complete string guide.* Reston, Va.: Music Educators National Conference.

Littrell, David, ed. 1977. *String syllabus.* Vol. 1. Washington, D.C.: American String Teachers Association.

Mark, Michael, and Charles Gary. 1999. *A history of American music education.* Reston, Va.: Music Educators National Conference.

Mitchell, Albert. 1924. *Violin class method.* Boston: Oliver Ditson.

Music Educators National Conference (MENC). 1994. *National standards for arts education: What every young American should know and be able to do in the arts.* Reston, Va.: Music Educators National Conference.

Turner, Kristin. 2001. A history of string programs. *American String Teacher* 51 (3):74–81.

Witt, Anne, Dean Angeles, et al. 1991. *Teaching stringed instruments: A course of study.* Reston, Va.: Music Educators National Conference.

ADDITIONAL RESOURCES

History of School Orchestras

Birge, Edward. 1966. *History of public school music in the United States.* Reston, Va.: Music Educators National Conference.

Gillespie, Robert, and Donald Hamann. 1998. The status of orchestra programs in the public schools. *Journal of Research in Music Education* 46 (1):75–86.

Mark, Michael, and Charles Gary. 1999. *A history of American music education.* 2d ed. Reston, Va.: Music Educators National Conference.

Value of Orchestra Programs in the School Music Curriculum

Gillespie, Robert. 1994. Our job: Understand and articulate the value of school orchestra programs. *American String Teacher* 44 (1):79–82.

Goodrich, Kathlene, and Mary Wagner. 2000. *Getting it right from the start: A guide to be-*

ginning and enriching a successful string orchestra program. Reston, Va.: American String Teachers Association.

Klotman, Robert. 2000. Why strings? *Music Educators Journal* 87 (3):44–46.

Klotman, Robert, Charles Avsharian, et al. 1988. *The complete string guide.* Reston, Va.: Music Educators National Conference.

Strategies for Defending the School Orchestra Program

Allard, Michael. 1989. *Razzle dazzle: Marketing the school orchestra.* Elkhart, Ind.: Glaesel Stringed Instrument Division, Selmer Company.

Benham, John. 1992. Forestalling budget problems. *Instrumentalist* 47:12–17.

Cutietta, Robert, Donald Hamann, and Linda Walker. 1995. *Spin-offs: The extra-musical advantages of a musical education.* Elkhart, Ind.: United Musical Instruments.

Gillespie, Robert. 1988. Is your program ready for attack? Building a defense for your orchestra program. *American String Teacher* 59(1):66–68.

———. 1992. The elementary pull-out crisis: Using research effectively. *American String Teacher* 42 (2):79–81.

Kendall, Sheila. 1997. Securing our string programs. *American String Teacher* 48 (2):47–50.

Music Educators National Conference. 1991. *Action kit for music education.* Reston, Va.: Music Educators National Conference.

Developing Community Support for the Orchestra Program

Culver, Robert. 1999. How to develop community-wide support for string study. *American String Teacher* 50 (1):48–54.

Gillespie, Robert. 1987. Getting the community behind your orchestra program. *American String Teacher* 37 (3):52–54.

The School Orchestra Curriculum

Allen, Michael. 1995. The national standards for arts education: Implications for school string programs. *American String Teacher* 45 (2):30.

Dabczynski, Andy. 1995. National standards for arts education: A golden opportunity for string teachers. *American String Teacher* 45 (1):73.

Dillon, Jacquelyn, and Casimer Kriechbaum. 1978. *How to design and teach a successful school string and orchestra program.* San Diego: Kjos Music Publishing Corp.

Straub, Dorothy. 1995. The national standards for art education: Context and issues. *American String Teacher* 45 (3):24.

Enhancing the School Orchestra Curriculum

Ballard, Keith. 2002. Mariachi: Ethnic music as a teaching tool. *Teaching Music* 52 (2):22–27.

Doan, Gerald. 1994. *Establishing school programs in chamber music.* New York: Chamber Music America.

Ensley, Jeanette. 1991a. The estudiantian of east Los Angeles. *American String Teacher* 46 (4):81–82.

———. 1991b. Hispanic student participation in school string programs. *American String Teacher* 46 (4):53–54.

Fisher, Sheldon. 1991. Walk right in—stroll right out. *American String Teacher* 46 (4):262–64.

Gillespie, Robert. 1992. New possibilities: Strings are strolling. *Music Educators Journal* 79 (1):252–53.

3
———

BEGINNING STRING
CLASS INSTRUCTION

GUIDING PRINCIPLES FOR TEACHING
BEGINNING STRING CLASSES

Careful Development and Review of Playing Skills

The beginning and second-year string classes lay the foundation for all future playing. The skills taught need to be carefully presented and reinforced so that the need for remedial instruction is limited. Much time must be spent reviewing previously introduced skills so that good posture, instrument and left-hand positions, bowing skill habits, and a high standard of intonation can be firmly established. These foundational skills must become so well established that they become habits. Careful attention to each aspect of students' playing skills in these early classes, reinforced with much review, gives students a solid basis for developing more advanced playing and listening skills in later classes.

Teaching Bowing and Left-Hand Skills Separately

Beginning string playing skills are complex. The right and left hands do something very different; that is, the left hand fingers while the right hand bows. This requires a high level of physical coordination. In the beginning string class, we recommend that bowing and left-hand skills first be taught separately. Once these skills are developed, along with note reading and aural discrimination skills, they can be combined. This sequence of instruction is discussed in detail in Chapter 6. Criteria for selecting methods books for teaching beginning playing skills in the string class are found in Chapter 10.

Teaching Different Learning Styles

Students' natural learning styles are different. Students who are visual learners often learn best by watching the teacher demonstrate or model skills. Tactile learners develop skills better through physically trying to imitate the skills modeled by the teacher on their own instruments, while auditory learners achieve more through listening. A first- or second-year string class will have students with all of these different learning modes, as well as global, sequential, analytical, and discovery learning styles.

Efficient Teaching of Playing Skills

Teachers need to adapt their instruction to the ways their students best learn. With beginning students, that means teachers must show, explain, and let students try the playing skills they are attempting to teach. Research suggests that students in early instrumental classes learn the most efficiently by watching teachers model the skills and then attempting to imitate on their instruments. String teachers will want to demonstrate the skill on a string instrument for the students and then give them an opportunity to try it.

Many skills necessary in playing string instruments require a high level of physical coordination. It is a good idea for the string teacher to break larger skills into smaller ones, model each of them, and then sequentially combine the smaller skills, leading to a more complex one. Finally, do not forget that the auditory learners are waiting for you to explain the skills and concepts that are presented in class! See Chapter 6 for more guidelines for effectively relating to and teaching first- and second-year students.

PERFORMANCE GOALS AND OBJECTIVES OF FIRST- AND SECOND-YEAR STRING CLASSES

During the first and second year of string class, instruction in bowing skills, instrument position and fundamental left-hand skills, music reading, and beginning aural skills need to be developed. The extent of students' skill development depends on the frequency of class meetings. If students have received instruction a minimum of two days a week, most of them, by the end of the second year of instruction, will be able to demonstrate at least the following basic performance skills.

Bowing Skills

- Acceptable bow hand shape
- Basic détaché stroke: bow parallel to bridge and acceptable tone production
- Basic string crossings
- Two-, three-, and four-note slurs
- Basic staccato stroke
- Acceptable hooked bowing
- Accurate bowing of basic rhythmic note and rest values
- Piano, mezzo forte, and forte dynamics

Instrument Position and Left-Hand Skills

- Acceptable body posture
- Acceptable instrument position

- Acceptable left-hand shape
- Play violin and viola finger patterns, cello extensions, and bass shifting required for D, G, C, and F-major scales [(Other scales such as B-flat major, A major, and g minor may be introduced if classes meet more than twice per week.) These keys are included in Chapter 4.]
- Play violin and viola finger patterns, cello extensions, and bass shifting for the d natural minor scale

Music Reading

- Name notes in major keys: D, G, C, F
- Name notes in the d natural minor scale
- Accurately sight-read musical examples in the major keys of D, G, C, F, and d natural minor, incorporating rhythmic note and rest values involving whole, dotted half, half, quarter, and eighth notes

Aural Skills

- Imitate raising and lowering a pitch by ear
- Imitate simple four-note pitch patterns by ear
- Imitate simple rhythms involving whole, dotted half, half, quarter, and eighth notes
- Imitate simple major and minor scales by ear
- Basic instrument tuning

STRATEGIES FOR DETERMINING PROPER INSTRUMENT SIZES

String instruments come in many different sizes. Determining the proper size is critical to the comfort and technical progress of the student. Each student needs to be sized individually because physical dimensions of students vary widely. As students grow, their instrument sizes need to be periodically reevaluated.

Violin and Viola

To determine the proper violin and viola size, place the instrument on the student's left shoulder in playing position. Then have the student extend her left arm underneath the instrument with the hand cupped around the scroll (see Figure 3.1). There should be at least five to six inches of space between the elbow and the center of the back of the instrument. If there is not, the student should play the next smaller instrument size.

Cello

When determining the proper cello size, first have the student adjust the length of the endpin so that the scroll is near the height of the player's nose (see Figure 3.2a). Then have the student sit and place his left hand on one string in

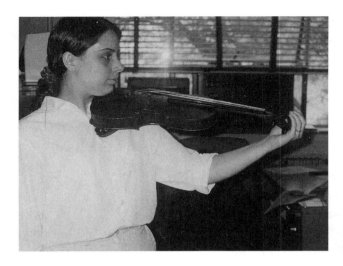

Figure 3.1 Instrument sizing for violin and viola.

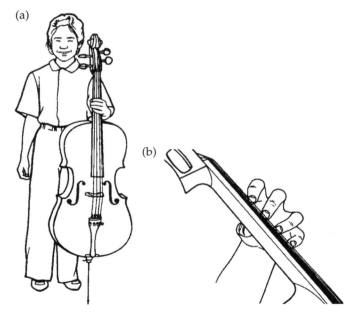

Figure 3.2 Instrument sizing for cello.

first position (see Figure 3.2b). The student should be able to comfortably play an interval of a minor third between the first and fourth fingers. If the player's hand is too small, the next smaller instrument size should be used.

Bass

First adjust the length of the endpin so that the nut of the bass is near the top of the student's forehead when standing (see Figure 3.3). Then have the student place her left hand on one string in first position. The student should be

Figure 3.3 Instrument sizing for play-ing the bass while standing.

able to easily play an interval of a major second between the first and fourth finger on the string. If this is not possible, a smaller instrument size is best.

PEDAGOGY FOR TEACHING INSTRUMENT POSITION

There are many ways to teach children how to hold their instruments. The fol-lowing four-step process may be used with all four string instruments in the heterogeneous class.

Violin and Viola

Our recommendation is that students first play the violin and viola while hold-ing the instrument in guitar position. It is easier for students to play the in-strument in this position while developing their left-hand shape. It also enables them to gradually develop their playing skills in shoulder position.

Introduce the parts of the instruments to prepare students to learn how to hold their instruments in playing position. Be sure students have some kind of shoulder support material on the back of their instruments. The purpose of the material is to help stabilize the instrument on a student's shoulders and to fill the space between his jaw and the top of his shoulder. The height of the shoul-der support material should allow the student's jaw to be parallel to the floor when his jaw is touching the chin rest. Many different shoulder support ma-terials can be used: commercial shoulder rests, foam rubber pads, and so on. Be sure the height of the support is proper and that the material is secured to the back of the instrument so it does not slide around. See Chapter 1 for more information and examples of different kinds of shoulder rests and materials that can be used.

As students are developing left-hand shape and fingering skills with the instrument in guitar position, gradually teach them how to hold their instruments in shoulder position. There are many ways to do so. The following is one method.

Begin by having them touch their left shoulder, collarbone, and side of the neck, which forms a triangle. Refer to it as the platform or shelf for the instrument. Also, have students touch the middle of their necks, as the button of the instrument will touch there when the instrument is in playing position. Then lead the students through the following four steps.

Step 1

Have students stand with their feet shoulder width apart. Ask students to turn their left feet to the ten o'clock position and step out one or two inches. They should adjust their body weight so that they are slightly leaning on the left foot. Some students may want to slightly turn the heel of their right foot toward the center of their body to be comfortable (see Figure 3.4a).

Step 2

Have the students hold their instruments parallel to the floor at eye level. Ask them to place their left hand on the high string bout to hold the instrument and to touch the instrument button with their right index finger (see Figure 3.4b).

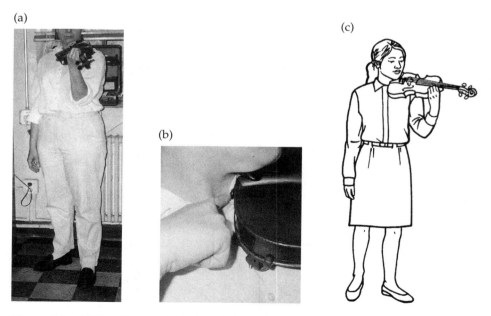

Figure 3.4 (a) Standing position for violin and viola. (b) Button position preparation for violin and viola. (c) Button positioning for violin and viola.

Step 3

Ask students to lift their instruments in the air and gently bring them down to their left shoulders without turning their heads. Instruct them to keep their left hands on the bout and to use their right hands to feel if their instrument's shoulder rest is resting comfortably on the platform or shelf. They should also touch the button to see if it is touching near the middle of their neck. The instrument scroll should be generally parallel to the floor and positioned over the left foot (see Figure 3.4c).

Step 4

Students are now ready to turn their heads so that the sides of their jaws touch the chin rest. Suggest that students check their instrument position by asking them to touch the end of their nose, top of the bridge, and scroll with the right index finger to see if they are generally in a straight line. The nose should be in the direction of the scroll when the instrument is in proper playing position (see Figure 3.4c). Walk behind students to see if there is a straight line between the tops of their heads and the bottoms of their spine to be sure that their body is in alignment. When students begin to play sitting down, check to see if their scrolls are parallel to the floor and that their feet are flat on the floor and positioned so that the frog of the bow can travel past the right side of their right legs.

Cello

A similar four-step process can be used to teach cello students how to properly hold their instruments. Students should learn the parts of their instruments at this time in preparation for this process.

Step 1

Ask students to gently remove their bows from their cases and put them in a safe place, and then remove the instruments from their cases. Adjust the length of the endpin so that the scroll of the cello is near the player's nose when standing (see Figure 3.5). With the endpin touching the floor, have the students balance their instrument about an arm's length in front of them with the student's right hand on the bout on the low string side of the instrument. The instrument scroll should point to the ceiling.

Step 2

The seat portion of the chairs student cellists will use should be flat and generally parallel to the floor. Have students sit on the front half of their chairs, with their feet placed flat on the floor, positioned underneath their knees, and spread far enough apart to accommodate the width of the cello. The height of the chair should allow the player's thighs to be generally parallel to the floor. The cello endpin should be directly in front of the student, one arm's length away (see Figure 3.6).

Figure 3.5 Determining length of cello endpin.

Figure 3.6 Chair and seated position for cello.

Step 3

Ask students to gently bring the instruments back to their bodies while keeping their heads looking forward. The cello should lean slightly to the left and rest comfortably on the upper torso of the player. The C string peg should be near the player's head behind the left ear. You may need to readjust the length or position of the endpin. Check to see if there is space between the neck of the cello and the student's neck, and between the back of the neck of the cello and the top of the player's shoulder. The student should be able to easily move her head side to side without bumping into the cello (see Figure 3.7).

Step 4

Students may now move their knees so that they touch the cello just below the "C" bout. The knees should gently balance the cello, with the instrument supported mainly by the body and endpin. The student's arms should be resting comfortably and freely at his side. Review Figure 3.7 once again.

Bass: Sitting Position

We recommend that students first learn to play the bass while sitting on a stool. This frees the young player's left hand so that shifting and vibrating is easier. Eventually, of course, students should learn how to play the bass standing as well. The following four steps may be used for teaching students to hold the bass while sitting. Students should learn the parts of their instruments at this time.

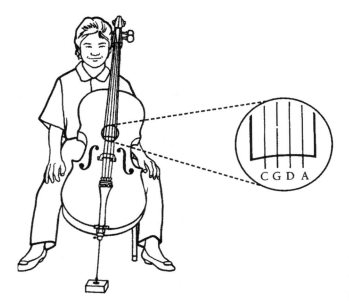

Figure 3.7 Instrument playing position for cello.

Step 1

A standard kitchen stool (two rungs for taller students, one rung for shorter students) or an adjustable, professional bass stool may be used (see Figure 3.8). The height of the stool should permit a student's left foot to rest comfortably on a rung of the stool, and allow the right foot to be flat on the floor with a slight bend at the knee. Shorten the legs to the proper height if a kitchen stool will be used.

Ask students to gently remove the bows from their cases and put them in a safe place. Have them remove the instruments from their cases. Adjust the length of the endpin so that the nut of the bass is near the top of the player's forehead when standing (see Figure 3.9). With the endpin touching the floor, have the students balance the instrument about an arm's length in front of them, with the students' right hand on the bout on the low string side of the instrument. The instrument scroll should point to the ceiling. Position the stool behind the student so that one leg of the stool is pointing straight ahead and the endpin is in front of the left stool leg. (Review Figure 3.8 once again.)

Step 2

Instruct the student to sit squarely on the front half of the stool, with her right foot on the floor and the left foot on a rung of the stool. Both coaxial bones should be on the stool, and the hip and legs should be flexible. The legs and knees should be placed far enough apart to accommodate the width of the bass. Students should be able to comfortably sit on the stool without the instrument.

Figure 3.8   Seated position for bass.

Figure 3.9 Determining length of bass endpin.

Step 3

Have students bring the bass back to their bodies without moving their heads. The bass should be rotated slightly to the right and leaning against the left side of their stomach. The instrument should lean into the center of the body, resting on the left thigh (see Figure 3.8).

Step 4

Check to be sure there is a slight space between the neck of the instrument and the player's neck. There should also be space between the back of the instrument's neck and the top of the player's shoulder, allowing the student to freely move his head from side to side without touching the instrument neck. The student's arms should be able to rest comfortably and freely at his side. See Figure 3.8 for the position of the bass.

Bass: Standing Position

Step 1

Students should learn the parts of their instruments at this time. Ask students to gently remove bows from their cases and put them in a safe place. Then have them remove the instruments from their cases. Adjust the length of the endpin so that the nut of the bass is near the top of the player's forehead when standing (see Figure 3.9).

Step 2

Instruct the students to stand with both feet flat on the floor and spaced far enough to accommodate the width of the bass. Place the endpin in front of the student's left foot, about one arm's length away. Have students balance the instruments with their right hands on the bout on the low string side of the instrument, about one arm's length away. Have the student move her left foot slightly forward. Flexible knees and free hip rotation are necessary as well.

Step 3

Have the student bring the instrument back to his body, rotating the bass slightly to the right and leaning the bass toward the body so that the upper bout rests against the left side of the stomach. The right back edge of the bass should rest on the player's left groin. The inside of the left knee should touch the back of the bass (see Figure 3.9).

Step 4

Check the balance of the bass by asking the students to drop their hands to their sides. The floor and the groin should balance the instrument. The bass should rest against the abdomen at an angle, with no further left-hand support needed. Check to see if the pitch A on the G string is over the left shoulder at eye level. See Figure 3.9 for the position of the bass.

ADDITIONAL INSTRUMENT POSITION TEACHING STRATEGIES

Rote teaching activities designed to develop students' playing skills are used frequently in string class instruction. The rote teaching strategies described in Chapters 3, 4, and 5 are commonly used in string classes throughout the country. They are based on the work of many experienced teachers and pedagogues, including Paul Rolland, Phyllis Young, Robert Culver, Irene Sharp, Margaret Rowell, Michael Allen, William Conable, Paul Robinson, and the authors of this text.

The following rote teaching strategies may be used to help students develop an acceptable body and instrument position.

All Instruments

Grow an Inch. Have students stand with feet shoulder width apart. Ask them to pull up an imaginary string attached to the top of their heads, so that their body is lengthened and free. This position allows the arms and hands to move freely for playing the instrument. Also try the same strategy with students sitting.

Puppet Shoulders. Have students quickly raise and lower both shoulders. This frees the shoulders and arms to move efficiently. This is a particularly good strategy for cello and bass students because of the temptation to twist one of the shoulders forward when setting the instrument in playing position.

Front Half of the Chair. Ask students to sit on the front half of their chairs with their backs away from the back of the chair. If students sit on the edge of the chair, this can stiffen the back and neck muscles.

Cello

Palms an' Knees. Have students place the palms of their hands on the tops of their legs while sitting with their feet placed flat on the floor. This sensitizes both the students and teachers to focus on the proper height of the chair for a student cellist. If the height of the chair is acceptable, the palms will generally be parallel to the floor.

Up and Light. Ask students to hang their hands at their sides with their instruments in playing position. Gently pull the cello neck away. The cello should move easily, because the knees should not be gripping the instrument. With the instrument away, check to see if the player's head, shoulders, and torso are aligned.

Jack-in-the-Box. Announce "Jack-in-the-Box." Instruct students to respond by standing quickly and easily. If their feet are placed flat on the floor and positioned correctly, they should be able to do so.

LEFT-HAND SHAPE: GENERAL GUIDELINES

Violin and Viola

Examine carefully the position of the thumb in Figure 3.10. Notice that the tips of the fingers are on the string, and the thumb is generally across from the index finger, resting on its side with the tip pointing up. When students gently tap the side of the fingerboard with their thumbs, the tapping motion allows their thumbs to rest on their sides at a location that is comfortable for their hand. Also notice that the base hand knuckle of the index finger is generally across from the top of the fingerboard.

Finally, notice that the left wrist is positioned comfortably away from the instrument, generally forming a straight line from the base hand knuckle to the elbow. In this position, the elbow will be movable and underneath the back of the instrument (see Figure 3.11).

Cello

Examine carefully the position of the fingers and thumb in Figure 3.12. Notice that all of the fingers are naturally curved, and the index finger is resting slightly on its side corner. The thumb is generally resting on its pad behind the second finger. The fingers should be equally spaced so that there is a half step between each finger.

Notice that the wrist and arm are in alignment. One way for students to find the best placement of the elbow is to have them alternate tapping the instrument nut and top of the bridge. When doing so, the elbow will naturally position itself at a place appropriate for the arm and hand in first position (see Figure 3.13).

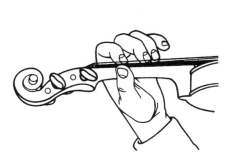

Figure 3.10 Left-hand position for violin and viola.

Figure 3.11 Left wrist and elbow position for violin and viola.

Figure 3.12 Left-hand position for cello.

Figure 3.13 Elbow position for cello.

Bass

Examine carefully the position of thumb and fingers in Figure 3.14. Notice that the thumb is generally behind the second finger and that the first finger is relatively straight. Notice the space between the index and long finger. The space between those two fingers should equal the space between the long finger and the pinky. Each interval should be one half step.

The arm and hand will be aligned, with a relaxed but generally straight wrist (see Figure 3.15).

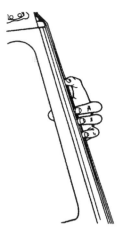

Figure 3.14 Left-hand position for bass.

Figure 3.15 Left arm and hand position for bass.

PEDAGOGY FOR TEACHING THE LEFT-HAND SHAPE

With string instruments, the index finger is referred to as the first finger, the middle finger as the second, the ring finger as the third, and the pinky, or little finger, as the fourth. To help students develop their left-hand shape, first introduce notes that use three or four fingers. It is also easier in this way for students to keep their proper hand shape when lifting fingers off to play different pitches, compared with adding fingers. The following rote teaching strategies may be used to help students develop an acceptable left-hand shape.

All Instruments

Top of the Hand Down. Have students learn to play descending tetrachords, scales, and musical fragments first before ascending lines (e.g., G-major descending tetrachords: violin and violas starting with three fingers on the D string for G, cellos four fingers on the D string, basses fingering F-sharp on the D string while playing open G).

   Tunneling. Have students slide all four fingers, or their third and fourth fingers together, up and down the length of the fingerboard between any two adjacent strings.

   Ridin' the Rails. Have students slide their fingers up and down one string. Hopefully their fingers will not become "derailed"!

   Doublin'. When students can bow two strings, have them finger pitches on one string while playing the next higher adjacent open string (no fingers on the string). This promotes curvature of the fingers.

   Taps. Have students lightly tap their fingers on one string and then combinations of strings. This will help the students curve their fingers and begin to coordinate fingering motions.

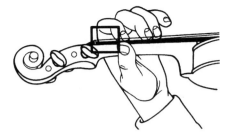

Figure 3.16 Left index finger shape for violin and viola.

Thumb Taps. Ask students to lightly tap their thumbs on the instrument neck while their fingers are on the strings. This should help remove tension and prevent squeezing the neck with the hand.

Violin and Viola

Square First Finger. Encourage students to shape their index fingers so that they form a square with the fingerboard. This helps allow all their fingers to be curved and gently poised over the fingerboard (see Figure 3.16).

Thumb Slides. Have students gently slide their thumbs along the side of the neck with their hands in playing position. When the thumb slides toward the second finger, their wrists will gently straighten, which will help promote a hand position that is at ease and generally in alignment with the arm (see Figure 3.17).

Pull Aways. Have students pull the sides of their hands away from the neck of the instrument while keeping their thumbs and fingers on the instrument. This promotes a relaxed left-hand position and encourages students not to squeeze the neck of the instrument when playing.

Strums. Have students strum across the strings with their fourth fingers while swinging their elbows. This helps the arm move freely from the shoulder joint.

Geminiani Chord. Geminiani was a Baroque string composter who frequently composed chords performed by placing one finger on each of the strings. Have students place their first fingertips on the lowest string, second fingertips on the next string, third fingertips on the next string, and their fourth

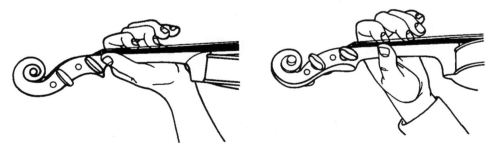

Figure 3.17 Thumb slides and position for violin and viola.

fingertips on the highest-pitch string. This will help them properly curve their fingers.

Fingertip Fingering. Remind students that they should be playing on the tips of their fingers.

Base Hand Knuckle Checks. Check to see if students' base hand knuckles are generally at the height of the top of the fingerboard. The base hand knuckle of students with longer fingers may be slightly lower.

Cello

Knuckle Knocks. Have students close their left hands and lightly tap the strings by raising and lowering the hand from the wrist joint. Instruct students to tap up and down the length of the fingerboard. This tapping motion from the wrist joint encourages the left hand to be relaxed from the wrist joint when playing.

Sodas and Fruits! Suggest to students that the general hand shape should be formed as though their hand is cupped around a pop can or a piece of fruit the size of an orange. Fingers should be rounded, and the thumb and index finger should form a C shape.

Finding Our Elbow. Ask students to alternate lightly tapping the bridge and the nut of the instrument. This will help the elbow position itself naturally so that the left hand may be properly placed on the string.

Bass

K Shape. Have students form the shape of a K on the string as in Figure 3.14. Notice that the string is the trunk of the K, and the index and pinky fingers form the other lines of the K.

C Clamp. Instruct students to shape their index finger and thumb like the shape of a C clamp (see Figure 3.18).

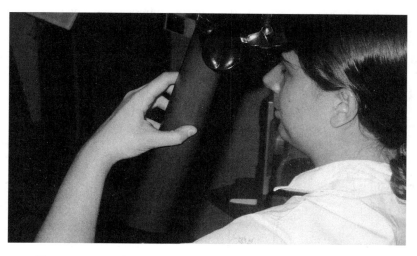

Figure 3.18   Left-hand index finger and thumb shape for bass.

PEDAGOGY FOR TEACHING PIZZICATO

As we stated previously, we recommend that bowing and fingering skills first be taught separately before they are combined. However, students can pizzicato simple scales and melodies while they are developing their bow hand shape and open string bowing skills. Pizzicato activities can start from the first day of instruction. Violin and viola students can pizzicato first in guitar position and later in playing position.

Violin and Viola

Instruct students to place the tips of their right thumbs at the corner of the fingerboard near their highest string and use their index fingers to pluck the strings. Students should pull the string to the side using the pads of their fingers (not the tip of the finger) to get the best sound.

Cello and Bass

Have students position the right side of their thumbs on the high~~/low~~ string side of the fingerboard, about two to four inches from the end. As with violin and viola, students should pull the string toward the adjacent string, using the pad of the finger to get the best sound.

PEDAGOGY FOR TEACHING BEGINNING FINGER PLACEMENT

The first keys that students learn in beginning string classes are D major and G major. As the class progresses, additional keys such as C major, F major, and d natural minor may be introduced. Students should play one-octave scales and arpeggios in these keys during beginning instruction.

Violin and Viola: The 2-3 and 1-2 Finger Patterns

Teaching finger patterns helps violin and viola students easily understand finger placement. The finger patterns describe the whole step and half step spacing between fingers. The 2-3 finger pattern is the first one introduced to students, followed typically by the 1-2 finger pattern.

The 2-3 finger pattern involves a half step between the second and third fingers, and a whole step between the first and second fingers and third and fourth fingers (see Figure 3.19). Notice that the fingertips are close to each other when forming a half step. The fingertips may or may not be touching, depending on the width of students' fingers.

The 2-3 finger pattern allows students to play the two major tetrachords in the D-major scale: whole step between the open D (no fingers on the D string) and first finger E, whole step between first finger E and second finger F-sharp, half step between second F-sharp and third finger G, and a whole step between third finger G and either fourth A or the open A string. The same 2-3 finger pattern may be used to play the second ascending tetrachord of the D-major scale on the A string. The 2-3 pattern is also used to play the G-major scale

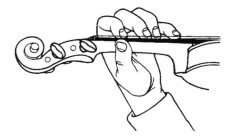

Figure 3.19   The 2-3 finger pattern for violin and viola.

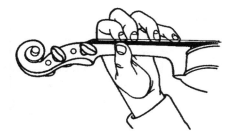

Figure 3.20   The 1-2 finger pattern for violin and viola.

starting on the open G string for both violin and viola, and a C-major scale on the viola starting on open C.

The 1-2 finger pattern involves a half step between the first and second fingers (see Figure 3.20). It is used in the tetrachord on the A string (open A, first finger B, second finger C natural) and the tetrachord on the D string (first finger E and second finger F natural) when playing the C-major scale starting on the G string. The 1-2 finger pattern is also used in the d natural minor scale, starting on the open D string.

Cello

Remember on the cello all fingers are spaced a half step apart, creating an interval of a minor third between the first and fourth fingers. The one-octave D, G, and C-major scales typically first introduced in beginning string classes are all fingered the same when starting on the open string for the tonic pitch (e.g., G major: G string—open G, first finger A, third finger B, fourth finger C; D string—open D, first finger E, third finger F-sharp, fourth finger G). As other major scales or tetrachords are introduced, the second finger is used. For example, to play a d minor tetrachord starting on open D, the second finger is used to play F natural. In an F-major scale, starting with a fourth finger F on the C string, the second finger is used to play B-flat on the G string.

Depending on how often the string classes are scheduled per week, cellists may begin to learn how to play the F-major scale beginning on second finger F on the D string during the first two years of instruction. This octave of the F major requires a backward extension for B-flat on the A string. Cello extensions and strategies for teaching them are presented in Chapter 4.

Bass

The distance between the first and fourth fingers is only a major second. This means that the bass player must learn how to shift to a higher position to play the D, G, and C-major scales that the other string students are learning if octave transpositions are to be avoided. We recommend that bass players learn their initial scales without switching octaves for each tetrachord to avoid inherent string crossing, tempo, and intonation problems.

The following are additional rote teaching strategies to help students learn basic fingering.

Block Fingering. Have students place the sounding finger and all lower number fingers on the string when first learning to finger pitches (e.g., playing G on the D string on violin and viola in first position with three fingers down rather than third finger only). This helps develop students' left-hand shapes. After the hand shape is well established, students may begin to use independent fingering.

Descending Scales. First introduce scales descending to help students develop left-hand shape, fingering motion, and finger placement between the first and fourth fingers, and to promote desirable left wrist and arm placement.

Descending Melodies. Emphasize melodies that begin with higher pitches and descend to lower pitches for shaping the left hand and establishing intonation within a hand frame. "Mary Had a Little Lamb" and "Joy to the World" are examples.

Simple Double Stopping. Have students finger a string while sounding the adjacent higher-pitched open string.

Finger Markers. Some teachers like to initially mark beginning students' fingerboards, indicating where students should place their fingers to help promote accurate intonation. Auto pinstriping, adhesive dots, or dots of Liquid Paper may be used. If a marking system is used, we recommend that as soon as possible, markers be removed gradually so that students will rely more on their ear than the marker.

BOWING INSTRUCTION: GENERAL GUIDELINES

The beginning of this chapter recommends that students develop body posture, instrument position, left-hand shape, and finger placement skills independent of bowing skills. Though instrument and bowing instruction should occur at the same time, beginning from the very first classes, the independent development of these skills allows students the opportunity to develop a level of mastery before trying to combine them. Remember that students may pizzicato the various scales and melodies they are learning as they are developing their bowing skills independently. See Chapter 6 for further discussion.

We recommend that bowing skills be taught sequentially because of their complexity. In beginning string classes, this involves first teaching bow hand shape, followed by instruction about simple détaché bowing, string crossings, and staccato and hooked bowing.

BOW HAND SHAPE: GENERAL GUIDELINES

We recommend that students first learn to hold the bow at the balance point so that their fingers and thumb may be relaxed while holding the bow. This also helps students understand that the instrument will help support their bow when they are playing.

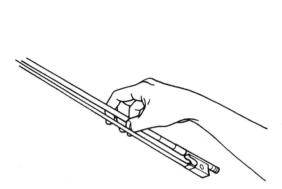

Figure 3.21 Bow hand shape at the balance point for violin and viola.

Figure 3.22 Bow hand shape for violin and viola.

Violin and Viola

Examine carefully Figures 3.21 and 3.22 and notice the following:

- The index finger rests on top of the bow stick near the second knuckle joint.
- The second finger is curved across from the thumb, is draped over the side of the bow, and touches the stick near the second knuckle joint.
- The third finger drapes over the side of the bow, and the fingerprint touches the concave side of the frog.
- The little finger is curved and its tip rests near the inner side of the bow stick.
- The thumb is across from the second finger forming an oval shape.
- The hand leans slightly on the index finger.

Cello

Examine carefully Figures 3.23 and 3.24 and notice the following:

- All fingers are naturally curved and draped over the side of the frog and bow stick.
- The index finger is draped over the bow stick near the first or second knuckle joints.
- The third fingerprint is near the U cutout of the frog.
- The fourth finger is near the eyelet of the bow.
- The thumb is curved, and the side of its tip rests across from the second finger.
- The hand is more perpendicular to the bow stick than upper strings.

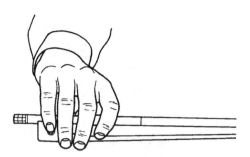

Figure 3.23 Bow hand shape for cello (view of the fingers).

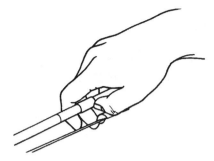

Figure 3.24 Bow hand shape for cello (view of the thumb).

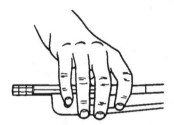

Figure 3.25 French bow hand shape for bass (view of the fingers).

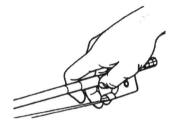

Figure 3.26 French bow hand shape for bass (view of the thumb).

Bass: French Bow

Examine carefully Figures 3.25 and 3.26 and notice the following:

- The shape of the hand is similar to the cello bow hand, but the fingers are positioned slightly more over the side of the frog.

Bass: German Bow

Examine carefully Figures 3.27 and 3.28 and notice the following:

- All fingers are naturally curved.
- The index finger and thumb form a circle.
- The second and third fingers are curved and positioned near the index finger.
- The fourth finger is located under the frog for support.

PEDAGOGY FOR TEACHING BOW HAND SHAPE

The following rote teaching strategies may be used to help students develop their bow hand shape.

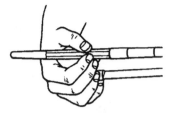

Figure 3.27 German bow hand shape for bass (front view).

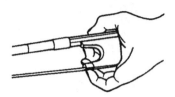

Figure 3.28 German bow hand shape for bass (back view).

All Instruments

Finger Bowing. Step 1: Have students hold their left index finger parallel to the floor in front of their face at the height of their chin. Step 2: Instruct students to place their right index finger on top of the left hand and let their other fingers hang on the left index finger. The thumb should not touch. Students should point their fingertips over the side. Step 3: Ask violin and viola students to tap their pinky on top of the left index finger. Step 4: Tell students to place their thumb tip across from their second finger, thumb knuckle curved outward. The thumb and the index finger should form an oval shape. Step 5: Have students move their bow hand formed on their left index finger to the place where it will be when bowing their instrument. Learning to shape their bow hand on an index finger allows students to incorporate the sense of touch when learning how to shape their fingers for bowing.

Pencil Bowing. Have students form their bow hand shapes on a pencil before placing them on the bow. This allows students to form their hand shape without having to balance the weight of the bow. Figure 3.29 shows an example of violin and viola bow hand shape formed on a pencil.

Straw Bowing. Have students form their bow hand on a straw. This encourages students not to squeeze or tense their hand because the straw is light and easily bends if pressure is applied.

Spyglasses and Telescopes. After students' bow hand shapes are formed, have them look through the spyglass or telescope shape formed by their long finger and thumb.

Eyes Closed! Have students form their bow hand with their eyes closed to help them focus on the *feel* of their bow hand when it is correctly formed.

Figure 3.29 Bow hand shape on a pencil for violin and viola.

Figure 3.30　Bow hand thumb shape on a pencil for violin and viola.

Balance Point Bows. Instruct students to form their bow hand at the balance point of the bow. This helps the bow hand to be relaxed while holding the bow.

Tap, Tap, Tap. Instruct students to tap their fingers lightly while forming their bow hand shape on a pencil, straw, or at the balance point of their bow. This helps relax the fingers and hand.

Bow Paths. Draw a line or an X on the students' fingers where the bow stick should touch. This helps students correctly position the bow in their hand.

Thumbs Up. Have students hold their bow with their bow hand. Ask them to turn the bow upside down so that the hair is facing the ceiling. Instruct them to check to see if their thumb is touching the bow correctly and if its middle knuckle is curved outward, forming an oval shape with their longest finger. See Figure 3.30 for an example of this hand position for the violin and viola when holding a pencil.

Thumb Bends. Step 1: Shape students' bow hands on a pencil, straw, or bow. Step 2: Ask them to turn their bow hands upside down by turning their hand. Step 3: Instruct students to bend their thumb slightly, along with all their fingers. The contact point of the thumb should stay the same while the thumb bends. This promotes flexibility throughout the fingers and thumb.

Violin and Viola

Flop Hand. Have students do the following steps. Step 1: Hold a pencil in the left hand at eye level. Step 2: Hang right-hand fingers over the top of the pencil, as shown in Figure 3.31. Step 3: Place the fourth finger on top of the pencil as shown in Figure 3.32. Step 4: Touch the tip of the right thumb on the pencil just opposite the second finger, forming an oval shape, as shown in Figure 3.33. Step 5: Lean the right hand toward the index finger, as shown in Figure 3.34. After completing Step 5, remove the left hand from the pencil.

Bass

Shelving! Step 1: Ask students to loosely hang their right hand at their side with their bow stick resting at the balance point on their fingers without the thumb touching. The fingers form a shelf on which the bow can rest. Step 2: Instruct students to slide their thumb tip across from their second finger, bending the knuckle outward. Step 3: Have students bring their hand up to their eyes and evaluate their bow hand shape.

Figure 3.31 Step 1 for forming bow hand shape.

Figure 3.32 Step 2 for forming bow hand shape.

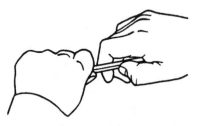

Figure 3.33 Step 3 for forming bow hand shape.

Figure 3.34 Step 4 for forming bow hand shape.

DÉTACHÉ BOWING: GENERAL GUIDELINES

Once students have developed their bow hand shapes they are ready to develop their first bow strokes. The first bow stroke that students learn is the détaché stroke. This stroke is produced by simply placing the bow on the string and pulling it back and forth. The bow hair should generally travel parallel to the bridge, touching the string about halfway between the bridge and fingerboard to get the best beginning sound. As bowing skills develop, students may begin to explore bowing closer or farther away from the bridge and fingerboard.

Examine carefully Figures 3.35, 3.36, 3.37, and 3.38. Notice the angle of the bow hair on the string. Notice also for each instrument the height of the elbow, its placement in relation to the body and instrument, and the curvature of the wrist and fingers. It is critical that students learn these correct positions when establishing their bowing skills.

The bow is divided into different sections, as illustrated in Figure 3.39. We recommend that students first learn to bow in the easiest part for their instrument: violins and violas in the middle, and cello and bass middle to lower half. As students master these areas of the bow, others may be emphasized.

PEDAGOGY FOR TEACHING DÉTACHÉ BOWING

The following rote teaching strategies may be used to help students develop their détaché bowing skills.

Figure 3.35 Position of bow on the string for violin and viola.

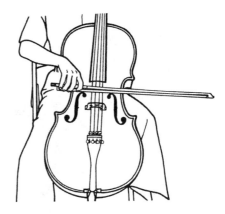

Figure 3.36 Position of bow on the string for cello.

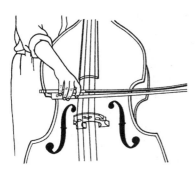

Figure 3.37 French bow position on the string for bass.

Figure 3.38 German bow position on the string for bass.

Tip   Upper Half   Middle   Lower Half   Frog

Figure 3.39 Different sections of the bow.

All Instruments

Shoulders, Arms, and Tubes! To help students develop their bowing skills away from their instruments, have violin and viola students hold a paper or plastic tube slightly above their left shoulder, place their bow in the tube, and begin bowing. Cello and bass students may hold a tube with their left hand at waist level, insert the bow in the tube, and begin bowing.

Instrument Tubing. Have students attach a paper or plastic tube to the top of the strings for students to bow through. The tube may be attached by tying two standard-sized rubber bands together, or one long rubber band may

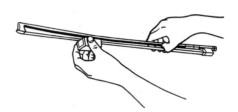

Figure 3.40 Bowing through a Tube (violin and viola).

Figure 3.41 Rosining the Bow (violin and viola).

be used. Place the rubber bands under the strings, and position the tube on top of the strings. Loop the ends of the rubber bands around the ends of the tube to fasten the tube to the strings. The tubes provide a path for the students' bows when they are first learning proper bowing motions. Straws can also be placed in the F holes to help guide the bow. See Figure 3.40 for both approaches.

Rosin Bowing. Have students hold their rosin in the left hand and bow across it. Violin and viola students may hold the rosin over the left shoulder where the bow would touch the strings when the instrument is in playing position. Cello and bass students may hold their rosin in front of them with their instruments in playing position. When rosining, they should gently pull their bow across the rosin only three or four times. Basses should pull only down bow motions across the rosin. See Figure 3.41 for a rosin bow example.

Lift, Set, Settle. Instruct students to lift their bow in the air above the strings, bring the bow down so that it rests on the string, and settle the bow by relaxing their right shoulder, elbow, wrist, and fingers.

Short Bows to Long Bows. Have students first learn to master shorter bow strokes and then gradually lengthen the stroke as their mastery develops.

Buddy Bowing. Pair students up with one student bowing and the other checking and guiding their bow so that it travels parallel to the bridge correctly.

Violin and Viola

Swingin' Out. Have students place their left index finger in the right elbow joint and gently swing their arm back and forth. This helps students develop the arm motion produced by the opening and closing of the elbow joint when bowing in the middle of the bow. See Figure 3.42.

Straws in the F Hole. Have students place a plastic straw in each instrument F hole and then bow near the straws as illustrated in Figure 3.43. This helps the bow to travel parallel to the bridge.

Figure 3.42 Swingin' Out Strategy (violin and viola).

Figure 3.43 Straws in the F Hole Strategy (violin and viola).

Bow Hand Shapes on the Go. Have students first learn their détaché bowing skills while holding the bow at the balance point. As students' bowing skills develop, gradually have them move their bow hand to the frog.

Cello

Ridin' the Rails. Have students hold their bow at the tip with their left hand and place the bow on the string near the tip. Then instruct students to slide their bow hand shape back and forth along the stick. This helps students learn the proper motion of the hand, wrist, and arm when they bow.

Traveling Down the Road. Have students hold the end of a yardstick, dowel, or PVC tube in front of them at the height where their strings would be when the instrument is in playing position. Then have them place their bow hand shape around the object and slide their hand back and forth along the stick. As they are moving their hand, check to see if the motion is in two steps. In Step 1, the motion with the hand moving away from the body is first initiated by the upper arm, followed by an opening of the forearm. In Step 2, when the hand is moving toward the body, the elbow should close first, followed by the upper arm. See Figure 3.44.

Bass

Swingin' to the Floor. Have students swing their right arm back and forth from their shoulder joint, allowing the elbow to bend only slightly so that the hand travels parallel to the floor. See Figure 3.45.

Frog to the Floor. Have students bow back and forth on their strings, keeping the frog parallel to the floor. This helps prevent the bow from traveling toward the fingerboard, particularly on the down bow stroke.

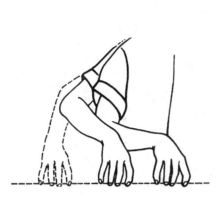

Figure 3.44 Traveling Down the Road Strategy (cello).

Figure 3.45 Swingin' to the Floor Strategy (bass).

BEGINNING STRING CROSSINGS: GENERAL GUIDELINES

It is important for students to move their arm to the new string level when they are changing strings. See Figures 3.46, 3.47, and 3.48 for illustrations. Notice that the string crossing motion is the opposite between high and low string instruments. Violinists and violists lower their arm when crossing to a higher-pitched string and raise their arm when crossing to a lower-pitched string. The motion is just the opposite for lower strings. Cellists and bassists raise their arm when moving to a higher-pitched string and lower their arm when going to a lower-pitched string.

PEDAGOGY FOR TEACHING STRING CROSSINGS

The following rote teaching strategies may be used to help students develop their string crossings skills.

All Instruments

Bridge Rocking. Have violin, viola, and cello students place their bow hair on top of the bridge at the balance point. Instruct them to rock the bow across the bridge. Basses may do so as well but will need to place their bows on the string at their normal contact point or at the end of the fingerboard, depending on the length of their arm. This shows students the distance between string levels for their instrument and helps them follow the natural curvature of the bridge when crossing strings. After students have mastered crossing at the balance point, have them try crossing at other parts of the bow.

Pencil Crossings. Have students insert a pencil between the bow hair and stick at the balance point. Violin and viola students may hold the bow over the left shoulder where the bow would be if they were playing; cello and bass stu-

Figure 3.46 String crossings for violin and viola.

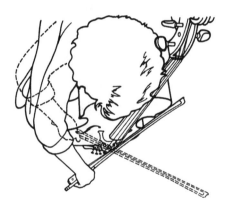

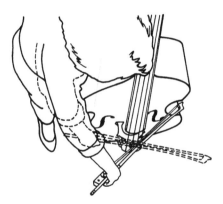

Figure 3.47 String crossings for cello.

Figure 3.48 String crossings for bass.

dents may hold the bow in front of them in their instrument playing position. Instruct students to rock the bow up and down as in a string crossing motion, first using large arm motions, then hand, and then fingers flexing only. This introduces students to the principle that string crossings can be done primarily by the arm, hand moving from the wrist joint, or fingers flexing, depending on the tempo and placement of the bow on the string.

Rest Crossings. Place rests between pitches that involve a string level change. This allows time for the student to execute a string crossing properly. Use longer rests first and then gradually shorten the amount of time for the string crossing motion as students develop their mastery of string crossings.

STACCATO AND HOOKED BOWINGS: GENERAL GUIDELINES

Staccato strokes begin with a pinch or slight depression of the bow stick, which is produced by leaning primarily the index finger into the bow stick. When the bow is pulled, the extra weight at the beginning of the stroke produces an accent. Immediately after the accent, the extra weight on the bow through the index finger should be released slightly. At the end of the stroke, the arm stops and another slight pinch of the index finger is added.

Once students have mastered the basic staccato stroke, they may hook or link two or more staccato notes in the same bow direction. This is commonly referred to as *hooked bowing*.

PEDAGOGY FOR TEACHING STACCATO AND HOOKED BOWINGS

The following rote teaching strategies may be used to help students develop their staccato and hooked bowing skills.

All Instruments

Pinched Bows. Have students practice pinching their bows by placing the bow on the string at the balance point and slightly leaning the index finger into the bow stick. It should be easy to see the bow stick go up and down while the bow hair stays on the string. Instruct students to try the pinching motion with their second finger, then their third finger, and finally their fourth finger. They will feel in their hand that the index finger is the easiest finger to produce the pinch. The other fingers together help the index finger, but the motion is led by the index finger. Have students practice their staccato bowing first using open strings and then review scales.

Doorknob. Using the analogy of the turning motion used when rotating a doorknob to open a door, lean the hand back and forth into the bow stick to start the staccato stroke.

Bow Pivots. Instruct students to lean their bow hand into the bow stick toward the index finger and pivot it by moving their bow hand closer and farther away from their body while keeping the same contact point of the bow on the string. After pivoting, the students can pull the bow to a different contact point and pivot again.

Hook and Pull. Ask students to place the bow on the string to lean slightly into the stick with their bow hand. Once the bow stick is depressed or "hooked," instruct students to pull it across the string. They may need to release some of the pressure on the bow between strokes if the sound is too scratchy.

Connect the Hooks. After students have leaned into the bow stick with their bow hand to hook the string, they may pull the bow to connect two or more staccato pitches in the same bow direction.

Loud Rests. Emphasize the silence necessary between the staccato notes by instructing students to play a loud rest between pitches.

PEDAGOGY FOR TEACHING SLURS

Slurs are produced on string instruments by smoothly pulling the bow in the same direction and connecting two or more different pitches. The following rote teaching strategies may be used to help students develop their slurring skills.

All Instruments

Trill Slurs. Have students pull their bow in one direction while trilling. This helps students coordinate pulling their bow in one direction while playing different notes with the left hand.

Hooking for Slurs. Have students first hook different staccato pitches in the same bow direction and then play the same notes legato while slurring.

AURAL SKILL DEVELOPMENT IN BEGINNING CLASSES: GENERAL GUIDELINES

The development of aural or listening skills in the string class is critical. Refining aural skills helps students play in tune by developing their pitch discrimination skills, as well as by helping them coordinate their right and left hands and memorize music. Well-developed aural skills lay the foundation for successful string playing by young students and may lead to interest in aural skills such as improvising, composing, and playing jazz, blues, and fiddling music.

PEDAGOGY FOR TEACHING BEGINNING AURAL SKILLS

In beginning string classes, students can learn how to raise and lower a pitch by ear and to match pitches. Echoing by ear what the teacher plays is one of the most effective ways to help beginning students' aural skills. The following are some examples of teaching strategies that can be used. Be sure that students cannot see the person playing what they are supposed to echo. In that way, students must use their ears to respond, not by watching the fingers of the performer. It is easiest if the leader stands behind or to the side of the class where students cannot see the player.

Sliding Pitches. Have students echo the pitch direction of the leader sliding her hand up or down the fingerboard.

Rolling Pitches. Have students echo the pitch direction of the leader by slightly rolling his finger on a pitch.

Four-Note Echoes. Have students echo four pitches played by the leader. Begin with four open string pitches, alternating styles, slurring, and rhythms. Once that is mastered, incorporate one other pitch that is a major or minor second above. Continue adding different pitches as students' skills develop.

We Get to Play Out of Tune! Once students can echo simple four-note patterns, the leader may begin deliberately bending or playing some of the pitches slightly out of tune. Students are required to echo the correct and incorrect pitches precisely as the leader played.

STRATEGIES FOR TEACHING INSTRUMENT TUNING IN BEGINNING STRING CLASSES

As students are learning the fundamentals of holding the instrument and bow, the teacher can be responsible for tuning the open strings that are being used in class. Be sure all violin, viola, and cello instruments have fine tuners that turn easily so that tuning can be done quickly and efficiently. Basses, or course, should have machine head pegs. Until students start learning how to tune their own instruments, we recommend that the teacher tune only the strings that students will use in class.

Once students can reliably hold their instruments, correctly produce desirable sounds on their instruments, and can discriminate differences in pitches learned by the aural skill instruction process described earlier, formal tuning instruction may begin. Many different strategies may be used. The following are some that the teacher may use:

- Play an open A string while turning its peg or tuner. Students must indicate if the string is getting higher or lower in pitch.

- Play an open A and have the students play their A string either with the bow or by plucking the string and compare it with the teacher's A. Have the students pluck their string while turning the tuner until it matches the teacher's.

- Play an A on an electronic tuner and have each student compare and turn the tuner accordingly.

- Repeat the previous strategies with other strings.

As students' ability to match the model develops in the beginning classes, the teacher may allow the students to quietly bow their strings and use their tuners (bass machine head pegs) to match the model. Teaching students to tune their instruments is done over a long period of time. The teacher must be patient and consistent and maintain a high standard of tuning. Students will only tune as accurately as they are taught and required.

PROBLEM SOLVING: BEGINNING STUDENTS' COMMON PLAYING PROBLEMS AND SOLUTIONS

The following table includes examples of some of the most common playing problems beginning string students will experience. Solutions are suggested for each problem and are described in detail earlier in the chapter.

Instrument	Problem	Solution
All	Collapsed right thumb on bow	Spyglasses and Telescopes
		Thumbs Up
		Thumb Bends
	Straight bow hand fingers	Tap, Tap, Tap
		Flop Hand
		Balance Point Bows
	Shortened body position	Grow an Inch
		Jack-in-the-Box
	Stiff string crossings	Bridge Rocking
		Pencil Crossings
		Rest Crossings
	Fingers flat on strings	Tunneling
		Taps
		Doublin'
	Bow not parallel	Shoulders, Arms, and Tubes!
		Instrument Tubing
		Buddy Bowing
		Rosin Bowing
		Lift, Set, Settle
	Left-hand spacing incorrect	Finger Markers
		Top of the Hand Down
	Right-hand fingers squeezing the bow stick	Tap, Tap, Tap
		Straw Bowing
		Pencil Bowing
		Balance Point Bows
	Harsh staccato	Pinched Bows
		Bow Pivots
		Doorknob
Violin and Viola	Collapsed left wrist	Thumb Slides
		Square First Finger
		Tunneling
		Fingertip Fingering
		Geminiani Chord
		Bass Hand Knuckle Checks
	Bow not parallel to the bridge	Straw in the F Hole
		Buddy Bowing
		Swingin' Out
		Instrument Tubing
		Bow Hand Shapes On the Go
		Lift, Set, Settle
		Shoulders, Arms, and Tubes!
		Instrument Tubing
	Left thumb too curved	Thumb Taps
	Squeezing left hand	Pull Aways
		Thumb Taps
		Bass Hand Knuckle Checks

(continued)

Instrument	Problem	Solution
Cello	Left elbow too high or too low	Bridge and Nut Tapping
	Shoulders twisted, not aligned	Puppet Shoulders
	Feet wrapped around chair legs	Jack-in-the-Box
		Shuffle feet
		Place feet flat on the floor
	Left wrist stiff	Knuckle Knocks
	Bow not parallel	Instrument Tubing
		Ridin' the Rails
		Traveling Down the Road
	Collapsed left wrist	Sodas and Fruits!
	Legs squeezing cello	Up and Light
Bass	Bow not parallel	Frog to the Floor
		Ridin' the Rails
		Shoulders, Arms, and Tubes!
		Instrument Tubing
		Traveling Down the Road
		Swingin to the Floor
	Left-hand finger spacing incorrect	K shape
		Finger Markers
	Bow skidding lightly across the strings	Lift, Set, Settle
		Use bass rosin
	Collapsed left wrist	C Clamp

4

INTERMEDIATE STRING CLASS INSTRUCTION

PERFORMANCE GOALS AND OBJECTIVES OF THIRD- AND FOURTH-YEAR STRING CLASSES

Third- and fourth-year string class performance goals and objectives are built on the bowing, instrument position and left-hand technique, music reading, and aural skills established in the first- and second-year string classes. Remedial work may be needed. However, by the end of the third and fourth year of instruction, the majority of students should be able to demonstrate the following performance skills.

Bowing Skills

- Consistent parallel bowing
- Smooth direction changes
- Acceptable tone production at different dynamic levels
- Moderate to faster tempo string crossings
- Slurs of more than four notes
- Basic martelé stroke
- Slow to moderate tempo spiccato strokes

Instrument Position and Left-Hand Skills

- Consistently lengthened and balanced body posture
- Consistently acceptable instrument position
- Consistently acceptable left-hand shape
- Violin and viola finger patterns, cello extensions, and bass shifting for F, A, D (violas and cellos beginning on the C string), and B-flat-major scales [Other scales, such E-flat major, may be introduced if students' first- and second-year classes meet more than twice per week.]

- Violin and viola finger patterns, cello extensions, and bass shifting for the g, a, c, and e natural minor scales
- Violin, viola, cello shifting between lower positions
- Consistently acceptable cello extensions
- Beginning vibrato

Music Reading

- Read and name notes in major keys: F, A, D, C, B-flat (E-flat optional)
- Read and name notes in the g, a, c, and e natural minor scales
- Accurately sight-read musical examples in the major keys of D, G, C, F, A, B-flat (E-flat) and d, g, a, c, e natural minor scales, incorporating rhythmic and rest values involving dotted eighth notes and rests, triplet eighth note patterns, an eighth note followed by two sixteenths or two sixteenths followed by an eighth note, a dotted eighth followed by a sixteenth, and syncopated rhythmic figures such as an eighth followed by a quarter and another eighth note

Aural Skills

- Imitate by ear four-note pitch patterns in the keys of D, G, C, F, A, and B-flat
- Imitate by ear simple rhythms involving whole, half, dotted half, dotted quarter, quarter, eighth, and sixteenth notes
- Play simple melodies by ear in multiple keys
- Demonstrate tuning involving harmonics and bowing two strings simultaneously

PEDAGOGY FOR TEACHING PARALLEL BOWING

Review the bowing strategies used in the first- and second-year classes (see Chapter 3). Additional strategies for intermediate students are the following.

Buddy Bowing. Pair students. Have one student bow and the other student observe, and help the player bow parallel by adjusting the stroke if necessary.

Lanes. Divide the distance between the bridge and the end of the fingerboard into five lanes. Number each lane. Have students practice bowing in each lane.

Letting the Air Out. Have students exhale on the down bow, while checking to see if their bow is traveling parallel to the bridge, and inhale on the up bow stroke.

Rockin' Bows. Have students rest their bow on the string at the frog or the tip. Ask students to pivot their bow by bending their fingers, wrist, and elbows.

Circle Bowing. Have students pull consecutive bow strokes in the same direction (e.g., all down bows). Be sure students' arms, wrists, and fingers are relaxed before beginning each stroke.

Bowing Parts. Have students practice bowing only in the lower half, middle, or upper half of their bows.

PEDAGOGY FOR TEACHING SMOOTH DIRECTION CHANGES

Changes in the direction of the bow (e.g., when the down bow stroke changes to the up bow stroke and vice versa) should be smooth and controlled. Bow hand fingers, thumb, and wrist need to be relaxed and able to react to the change of direction.

Statue of Liberty. Have students extend their arm in the air, with the bow tip pointing straight up, and flex their fingers.

Balancing and Rubbing. Have students place their bows on the string at the balance point with their bow hand near the balance point. Instruct students to make short strokes at the balance point by flexing their right-hand fingers and wrist.

Multiple Flexes. Have students practice several finger and wrist flexes at either end of the bow while bowing.

Two-Handed Pulls. Have cello students place their bow on the string. Their left hand should hold the bow at the tip with their right hand positioned at the frog. Instruct students to use both hands to pull their bows back and forth on the string.

PEDAGOGY FOR TEACHING TONE PRODUCTION
AT DIFFERENT DYNAMIC LEVELS

Intermediate students should understand the relationship between bow speed, weight, and contact point to begin to refine their sound production. Review the basic sound production principles for string instruments. Use the following intermediate teaching strategies to refine students' tone production, including different dynamic levels.

Give Me an SWS! Have students vary their bow speed, weight on the bow, and sounding point (the contact point of the bow on the string), and any combination, to produce different dynamic levels.

Lanes. Divide the distance between the bridge and the end of the fingerboard into five lanes. Number each lane. Have students practice bowing in each lane.

Miles per Hour. Use the analogy of miles per hour to vary the speed of students' bow strokes—for example, five miles per hour (very slow), thirty-five miles per hour (moderately fast), or seventy miles per hour (very fast).

Pounds. Use an analogy of pounds to have students vary the weight they put on the bow to change dynamic levels—for example, two pounds on the bow for a light, piano dynamic, twenty-five pounds for a mezzo forte dynamic, and fifty pounds for a forte dynamic.

Down Equals Up. When dynamic changes are not required, students' down bow sound should equal their up bow sound. Have students close their eyes and listen to their sound production and compare their down and up bow sounds. Instruct students to adjust their bow speed, contact point, or weight on their bow if the sound of the down bow stroke is different from their up bow.

PEDAGOGY FOR TEACHING MODERATE-TO-FASTER TEMPO STRING CROSSINGS

String crossings for intermediate students should be smooth as they occur at moderate tempos in all parts of the bow. Students' right elbows, wrists, and bow hands should be relaxed and free to flex. As the tempo of string crossings increases, students should use less arm motion and more wrist and bow hand motion. Use the following intermediate teaching strategies to develop their moderate tempo string crossings.

Finger Teeter-Totters. Have students place their bows on the string and practice crossing strings by waving their hands from the wrist joint. While bending their fingers, there should be only slight motion from the arm during the crossing.

Variable Speed Crossings. Rehearse students crossing strings at different speeds. Remind them that the faster the string crossing, the smaller the wrist, hand, and finger motion.

Variable Place Crossings. Have students cross strings in all parts of the bow.

PEDAGOGY FOR TEACHING SLURRING MORE THAN FOUR NOTES

Intermediate students should be able to easily slur four-, six-, and eight-note passages. Help them develop their slurring skills by using the following teaching strategies.

All the Way Up, All the Way Down. Rehearse students playing one-octave scales, slurring all ascending pitches in one bow and all descending pitches in one bow.

Trilling Slurs. Have students slur while trilling.

PEDAGOGY FOR TEACHING MARTELÉ BOWING

Martelé bowing involves an accent at the beginning of the stroke, immediately followed by a release of weight on the bow. There should be silence between the martelé strokes. The following teaching strategies are designed to develop students' martelé bowing skills.

Index Finger Pinches. Have students place the bow on the string with the bow held only by the index finger and thumb. Instruct students to lean their index finger into the bow stick. Alternate the lean with a release of weight on the bow. Students should see their bow stick move slightly up and down while resting on the string.

All Finger Pinches. Use a variation of the Index Finger Pinches strategy by asking students to pinch the bow stick with all four fingers placed on the bow stick.

Pinch, Pull, Release. Demonstrate to students that the martele stroke involves a series of three steps: (1) the bow hand leans slightly into the bow stick, (2) the bow is pulled, producing an accent, and (3) there is an immediate release of weight so that the bow moves easily.

Pinch and Glide. Use these words to reinforce the attack stroke sequence.

Pizzicato Martelés. Ask students to imitate the sound of a pizzicato note with the sound of the accent that is a part of the martelé stroke. Rehearse students alternating pizzicato with martelé strokes.

Fingered Martelés. Rehearse students playing simple scales played with a martelé stroke on each pitch.

PEDAGOGY FOR TEACHING BASIC SPICCATO

Spiccato is a stroke that involves bouncing the bow on the string. At slow to moderate tempos, the bounce occurs in the lower half of the bow. Before students begin learning spiccato bowing, they first must have smooth, flexible direction changes and the ability to cross strings while flexing their fingers and bending their wrists. Spiccato is produced in an arclike motion with a relaxed elbow and shoulder, wrist joint, and fingers.

Balance Point Rub. Have students place the bow at the balance point with their bow hand positioned on the bow stick near the balance point. Instruct students to move the bow back and forth on the string primarily using their fingers. The arm should move only slightly. The wrist should bend, and the bow should travel parallel to the bridge.

To the Frog We Go. Once students can accomplish the Balance Point Rub, have them gradually move their bow hands from the balance point to the frog while flexing the bow hand.

Balance Point Bounce. Have students bounce the bow near the string while holding the bow at the balance point. Rehearse students alternating moving the bow on the string by flexing their fingers and bouncing the bow on the string.

Bouncing All the Way. Lead students through this three-step sequence: (1) move the bow on the string at the balance point, primarily by flexing the wrist and fingers, (2) bounce the bow at the balance point with a similar motion, and (3) gradually move the bow hand on the stick to the frog while repeating Steps 1 and 2.

Heard But Not Seen. Use this phrase to remind students that the bouncing motion for the basic spiccato stroke should be small. The bow should bounce close to the string.

Multiple Bounces. After students have learned the basic spiccato stroke on open strings, give them opportunities to bounce fingered pitches. Begin by having them first bounce each pitch at least four times before proceeding to another pitch. As students' spiccato skill develops, they can use fewer bounces per pitch. The skill to bounce individual pitches in a spiccato passage is very complex. Begin with multiple bounces on each pitch to coordinate the left hand with the spiccato stroke, and then gradually lower the number of bounces per pitch as students' skills develop.

PEDAGOGY FOR TEACHING CONSISTENT LENGTHENED AND BALANCED BODY POSTURE

Intermediate students should play with a consistently relaxed, lengthened, and balanced body position. Students should also be able to move freely in reaction to their bow stroke. Continually review the body posture strategies described in Chapter 3 for each step in helping students establish their body and instrument position. The following are some additional strategies to use with intermediate students.

Crunches. Review the Grow an Inch strategy (Chapter 3) for beginning students. Contrast a lengthened body position by having students attempt to play with shrugged shoulders, tensed neck muscles, and chins pulled forward. Then have students play with a lengthened and relaxed body position.

String Flying. Have students (1) sit in playing position without their instruments, (2) close their eyes, (3) mimic the playing motions involved in playing their favorite piece while moving their bodies (e.g., leaning from side to side, violin and viola students bending their knees, and so on), and (4) open their eyes and move their bodies while playing open strings or their favorite piece. Instruct students to move their bodies with the bow stroke: lean from the left to the right on the down bow and from right to left on the up bow. Students should be encouraged to move freely while playing.

Breathing and Playing. Instruct students to focus on their breathing while playing. Inhaling and exhaling while playing frees and relaxes the body, which is crucial for desirable tone production. Help students focus on their breathing by having them practice playing open strings while exhaling on the down bow stroke and inhaling on the up bow stroke.

PEDAGOGY FOR REFINING INSTRUMENT POSITION

Intermediate students' instrument position should be well established. Students should be able to demonstrate intermediate bowing, left-hand skills, and music while maintaining a desirable instrument position. Periodically review the teaching strategies for establishing students' instrument position in Chapter 3. Use the following teaching strategies to develop students' ability to maintain an acceptable instrument position while playing for longer lengths of time and with more advanced left-hand skills.

Instrument Position Checkpoints. Develop a list of checkpoints that may be used to evaluate students' instrument positions while they are playing intermediate level music. See the following table for some examples.

Instrument	Position Checkpoints
Violin/Viola	Body remains lengthened when the instrument is brought to the body.
	Center line of back of the instrument rests near the shoulder.
	Instrument is supported by shoulder and collarbone and is gently stabilized by the left hand; elbow is movable.

Instrument	Position Checkpoints
	Button of instrument is positioned slightly left of the Adam's apple or center of neck.
	Mandible or jawbone rests on chin rest; nose points toward scroll.
	Instrument is generally parallel to the floor when left hand is in lower position.
	Scroll and left elbow are over left foot.
	Knees and legs are flexible to react to bow stroke.
Cello	The instrument touches the chest and is supported by the body.
	The knees gently cradle the instrument.
	The endpin is adjusted so that (1) the bottom of the scroll is normally one to three inches from the top of the shoulder (about the width of three fingers), (2) the C peg is located near the back of the student's neck, and (3) the instrument bouts are slightly above the student's knees.
	The cello is slightly slanted to the student's left. The line of the strings crosses the axis of the body at a slight angle.
	The cello is tilted slightly so that it is possible to bow on both the A string and the C string without hitting the legs.
Bass (standing)*	The right back edge of the bass should rest on the player's left groin.
	The instrument should be balanced by the body; only the floor and the groin should support the bass.
	The pitch A on the G string should be over the left shoulder at eye level.
	The bass should rest against the abdomen at an angle, with no further left-hand support needed.
	The inside of the left knee should touch the back of the bass.
	The hip and legs should be flexible.
Bass (sitting)*	Both feet should support the bass—the right foot by the floor and the left foot by the rung of the stool.
	The instrument should lean into the center of the body, resting on the left thigh.
	Both pelvic bones should be on the stool.
	The hip and legs should be flexible.

*Instrument position goal for bass: Adjust instrument so that both hands and arms are comfortable.

Instrument Buddies. Pair off students. Have one student play and the other student touch the scroll of the other student's instrument. A proper instrument position should be maintained, regardless of the difficulty of the music or its length.

Timing. Challenge students to play for longer and longer periods of time while keeping an acceptable instrument position. Use a watch to time how long students can play intermediate level music and keep their instrument positioned properly. Then gradually lengthen the time, building up students' physical endurance.

INTERMEDIATE LEFT-HAND SKILLS: GENERAL GUIDELINES

Intermediate students' left-hand techniques involve those skills required to play the F, A, D (violas and cellos beginning on the C string), and B-flat-major scales, and g, a, c, and e natural minor scales. Frequently review the teaching strategies in Chapter 3 for establishing students' left-hand position and fundamental skills to play the D, G, and C-major scales. Students should be able to demonstrate a relaxed and properly shaped left-hand shape before beginning to develop intermediate skills. Refer to Chapter 3 for the beginning D, G, and C-major and d-minor scales and arpeggios. Fingerings are provided. The F-major scale appears in both Chapters 3 and 4 because it is sometimes included in the curricula for string programs with first- and second-year classes that meet three or more times a week.

Figure 4.1 shows intermediate scales and arpeggios with fingerings.

Figure 4.1

G-Major Scale and Arpeggio

G-Major Scale and Arpeggio

D-Major Scale and Arpeggio

Figure 4.1   (*continued*)

D-Major Scale and Arpeggio

A-Major Scale and Arpeggio

A-Major Scale and Arpeggio

F-Major Scale and Arpeggio

F-Major Scale and Arpeggio

B-flat-Major Scale and Arpeggio

Figure 4.1 (*continued*)

D-Minor (Natural) Scale and Arpeggio

D-Minor (Natural) Scale and Arpeggio

G-Minor (Natural) Scale and Arpeggio

G-Minor (Natural) Scale and Arpeggio

Violin and Viola

Intermediate violin and viola skills include the following:

- the 1-2 finger pattern (half step between the first and second fingers) on the G and E strings
- the open-hand finger pattern (whole steps between first and second fingers and second and third fingers)
- the high third finger and low fourth finger pattern (half step between the third and fourth fingers)
- the introduction of third position, shifting, and vibrato

The 1-2 (half step between the first and second fingers) finger pattern in first position scales occurs on the violin G string in the B-flat-major scale and the g natural minor scale; the 1-2 finger patterns on the E string in first position appear in the upper octave of the G-major scale and g natural minor scales.

The open-hand finger pattern involves moving the first finger back so it is positioned close to the nut of the fingerboard. A half step is formed between the first finger and the open string and a whole step between all other fingers. The open-hand finger pattern occurs in the first position of the violin in the F-major and B-flat-major scales, and the d and g natural minor scales.

The 3-4 finger pattern involves a half step between the third and fourth fingers and whole steps between all other fingers. Examples include the A-major scale, beginning on the G string on violin and viola, and upper octave first position B-flat scale on the E string on violin.

Third position on the violin and viola involves placing the first finger of the left hand on the pitch that is played with the third finger in first position. For example, the first finger sounds the pitch G on the D string that is played with the third finger in first position. Notice the placement of hand and notes in Figures 4.2 and 4.3.

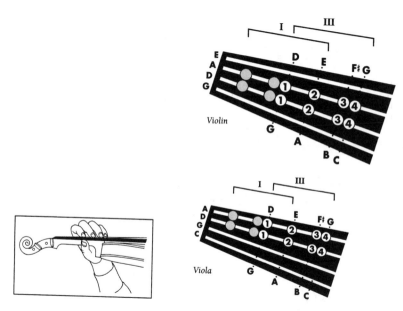

Figure 4.2   Third position for violin and viola.

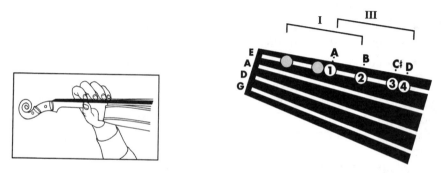

Figure 4.3   Third position on the E string for violin.

Cello

Cello intermediate left-hand skills include backward and forward extensions and the introduction of fourth position. Backward extensions involve cellists extending their first finger back a half step from first position. The first finger extends backward so that there is a whole step between the first and second fingers. When extending backward, the player should move the elbow and forearm forward and roll the thumb slightly on its pad, allowing the side of the first finger to contact the string. This enables the first finger to extend backward far enough to play in tune. The pitches B-flat on the A string, E-flat on the D string, A-flat on the G string, and D-flat on the C string are played with backward extensions.

Notice in Figure 4.1 that the backward cello extension is involved in playing the B-flat-major scale, the d natural minor scale, and the g natural minor scale. See Figure 4.4 for an illustration of the proper hand position when playing a backward extension.

The following checkpoints may be used to evaluate your cello students' backward extensions:

- First finger moves a half step toward the end of the scroll.
- The side of the first finger touches the string.
- The thumb rolls as the first finger extends backward.
- The elbow moves toward the floor and instrument.
- A whole step is formed between the first and second fingers.

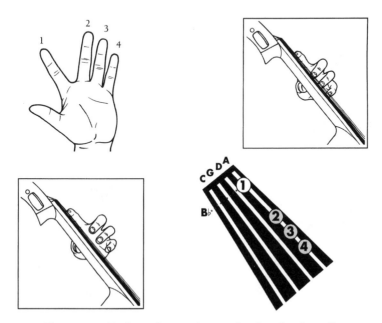

Figure 4.4 Backward extension on the A string for cello.

Forward extensions enable cellists to play a whole step between their first and second fingers. By extending their hand forward from first position, the interval of a major third is formed between the first and fourth finger. In extended position, cellists may play a D-sharp on the A string, G-sharp on the D string, C-sharp on the G string, and F-sharp on the C string. When extending, cellists should open their hand between the first and second fingers so that there is a whole step between the fingers. Students should move their second, third, and fourth fingers, and thumb, toward the bridge while keeping their first finger on the string. The thumb should move with the hand so that it remains behind the second finger in this new extended position. The second finger now sounds the pitch that was played with the third finger in regular first position.

As a part of the extension, the elbow should move forward at the same time, which helps the second finger extend so that there is a whole step between the first and second fingers.

See Figure 4.5 for an illustration of the proper hand position when playing a forward extension.

The following are checkpoints to help you evaluate your cellists' forward extensions:

- The hand opens between first and second fingers.
- There is a whole step between first and second fingers.
- The thumb moves with the hand, positioned behind the second finger.

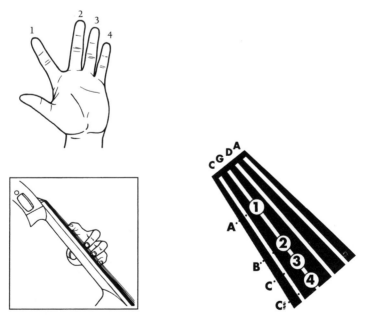

Figure 4.5 Forward extension on the G string for cello.

 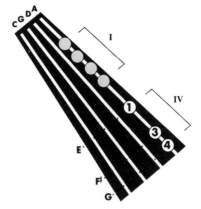

Figure 4.6 Fourth position for cello.

- The first finger contact on the string remains the same, but the finger rests more on its side in extended position.
- The elbow moves toward the floor and instrument.
- The fourth finger is curved.

Fourth position, and sometimes third position as well, is introduced as a part of cello intermediate skills. For example, fourth position is used in the G-major scale when starting the scale on the D string, as shown in Figure 4.1. Figure 4.6 illustrates the left hand in fourth position on the cello. Notice that the thumb pad is placed in the saddle or cradle of the neck of the instrument.

Refer to Figure 4.5, which illustrates cello forward extensions. These extensions are used when playing the D-major scale beginning on the C string and the A-major scale beginning on the G string.

Double Bass

Intermediate double bass skills involve new positions and continued development of shifting skills introduced during the first two years of instruction. New positions include second, second and a half, fourth, fifth, and fifth and a half position, and new pitches in first position (e.g., B-flat on the G string and G-sharp on the E string). Figures 4.7, 4.8, 4.9, 4.10, 4.11, 4.12, and 4.13 illustrate the intermediate positions and pitches introduced on the bass in order to play the scales in Figure 4.1.

Study the double bass scales and their fingerings and positions in Figure 4.1 to prepare to teach intermediate left-hand skills.

Review with students the teaching strategies in Chapter 3 for establishing the left-hand shape and introducing higher positions and shifting for the double bass. Once those skills are mastered, introduce the following strategies for developing intermediate skills.

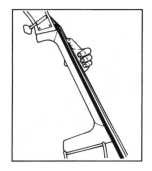 

Figure 4.7   Half position B-flat on the A string for bass.

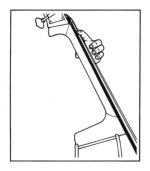 

Figure 4.8   Half position F-natural on the E string for bass.

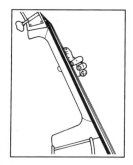 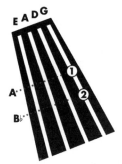

Figure 4.9   First position B-flat on the G string for bass.

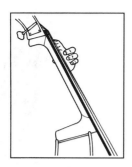 

Figure 4.10 Half position G-sharp on the G string for bass.

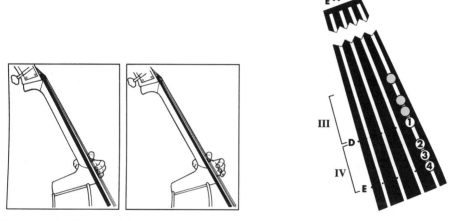

Figure 4.11 Third and fourth positions on the G string for bass. (Note: The entire fingerboard is not shown, as indicated by the break. Use third position as a guide to find fourth position.)

Figure 4.12 First position E-flat on the D string for bass.

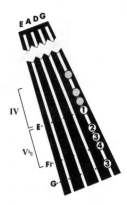

Figure 4.13   Fifth and a half position and harmonic on the G string for bass. (Note: The entire fingerboard is not shown, as indicated by the break. Use fourth position as a guide to find fifth and a half position.)

PEDAGOGY FOR REFINING LEFT-HAND SHAPES

Review the teaching strategies in Chapter 3 for establishing students' left-hand shapes. Once students have established a consistently proper left-hand shape while playing, the following intermediate strategies may be introduced.

Doublin' Up. Have students practice playing simple double stops. This involves playing two pitches at the same time. One pitch is an open string and one pitch is fingered. On violin, viola, and cello, have students finger and bow a pitch on a higher string while also bowing an adjacent lower open string. Basses should bow and finger a pitch on a lower string while also bowing an adjacent higher-pitched open string.

Add a Note. Lead students through a descending scale, starting at the top of the scale, and then ascend the scale, adding one pitch at a time. For example, in the D-major scale, students would play the following pitch pattern: DC#D, DC#BC#D, DC#BABC#D, DC#BAGABC#D, DC#BAGF#GABC#D, DC#BAGF#EF#GABC#D, DC#BAGF#EDEF#GABC#D.

Tappin'. Have students, independently and in groups, practice tapping their fingers on one string and then on multiple strings.

Anchor and Slide. Instruct students to place all fingers on one string. They should keep one or more fingers on a string while sliding others. Eventually some fingers may be positioned on one string, while remaining fingers slide on other strings.

Anchor and Tap. This is the same strategy as Anchor and Slide except that the fingers are lightly tapped on the string.

PEDAGOGY FOR TEACHING CELLO EXTENSIONS

Extending Backward. Lead students through the following sequenced steps. Instruct them to (1) hold their right arm vertically in the air in front of them to act as a fingerboard, (2) place their left hand on their arm as if playing on the fingerboard in first position, and (3) practice extending their first finger backward toward their right hand while keeping their other fingers down. Students' index finger should straighten out, their thumb should pivot, and their fingers should lean slightly backward. Once this motion is learned, the students can transfer it to the instrument fingerboard. Instruct them to practice the same motion on the fingerboard—first with pizzicato and then with bowed pitches.

Extending Forward. Lead students through the following sequenced steps. Instruct them to (1) hold their right arm near chin level and positioned parallel to the floor; (2) place their left hand on their arm, shaped as if playing in first position (the left hand should hang on their right arm. The thumb should be positioned behind the second finger but hanging underneath the arm); (3) practice opening and closing the space between their first and second fingers. The first finger should pivot. The second finger should alternate between moving closer and farther from the index finger. The thumb should move with the hand, touching underneath the arm and remaining behind the second finger; (4) practice Step 3 on the string; (5) continue the motion involved in Steps 3 and 4 and pizzicato the pitches played by the first finger, extended second finger, and fourth fingers; (6) repeat Step 5, bowing the pitches.

SHIFTING: GENERAL PRINCIPLES

Shifting involves sliding the left hand smoothly and lightly on the string to a new location. The thumb should travel with the hand. When shifting, students must be careful to maintain their left-hand shape. The speed of the shift should be controlled and consistent. The hand must not be jerked from one position to the next. Encourage students to lighten the weight of their left hand on the string before and during the shift.

Students should gently stop their bow before moving their left hand when shifting between notes that are not slurred. In shifts between notes that are slurred, students may slow their bow down and lighten the weight on the bow. This helps minimize the sound of the finger sliding on the string during the shift.

A basic shifting principle is that the hand should shift on the last finger that was down in the old position. The hand should shift on that finger to the new position. Then the new finger in the new position should be placed on the string. This principle of shifting on the old finger (last finger used in the previous position) to the new position is used in most shifting passages. The shifting finger is sometimes called the transport finger. It is used to transport the hand from one position to another. See Chapter 5 for more melodic and expressive shifting. The following illustration (Figure 4.14) shows an example of a shift on a transport finger.

Figure 4.14 Shifting on a transport finger to a new position.

Intermediate shifting skills involve violin and viola players shifting to third position. In ascending shifts, players should slightly close their arm at the shoulder joint and close their elbow joint; in descending shifts, players should slightly open their arm at the shoulder and open their elbow joint.

Cello intermediate shifting skills involve students shifting to and from fourth position and sometimes third position. During ascending shifts, the arm should open slightly from the shoulder joint and the elbow joint should open; during descending shifts, the arm and elbow joints should close.

Basses are already shifting at least to second position during the first two years of instruction. Intermediate skills for the double bass involve shifting to half, third, and fifth and a half positions. When shifting among these positions, bass students should keep their second finger behind their thumb, and their wrist, hand, and arm should be generally in a straight line.

When students are first developing their shifting skills, have them simply slide their hand up and down the fingerboard to refine their general shifting motions. As their skill develops, have students pizzicato specific notes when shifting to specific pitches that are located in different positions. Finally, have students bow while shifting, first without slurring and later slurring between pitches that involve a shift.

Placing a dash before a finger number in a new position helps students remember to shift. Notice in Figure 4.1 a dash (-) before a finger number indicating a shift.

PEDAGOGY FOR TEACHING SHIFTING

Evaluate students' general left-hand skills before beginning to focus specifically on developing their shifting skills. They should be able to play a Grade 1 and easier Grade 2 piece (see Chapter 10 for examples) while maintaining an acceptable left-hand shape.

The following pre-shifting teaching strategies are designed to help students relax their left hand and thumb when shifting, develop their right-hand and left-hand coordination, and prepare them for developing their fundamental and intermediate shifting skills.

Sliding between Strings. Have students slide their fingers up and down the fingerboard between any two adjacent strings. Watch students' thumbs to be certain they are moving with the hand and that students are maintaining their general hand shape while sliding between the strings.

How Many Harmonics Can You Find? Challenge students to move their hands up and down the length of the fingerboard to find as many harmonics as they can. Students should be able to find at least three or four harmonics at the intermediate level of playing.

Tunneling. Ask students to place their fingers on one string so that a tunnel is formed over an adjacent string (e.g., violin and viola students place their fingers on the D string, forming a tunnel over the A string). Have students shift up and down the fingered string while sounding the string that is tunneled. (Note: It is easiest for students to first pizzicato the tunneled string. Later they can bow the string while shifting on the tunneled string.)

Sliding Geminiani Chords. Have students position one finger lightly on each of the four strings and slide their hands up and down the fingerboard.

One-Finger Scales. Have students play scales using the same finger for each note. Encourage students to play each tetrachord on a different string. Check to see that students are maintaining their hand shape and moving their thumb with their hand when shifting to each new pitch. Have students first pizzicato the scales. As students' shifting skills develop they can bow the scales while shifting.

One-Finger Melodies. Have students select an easy review melody and play it using the same finger for each pitch.

Paper Slides. Have students place tissue paper on their fingerboard, below the strings. Ask them to slide their hands up and down the fingerboard with their fingers on the tissue paper. This strategy should help students' left hands relax and slide lightly on the string while shifting.

Tap and Slide. Have students tap their thumbs lightly before shifting. This should release some of the weight on the thumb and fingers as the hand prepares to shift.

Shuttle Shifts. Have students shift on one string while they pizzicato an adjacent string (e.g., shift on the D string with the first and second fingers while plucking the A string with the fourth finger).

VIBRATO: GENERAL PRINCIPLES

Once students have developed shifting skills between lower positions (positions between first and fourth on the violin, viola, and cello, plus half position on the double bass), especially shifted pitches that are slurred, they are ready to develop their basic vibrato skills. Students must have well-developed independence of hands to be able to bow pitches that are vibrated.

Vibrato on string instruments involves slightly changing the string length by rolling the left hand on the string. Vibrato motion is generated by moving the arm and hand as a unit on the cello and bass. On the violin and viola, the arm and hand can move either as a unit or independently. Vibrato motion is measured by its speed and width: the lower the pitch, the slower and wider the vibrato motion.

Rolling the fingertip on the string while flexing the first knuckle joint produces violin and viola vibrato. It is critical that the first knuckle flex. It is the bending of the knuckle joint that causes the pitch change in vibrato. The flex or bend of the knuckles is caused either by waving the hand from the wrist joint or by moving the arm and hand as a unit. These two different vibrato motions are referred to as hand and arm vibrato. Vibrato generated by the hand waving is often referred to as wrist vibrato. Hand (wrist) and arm vibrato are equally valuable. Introduce both motions to students. Some will find one of the motions easier than the other. Allow each student to first develop the type she finds easiest. Eventually students should be able to execute both types.

Upper string instrument vibrato often takes longer to develop than lower strings because of the complexity of the motions involved. Encourage students to be patient and careful in working on their vibrato. They will be successful if they spend the necessary effort and concentration.

Cello and bass vibrato involves rolling the finger on the string by moving the arm and hand in a straight line. The arm and hand act as a unit. When sustaining pitches are vibrated, it is permissible for the thumb not to touch the back of the neck, if the player wishes.

Vibrating properly on a string instrument is a complex skill. It is best developed gradually over an extended period of time. A little vibrato practice incorporated into classes over many months is much more effective than concentrating on vibrato motions during a few weeks of instruction. Spend only a few minutes per class working on developing students' vibrato motions so that incorrect motions, frustration, and excessive left-hand tension does not occur.

PEDAGOGY FOR TEACHING VIBRATO

Student vibrato motions should first be slow and wide. As vibrato develops, the motion can easily be refined using the following four-step vibrato teaching sequence taken from *Essential Technique for Strings* (published by Hal Leonard Corporation, used with permission, copyright 1997, all rights reserved).

Step 1

Violin and Viola

At the Bout. Have students place their third fingers on top of the violin or viola, with their hand against the bout, as illustrated in Figure 4.15. Instruct them to wave their hands for hand vibrato or move their arms for arm vibrato. For hand vibrato, the wrist should always touch the bout in Step 1; for arm vibrato, the wrist should remain straight as it moves away from the bout. For both vibrato types, the first knuckle joint of the finger should bend. It is helpful if the fingernail touches the side of the fingerboard while practicing At the Bout. Once students have mastered the motion with their third finger, have them try other fingers. Only one finger at a time should be used. Then have students place their instruments in playing position on their shoulders and continue practicing the motions. Check that the motion is parallel to the side of the fingerboard at all times.

Cello and Double Bass

The Slide. Cello and bass vibrato motion is produced by a combination of sliding and pivoting. "To develop these motions, first have students place their second fingers on the A string, with their thumbs behind the neck, opposite the second finger. The thumb may or may not touch the neck. Have students slide their fingers up and down the string, covering the distance of about three half steps, then gradually shorten the distance, from two half-steps to finally one half-step. Be sure the thumb slides with the hand, eventually touching the neck" (p. 226). See Figure 4.16.

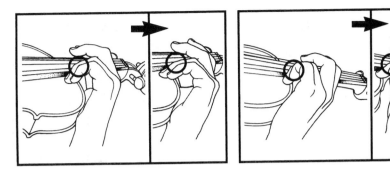

Figure 4.15 Step 1 for violin and viola vibrato: At the Bout, using hand vibrato (left) and arm vibrato (right).

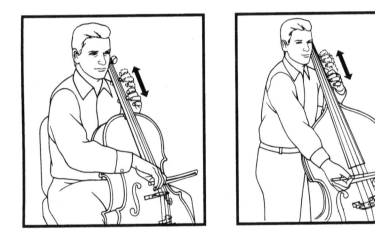

Figure 4.16 Step 1 for cello (left) and bass (right) vibrato: The Slide.

"After students have mastered The Slide, have them hold their bow at the balance point and bow above the strings while sliding, beginning to coordinate the right and left hands. Eventually have them bow on the string while sliding their left hand along the string" (p. 226). Refer to Figure 4.16.

Step 2

Violin and Viola

On the String. While they are in playing position, have students place their fingertips on the D string or A string and continue their vibrato motion. Their wrists should always touch the bout if hand vibrato motion is used; the wrist should bump away from the bout if arm motion is used. Check to see if the first knuckle joint of the vibrating finger is flexing. See Figure 4.17.

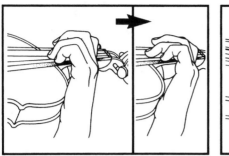 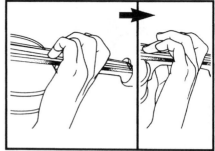

Figure 4.17 Step 2 for violin and viola vibrato: On the String, using hand vibrato (left) and arm vibrato (right).

Cello and Double Bass

The Pivot. Once lower string students have mastered the sliding motion, which prepares them for vibrato, they are ready to begin learning the pivoting motion involved in vibrating. Keeping their left-hand fingers moderately straight, students should touch their collarbones with the end of their second fingers, as illustrated in Figure 4.18. Students should pivot or rotate their arm while keeping their elbow motionless. "Check that students' forearms are rotating without moving their elbow up and down" (p. 227). See Figure 4.18.

If necessary, students may practice The Pivot motion with elbows touching a wall as illustrated (see Figure 4.18). Elbows should not move on the wall. This teaching strategy encourages proper pivoting motion.

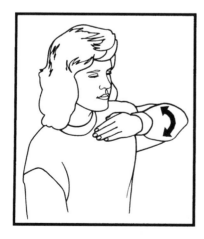 

Figure 4.18 Step 2 for cello and bass vibrato: The Pivot (left) and checking the pivoting motion against the wall (right).

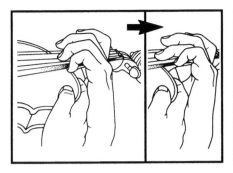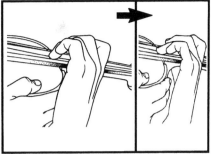

Figure 4.19 Step 3 for violin and viola vibrato: Lend a Helping Hand, using hand vibrato (left) and arm vibrato (right).

Step 3

Violin and Viola

Lend a Helping Hand. Violin and viola students should place two fingers of their right hand on the bout as illustrated in Figure 4.19. Hand vibrato students should touch their left wrists with their fingers and continue practicing their vibrato motion on the string. Arm vibrato students should touch their left wrists with their fingers, but should alternate moving their hand toward and away from them by moving their arm. The wrist should remain straight, and the arm should move from the elbow joint. Be sure that students' vibrating finger knuckles are bending.

Cello and Double Bass

Pivot and Bow. Have students continue practicing their pivoting motion. Once the motion is mastered, have them air bow above the string while pivoting. Consider having students hold their bows at the balance point when bowing in the air above the string to avoid cramping their bow hand. Once students can pivot while air bowing, have them begin to bow an adjacent open string while pivoting (e.g., bowing the open A string while pivoting on the D string). Students should first pull faster bows to help the left hand continue to pivot properly and then gradually slow down the bow speed for playing longer bow strokes. See Figure 4.20.

Step 4

Violin and Viola

Back Down the String. Instruct students to move their left hands to first position. "Have them touch their left arms just below their wrists with their right hand fingers as illustrated" (p. 229). The right hand fingers serve as a bout, as the wrist was a bout when vibrating in higher positions was first learned.

"Students should then practice their vibrato motions. If they are attempting hand (wrist) vibrato, be sure that their arms and wrists are relaxed, but not

Figure 4.20 Step 3 for cello (left) and bass (right) vibrato: Pivot and Bow.

moving; if they are attempting arm vibrato, be sure that their hands and arms remain in a straight line as they are moving their arms back and forth. For both vibrato types it is critical that the first knuckle joint of the vibrating finger flexes (bends)" (p. 229). As students master the vibrato motion with their third finger, have them practice vibrating with other fingers. See Figure 4.21.

"It is helpful if students vibrate with their vibrating fingers only touching the string. Also, their base hand knuckles may lightly touch and slide along the neck of the instrument while vibrating, or not touch at all. Once students have mastered the vibrato motion with right hand fingers touching, they should gradually remove their right hand fingers. If students are able to continue vibrating properly, they are ready to begin bowing while vibrating. If not, students should continue practicing their vibrato motions before adding the bow" (p. 230).

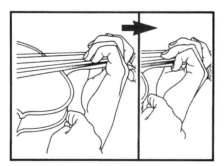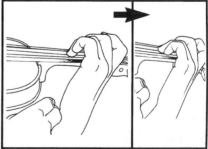

Figure 4.21 Step 4 for violin and viola vibrato: Back Down the String, using hand vibrato (left) and arm vibrato (right).

Cello and Double Bass

You've Made It! "Once students have mastered bowing an open string while vibrating with a proper motion on another string, they are ready to bow vibrating pitches. With their left thumbs behind the neck of the instrument, they should place their second fingers on the string in first position (second-finger C-natural on the A string for cello, and second-finger B-flat on the G string for bass). Students should begin bowing while vibrating" (p. 230). Once this is mastered, students are ready to begin using other fingers. See Figure 4.22.

In addition to this four-step teaching process, the following are some of the other rote strategies that may be used to develop students' basic vibrato skills on all four string instruments.

Tissue Vibrato. Place tissue paper between the strings and fingerboard. Have students practice their vibrato motions with their fingers on the strings and tissue paper. The tissue paper helps relax students' hands.

Air Vibrato. Have students practice their vibrato motions in the air, away from their instruments.

Neighbor Bowing. Divide students into groups of two. Have one student bow while the other vibrates.

Vibrato Harmonics. Have students play a harmonic and then slide or roll their finger lightly on the string above and below the pitch.

Movin' Those Feet While Vibrating. Ask students to tap a toe or foot while vibrating, with one foot motion per vibrato motion. This allows students to practice together their vibrato motions at the same tempo.

Vibrating to the Click. Use a metronome to coordinate students' vibrato motions when they are practicing as a class. Incorporate one vibrato motion per click. Encourage students to tap their toes or feet with the metronome click. Find the tempo at which all students vibrate properly, and gradually increase the tempo on the metronome at each class meeting.

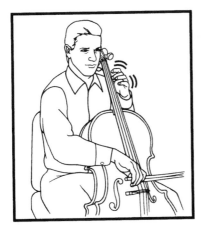 

Figure 4.22 Step 4 for cello (left) and base (right) vibrato: You've Made It!

DOUBLE BASS PIVOTING: GENERAL GUIDELINES

One of the most recent developments in double bass playing is pivoting with the left hand on the thumb. When passages fall a half step above or below the normal hand shape, bass players normally shift to those pitches. However, some bass players believe that in third position or above, the performer should experiment with rolling or pivoting on the thumb to those pitches rather than shifting. This involves rolling the hand on the thumb backward or forward instead of moving the location of the thumb on the neck as in shifting.

Give students an opportunity to experiment with pivoting their left hands in higher positions. They may find the motion easier and more efficient than always shifting to pitches nearby. If they are studying privately, defer to the opinion of their private teacher to determine if and when students should pivot.

PEDAGOGY FOR DEVELOPING INTERMEDIATE AURAL SKILLS IN THE SCHOOL ORCHESTRA

In addition to developing students' intermediate bowing and left-hand skills, developing their aural skills is also critical. Intermediate aural skills include developing students' abilities to do the following:

1. match pitch patterns found in the more complex scales, such as the F, B-flat, and A-major scales and their relative minor scales
2. match double stops
3. play melodies by ear
4. perform and understand ensemble primary chords

Continue to review students' pitch-matching skills, introduced during the first and second years of instruction. Consider using the following teaching strategies to develop students' intermediate aural skills.

Intermediate Pitch Matching

Four-Note Echoes. Have students echo four pitches played by the leader, as during the first two years of instruction (see Chapter 3). Incorporate pitches in the F, B-flat, and A-major scales, including pitches on the C string for the viola and cello, and the E string on the violin and bass. Also include fragments from the g, a, and e natural minor scales. As students' pitch-matching skills develop, include different bow strokes, tempos, and dynamics in the echoes. Also include some pitch patterns that involve shifting and vibrato.

Matching Arpeggios. Have students match arpeggios by ear from the D, G, C, F, and B-flat-major scales and their relative minors.

Finding Octaves. Have students find as many octaves of the same pitch by ear (e.g., finding four Ds on their instruments).

Matching Leaps. Have students, by ear, match pitch patterns that include intervals of a major or minor third (or both major and minor).

Matching Octaves. Have students echo pitch patterns in an octave different from the leader's pattern.

Six-Note Echoes. Once students can reliably match four-note echoes, begin to incorporate six- and eight-note patterns for students to imitate by ear.

Altered Melodies. Have students imitate, by ear, familiar melodies that contain altered pitches (e.g., "Happy Birthday" melody in minor).

Section Matching. Challenge each instrument section to compose its own fragment to play as a group for the rest of the class to echo.

Matching Double Stops

As their pitch-matching skills advance, intermediate students can develop the skill to match more than one pitch played at a time. Begin by using the following teaching sequence to develop their skills to match simple double stops (two notes played at the same time with one of the pitches an open string). Play and have students match the following:

1. open strings played separately and together
2. an open string and a pitch played with the first finger in first position on an adjacent string [Play the pitches separately first and then together for students to echo.]
3. an open string and a pitch played a minor or major second above the open string of an adjacent string [Play the pitches separately first, and then together, for students to echo.]

Matching Octave Doubles. Have students find and play simple octave double stops (e.g., one pitch is an open string, and the other pitch is a fingered pitch an octave higher or lower).

Tuning Section Doubles. Have one section play a scale or short passage in one key, while another section of the orchestra, or the rest of the orchestra, sustains the tonic of the key.

Play Melodies by Ear

Challenge students to play melodies by ear. Playing melodies by ear should be introduced in beginning classes. Intermediate skills involve giving students different starting pitches of a melody so that they must transpose it to different keys by ear.

Melodies that are familiar to the students are the best to use (e.g., "Jingle Bells," "Happy Birthday," "Row, Row, Row Your Boat," "Wedding March," "America the Beautiful," "Good King Wenceslas," "For He's a Jolly Good Fellow," "Home on the Range," "Deck the Hall," and "Joy to the World").

Perform and Understand Ensemble Primary Triads

As students' abilities to match pitch patterns in multiple keys and simple double stops by ear increase, they will have enough aural training to prepare them to perform harmonic chord progressions and increase their harmonic listening skills. Begin by explaining to students how primary triads are formed. Write the pitches on the board in the tonic, subdominant, and dominant chords of familiar keys. Describe how the chords are formed. Play the chords for students on a keyboard if one is available. Once students understand how the chords are formed, they can be given opportunities to perform the chords as an ensemble. Use the following teaching strategies, beginning with the chords as an ensemble. Begin with the chords in D major and then G major.

Ensemble Primary Chords. Assign one pitch of the tonic triad to each string section. In the easiest formation, ask students to play the pitches in first position on their instruments. Give basses and cellos the root of the chord, the violas and second violins the third of the chord, and the first violins the fifth of the chord. Have students play the pitches at the same time to sound the chord. Repeat the process, creating the subdominant and dominant chords in root position.

Change Up Ensemble Primary Chords. Form inversions of the primary chords by giving the third or fifth of the chords to the basses and cellos.

Finger Signals. Have the leader hold up fingers indicating the chords the orchestra is supposed to play (e.g., one finger for the primary chord, four fingers for the subdominant chord, and five fingers for the dominant chord).

Primary Chords by Ear. Play primary chords on the keyboard and have the orchestra listen and then echo. One pitch of each chord should be assigned to the same instrument section (e.g., the root of the third always played by the cellos and basses, the third always played by the violas).

Chords on the Board. Write a primary chord progression on the board and have the orchestra perform it.

Student-Led Chord Progression. Choose the key and write on the board the chord symbols for primary chords. Select a student to point to each chord as the orchestra plays them.

INTERMEDIATE INSTRUMENT TUNING

Continue reviewing the instrument tuning strategies described in Chapter 3. Then introduce and regularly review the simple double stop pitch-matching strategies described in this chapter. Also, have violin, viola, and cello students practice bowing two open strings together with a light bow stroke. Violin and viola students should play in the upper half of the bow, cellos in the middle or lower half. Show basses how to place their left hands in fourth position, and match the harmonic under their fourth finger on one string to the first finger on the adjacent string. The two harmonics should sound the same when the strings are in tune with each other.

As students are learning to tune, frequently play for them two strings together that are in tune and out of tune. Violin, viola, and cello students need to learn to discriminate aurally between open strings that are accurately tuned a perfect fifth apart, and when the strings are not in tune with each other.

Once students are competent with the previous skills, establish one of the following tuning routines.

Sample Tuning Routine 1

- Model A pitch is sounded by a student, teacher, or electronic tuner.
- All instruments tune A strings quietly to the model.
- All instruments tune D strings to A strings.
- All instruments sound and compare D strings.
- All instruments tune G strings to D strings.
- All instruments sound and compare G strings.
- Violas and cellos tune C strings to G strings.
- Violas and cellos sound and compare C strings.
- Basses tune E strings to A strings.
- Basses sound and compare E strings.
- Violins tune E strings to A strings.
- Violins sound and compare E strings.

Sample Tuning Routine 2

- Model A is sounded by teacher, student, or electronically.
- Basses tune their harmonic A on the D string to the model A.
- Basses use harmonic tuning to compare each string.
- Continue with Tuning Routine 1.

PROBLEM SOLVING: INTERMEDIATE STUDENTS' COMMON PLAYING PROBLEMS AND SOLUTIONS

The following table provides examples of some of the most common playing problems intermediate students experience. Titles of various teaching strategies described in this chapter are suggested to solve problems.

Problem	Solution
Harsh détaché tone	Give Me an SWS!
	Pounds
Bowing not parallel to the bridge	Lanes
	Buddy Bowing
	Rockin' Bows
Uneven sound production	Miles per Hour
Scratchy direction changes	Balancing and Rubbing
Stiff faster string crossings	Variable Speed Crossings
	Variable Place Crossings
Harsh staccato tone	Pinch, Pull, Release
	Pinch and Glide
No accent at beginning of	Index Finger Pinches
martelé or staccato strokes	All Finger Pinches
	Pizzicato Martelés

(continued)

Problem	Solution
Harsh, stiff spiccato stroke	Balance Point Rub
	To the Frog We Go
	Balance Point Bounce
	Heard But Not Seen
Body slumping while playing	Crunches
	String Flying
Instrument slouching	Crunches
	String Flying
	Timing
Flat fingers on string	Doublin' Up
	Tappin'
Violin/viola: Fourth finger flat	Add a Note
Tense left-hand fingers	Tappin'
	Anchor and Slide
	Anchor and Tap
Cello: Extending between third and fourth finger	Left hand hangs down from first finger on the right arm. Open web between first and second fingers.
	Open web between first and second finger on arm, then string, then with pizzicato, and then by bowing between first finger and extended second finger.
Tense shifting	Sliding between Strings
	How Many Harmonics Can You Find
	Paper Slides
Hand shape changes during shift	Sliding Geminiani Chords
	Shuttle Shifts
Thumb does not move with the hand when shifting	Tap and Slide
	One-Finger Scales
Violin/viola: Wrist waving while vibrating	Four-step sequence
Tense vibrato motion	Tissue Vibrato
	Air Vibrato
	Vibrato Harmonics
Uncontrolled vibrato speed	Movin' Those Feet While Vibrating
	Vibrating to the Click
Cello/bass: Elbow/hand lowers while vibrating	Steps 1 and 2 from four-step sequence

5

ADVANCED STRING
CLASS INSTRUCTION

GOALS AND OBJECTIVES OF ADVANCED PLAYING SKILLS

Once students have mastered intermediate performance skills, as described in Chapter 4, they are ready to learn more advanced ones. These would typically occur in the high school orchestra if students had received three or four years of prior instruction. The goals and objectives of advanced bowing, left-hand, and aural skills include the following:

Bowing Skills

- Expressive détaché
- Louré (portato)
- Sul tasto
- Ponticello
- Controlled tremolo
- Collé
- Fast string crossings
- Expressive spiccato
- Sautillé

Left-Hand Skills

- Refined two-octave scales through four sharps and four flats
- Introduction of three-octave scales
- Refined shifting
- Refined vibrato

Aural Skills

- Advanced pitch-matching skills
- Ability to play melodies by ear in multiple keys

- Ability to perform and understand ensemble secondary chords
- Ability to select chords by ear to accompany scales
- Ability to demonstrate more advanced improvisation skills

PEDAGOGY FOR TEACHING EXPRESSIVE DÉTACHÉ BOWING

Review the teaching strategies for developing the intermediate détaché bow stroke in the third- and fourth-year classes (see Chapter 4). Once students have achieved these skills, they are ready to refine their détaché bowing to play more expressively. Use the following activities to help students develop their expressive détaché bowing.

Expressive Dynamics. Lead students to experiment with different crescendos and decrescendos throughout the bow, (e.g., one long crescendo on the up bow and one decrescendo on the down bow, two crescendos/decrescendos per bow, and so on). Vary the tempo and dynamic ranges involved.

Subito Dynamic Changes. Have students practice sudden dynamic changes, first on open strings and then with fingered pitches. Have students explore differences between forzando and forte piano. A forte piano involves leaning on the bow stick slightly, followed by a release; a forzando involves more of an accent at the beginning of a stroke, followed by a quick release.

Timed Bowing. Time the length of students' bow strokes. Begin with faster bows (e.g., bowing from the frog to the tip in fifteen seconds). Gradually increase the length of time until students can maintain one bow stroke from the frog to the tip, or tip to the frog, in one minute.

Equal Sound Throughout. Ask students to close their eyes while bowing and listen to the sound of their down bow stroke compared with the up bow stroke. Challenge them to maintain the same sound throughout the length of the stroke and to produce an equal down and up stroke. This typically involves increasing the weight of the bow stroke toward the tip and decreasing the weight toward the frog.

Changing Speeds with Clicks. Have the orchestra practice with a metronome to increase its ability to maintain the same bow speed or change it at will. Begin with the metronome at 60, and have students play one bow length with four clicks to the stroke on both the down and up bow. Then begin to increase the number of clicks per bow stroke (e.g., five clicks per stroke, six clicks per stroke). Eventually change the number of clicks between the down and up bow strokes (e.g., five clicks on the down bow and six clicks on the up bow, and so on).

PEDAGOGY FOR TEACHING LOURÉ (PORTATO) BOWING

Louré bowing involves two or more notes that are hooked or linked together with only a slight pause or articulation between the notes. Another common term for louré is portato. Students should lean their hand on the index finger slightly to create the pause between the hooked pitches. Review the strategies for developing stopped bow stroke skills introduced at early levels (see Chapters 3 and 4). Then use the following strategies to help students develop skills for louré bowing.

Wavy Bows. Have students press and release their hands on the bow as they are playing a long stroke. The bow stick should go up and down slightly while the bow hair stays on the string. Students should lean slightly on the index finger when depressing the stick. As students' skill develops, have them stop their bows momentarily between the release of one wave and the lean starting the next wave.

Hooked Staccato vs. Louré. Have students alternate groups of pitches that are performed with hooked staccato strokes and then with louré strokes. Show students how both strokes are similar (staccato involves more weight at the beginning of the stroke and less release of the weight compared with louré). Staccato is an accented stroke. Louré is not.

Scaling Styles. Have students play scales while alternating different bow strokes (e.g., ascending first tetrachord legato, ascending second tetrachord staccato, descending first tetrachord louré, descending second tetrachord spiccato).

Theme from Beethoven's Symphony No. 7. Play a recording, demonstrate, or show students the opening melody of the first movement of Beethoven's Symphony No. 7. This is a musical example of a melody that uses louré bowing (see Figure 5.1). Have students practice playing the melody with louré bowing.

PEDAGOGY FOR TEACHING SUL TASTO BOWING

Sul tasto bowing involves a very light bow stroke performed over the fingerboard with flat bow hair, with a faster bow speed, in the upper half of the bow. Sul tasto bowing appears often in music by impressionistic composers such as Debussy and Ravel. The following strategies will help students learn to play this bow stroke.

Fingerboard Lanes. A sound production teaching strategy introduced to intermediate students in Chapter 4 divided the string between the bridge and the fingerboard into various bowing lanes or paths. Now add lanes over the end of the fingerboard that students can use for sul tasto bowing (e.g., lane 6 is at the end of the fingerboard and lane 7 farther down the fingerboard).

Sul Tasto Dynamics. Sul tasto bowing is performed at a very quiet dynamic level such as piano or pianissimo. Have students play with their bows on the string over the fingerboard and experiment while trying to play loud dynamics. They will suddenly realize that sul tasto bowing must be performed with a soft dynamic. When weight is added to the bow over the fingerboard, the sound produced will be muffled, scratchy, and unpleasant.

PEDAGOGY FOR TEACHING PONTICELLO BOWING

Once students have learned to play accurately with sul tasto bowing, it is easy for them to learn to play ponticello bowing. In short, ponticello bowing is sul

Figure 5.1

Theme from Symphony No. 7   Ludwig van Beethoven

tasto bowing next to the bridge. The bow hair is placed flat on the string either slightly touching the bridge or immediately next to the bridge. The bow
is pulled fast with little weight placed on it. The eerie sound produced is used
to produce chilling or suspenseful sound effects. Composers will write the word
ponticello, or its abbreviation, *pont.*, over notes to played with a ponticello bow
stroke. The following practice strategies will help students to develop their
ponticello bowing.

Lane 5. Number the lane near the bridge as lane 1. Then divide the distance
between lane 1 and the fingerboard into five lanes. Have students practice their
ponticello bowing in lane 1. Once that skill is mastered, have them begin alternating lane 1 with the other lanes between the bridge and fingerboard.

Ponticello vs. Sul Tasto. Compare ponticello and sul tasto bow strokes for
students. Point out that both are light bow strokes, performed with flat bow
hair, with a fairly fast bow speed. Point out to students that the major differ-

ence between the strokes is the location of the bow hair on the string: ponticello is near the bridge, and sul tasto is on or near the fingerboard.

The Recipe. Use an analogy of adding ingredients in a food recipe to produce a ponticello bow stroke: add flat bow hair, faster bow speed, no weight on the bow, and bow location next to the bridge and ponticello bowing is produced!

PEDAGOGY FOR TEACHING CONTROLLED TREMOLO BOWING

Short passages involving tremolo bowing can be easily performed by younger players by having them stiffen their arms and wrists while moving the bow quickly back and forth on the string with short bow strokes. However, more skill is needed to play a longer tremolo passage and to refine the speed and sound of tremolo.

Tremolo bowing is usually performed in the middle to upper half of the bow. It may be produced either by waving the bow hand from the wrist or by moving the entire arm, wrist, and hand as a unit. Tremolo produced by waving the hand works well for longer passages of tremolo bowing and for those passages that require quiet, soft dynamics. Tremolo produced by moving the arm, wrist, and hand as a unit can produce louder, shorter tremolo passages.

Tremolo is indicated by three ledger lines on a pitch (♪.) Sometimes a composer wants a specific number of tremolo strokes per pitch (referred to as measured tremolo). If the composer does not indicate the number of tremolo strokes, it is up to the conductor's interpretation.

The following strategies will help students develop their tremolo bowing skills.

Hand Waving Tremolo. Have students place their bows lightly on the string in the upper half of the bow. Instruct them to wave their hands from their wrist joint, quickly moving one or two inches back and forth on the string. Request students to experiment with different tremolo speeds and dynamics. Once the skill is mastered, have students practice playing scales with tremolo bowing on each pitch.

Loud, Fz, *and* Fp *Tremolos.* Show students how to play loud tremolo bowing by keeping the arm, wrist, and hand in a straight line while moving the bow quickly back and forth on the string with a loud dynamic. Have students imitate. Practice forzando (*fz*) within forte piano (*fp*) dynamics by pulling the bow faster and longer on the first stroke, followed by tremolo bowing.

Alternating Arm to Hand Tremolo, Accented, and Fp *Tremolo.* Practice with students alternating tremolo motions performed by their arm and then by their hand. Once that skill is mastered, have them practice playing forte piano tremolo pitches by first pulling the bow fast and heavy with the arm, immediately followed by a light hand-wave tremolo. Have students practice *fp* tremolo motions on each pitch of a scale. Then students can practice accented tremolos by slightly pulling the first tremolo stroke longer and by using an accent at the beginning.

PEDAGOGY FOR TEACHING COLLÉ BOWING

Collé is a short, accented stroke that is performed by placing and lifting the bow on the string using only the fingers of the bow hand. Little arm motion is involved. The hand should move freely from the wrist joint. There is an accent at the beginning of the stroke on the string, followed by the fingers lifting the bow off the string slightly. This stroke encourages the hand and fingers to bend and flex while playing. It also helps lower strings on the viola, cello, and bass (e.g., the C string on the viola and cello and the E string on the double bass) to sound immediately at the beginning of a stroke. Strategies such as the following will help develop students' collé strokes.

Frog Collé. Have students practice short collé strokes at the frog of the bow. Have them first practice the strokes all down bow, then all up bow, and finally alternate bow directions. Check that students use primarily their fingers to lift and set the bow for each stroke.

Pizzicato Collé. Demonstrate for students the similarity in sound of a short, accented collé stroke and the sound of a loud pizzicato produced near the bridge. Both sounds are quite similar. Have students work to make the collé strokes sound like their pizzicato.

Lower Collé. Have students practice their collé bowing motions (the set and lift with the fingers) in different places on the string in the lower half of the bow.

PEDAGOGY FOR TEACHING FAST STRING CROSSINGS

Faster string crossings follow this principle: the faster the string crossing, the less arm motion and more wrist and hand motion involved. Also, the faster the string crossing, the smaller the motion. Faster string crossings are performed most easily near the balance point or middle of the bow.

Review the intermediate skill string crossing teaching strategies described in Chapter 4. Once those strategies have been reviewed and mastered, introduce the following more advanced strategies. Be sure to practice all strategies using crosswise motions and counterclockwise motions, both on the beat and before the beat.

Metronome Crossings. Use a metronome to coordinate the speed of string crossing warm-ups in class. Determine which strings will be crossed. The sound of the string crossings should be in unison. One click on the metronome should equal one string crossing. Gradually increase the speed of the metronome, reminding students to decrease their arm motion while increasing their hand and wrist motions as the tempo increases. Ask students to begin crossing at the balance point of their bows and eventually in other places in the bow.

Foot Crossings. Have students tap their feet or toes to the beat while practicing string crossings. One foot or toe tap equals one string crossing. Change the speed of the crossings by changing the speed of the taps.

Slurred String Crossings. Practice with students slurring across strings—first across two strings, then three strings, then all four strings. Begin with slower tempos and gradually increase to help students coordinate their motions. Once motions have been mastered on open strings, have them begin adding fingered pitches to their practice routine.

PEDAGOGY FOR TEACHING EXPRESSIVE SPICCATO

After students have developed their intermediate spiccato bowing skills (see Chapter 4), they are ready to develop an array of different spiccato strokes to match the expressive qualities of an off-the-string passage of music. For example, once students can control the basic bounce of the bow on the string, they can begin experimenting with different lengths of the bow on the string during the bounce, and with different heights of the bounce. Eventually students should be able to play an entire palette of spiccato sounds from short and percussive to longer, more lyrical bounces.

Begin by reviewing spiccato learning strategies in Chapter 4, and then proceed to teaching the following more advanced spiccato skills.

Trampoline Bounces. Begin by having students bounce their bows high off the string by rotating their right arms and hands. While keeping the same tempo, students should gradually move the bow bounces to the balance point of the bow or slightly below. Once at the balance point or slightly below, students should begin adding a short back-and-forth motion to the stroke. Have students experiment with different heights of the bow dropping on the string. Different heights produce different spiccato sounds: the larger the drop or lift, the more percussive the stroke.

Add-a-Lift. Instruct students to play with a light détaché stroke on the string at or slightly below the balance point of the bow. Students' fingers (including the thumb) and their wrists should react to the strokes on the string by slightly bending or flexing. Once students have demonstrated this motion, ask them to add a small lift to the stroke. Have students experiment with different lengths of the bow on the string between lifts.

Brush Strokes. Spiccato strokes that involve the bow on the string for longer periods of time between lifts are often called brush strokes. These brush strokes involve dropping the bow on the string from a height very close to the string, pulling the bow on the string, and then slightly lifting the bow. The motion is analogous to the movement involved in painting a wall with a paintbrush. Have students experiment with different heights of the lift and drop of the bow on the string, and with the length of the bow stroke on the string.

Heard But Not Seen. To refine students' spiccato strokes, ask them to practice their spiccato bounces with their eyes closed. Instruct them to listen carefully to the glance of the bow hair hitting the string. With their eyes closed, they can experiment with the different motions involved in producing an array of different bounce sounds, from long brush strokes to short, percussive strokes.

Alternating On to Off. Have students practice on the string and gradually alternate with off-the-string bounces. Begin with four strokes on the string, followed by four spiccato bounces, then advance to four on the string to six off-

Figure 5.2 Diagrams representing different heights and lengths of spiccato strokes.

the-string strokes, four on the string to eight off-the-string bounces, and so on. By returning each time to a few strokes on the string, the students' hands may relax so that their fingers and hands can react to the bounce when the bow is bounced once again.

Bounces on the Board. On the board, draw diagrams that represent different heights of the drop and lift of the bow and different lengths of the bow on the string in spiccato bowing, as shown in Figure 5.2.

Foot and Metronome Bounces. Have students tap their feet or toes to the click of a metronome in class: one bounce per click, then two bounces per click, then four bounces per click, and so on. Also, you may gradually increase the speed of the metronome.

Downs and Ups and Ups and Downs. Start spiccato warm-up passages or teaching strategies with the first bounce on a down bow. Once the motions are mastered, repeat the same activities beginning with an up bow.

String Crossings Bounces. Practice placing an adjacent open string bounce between each fingered pitch in a warm-up exercise or music passage. This helps students learn the slight hand and arm motions involved in both crossing strings and in bouncing among different strings.

Scales Are a Bouncin'. Practice playing scales with different types of spiccato bounces, with some pitches more percussive and others more brushed.

On the String First. Once spiccato motions are learned and refined, students are ready to use the strokes in their music. Be sure to give students the opportunity to first learn passages on the string to secure the left hand before adding the spiccato bounce. Great physical coordination is needed to bounce individual pitches in a musical passage. Once students' left-hand fingering is mastered, they are ready to add a spiccato bounce.

TWO-OCTAVE SCALES THROUGH FOUR SHARPS AND FOUR FLATS: GENERAL GUIDELINES

Review the teaching strategies for developing intermediate body position and left-hand skills (see Chapter 4). Once students have achieved these skills, they are ready to refine and extend their abilities so that they can adequately perform orchestral repertoire of publishers' music Grades 3 through 5.

Begin by reviewing the two-octave G, D, A, and B-flat-major scales (see Chapter 4). Then introduce the following additional two-octave major scales: C, F, and E-flat. As students are learning these scales, also introduce the following two-octave minor scales: a, e, d, g, and c. Figure 5.3 shows fingerings and fingerboard positions that may be used when playing each of the scales.

Figure 5.3

Figure 5.3   *(continued)*

E-flat-Major Scale

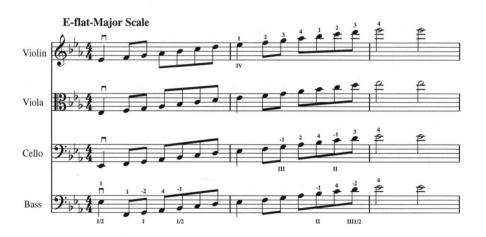

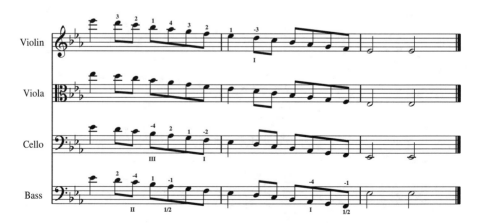

A-Natural Minor

A-Harmonic Minor

A-Natural Minor

Figure 5.3 (*continued*)

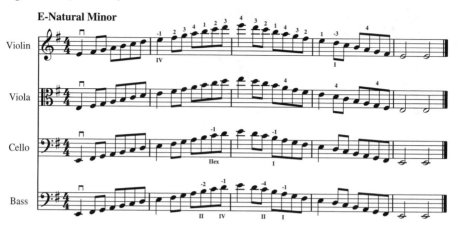

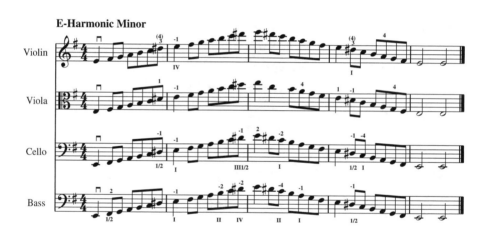

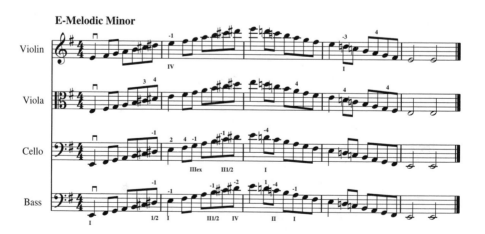

D-Natural Minor

D-Harmonic Minor

D-Melodic Minor

Figure 5.3   *(continued)*

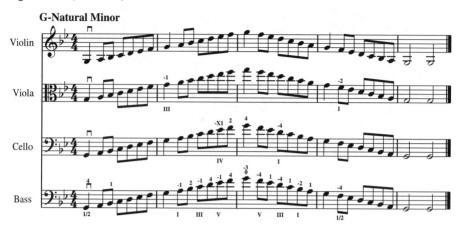

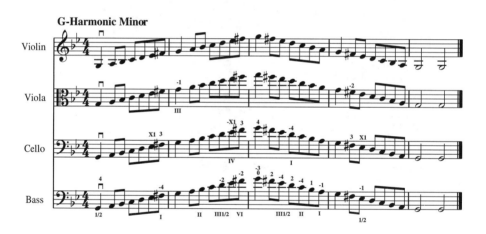

C-Natural Minor

C-Harmonic Minor

C-Melodic Minor

INTRODUCING THREE-OCTAVE SCALES: GENERAL GUIDELINES

Once students have mastered more advanced two-octave scales, they are ready to learn to play three-octave scales. Advanced high school orchestra, youth orchestra, regional, and all-state literature involves passages that include the upper registers of the instrument. Begin by having students practice each of the three octaves separately. As students become more comfortable with the upper octave, they may add the other octaves to form a three-octave scale. Use different slurring patterns, rhythms, articulations, and tempos as you rehearse the scales.

Figure 5.4 shows fingerings and fingerboard positions that may be used to play each of the scales in some of the keys most common to more advanced orchestral literature.

Figure 5.4

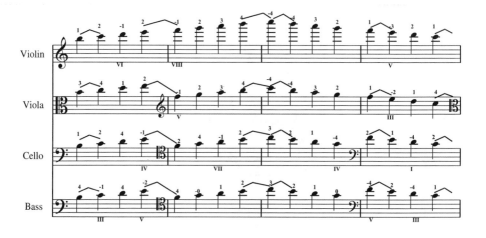

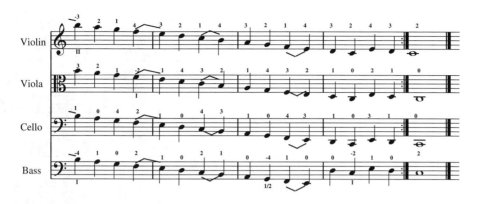

G-Major Scale

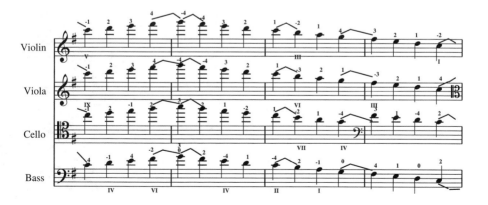

Figure 5.4 (*continued*)

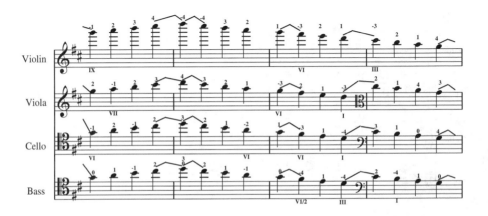

A-Major Scale

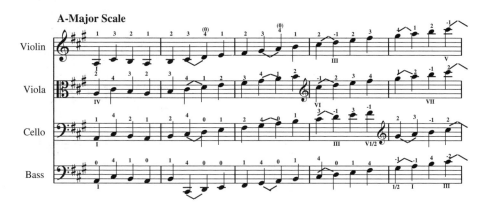

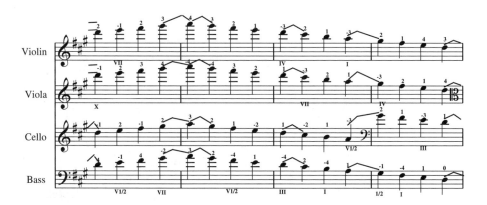

Figure 5.4   *(continued)*

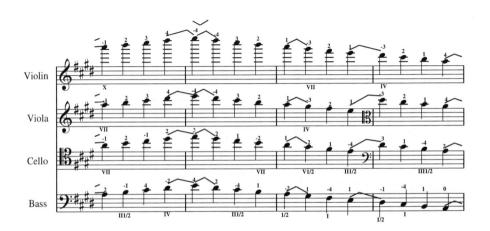

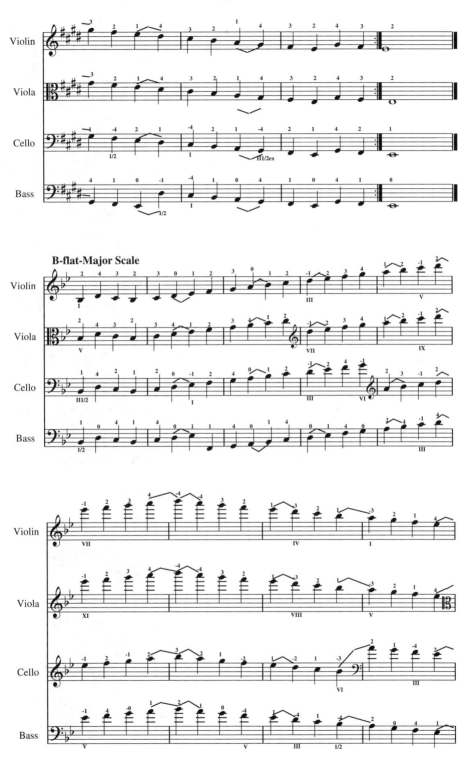

B-flat-Major Scale

Figure 5.4 (*continued*)

A-Melodic Minor Scale

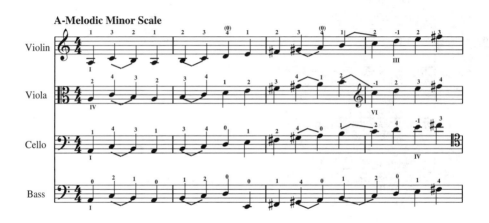

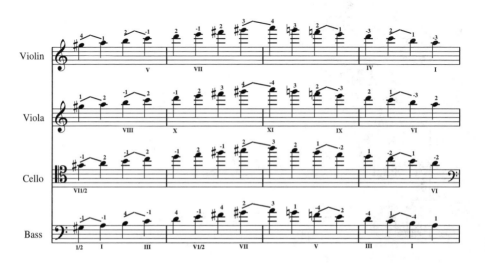

D-Melodic Minor Scale

Figure 5.4   (*continued*)

C-Melodic Minor Scale

Figure 5.4 (*continued*)

PEDAGOGY FOR REFINING SHIFTING

Review the shifting teaching strategies described in Chapter 4. Once students understand and can demonstrate fundamental shifting skills, use the following teaching strategies to refine them.

Checkpoints, Checkpoints. Use the following checkpoints to evaluate students' shifting skills:

1. The thumb travels with the hand.
2. A transport or guide finger is used when shifting.
3. The finger travels smoothly and lightly on the string during the shift.
4. The bow stops briefly between shifting notes that are not slurred.
5. The weight of the bow on the string lightens slightly during shifts between slurred pitches if attempting to diminish some of the shifting sound.
6. The left-hand shape generally stays the same during shifts involving positions one, two, three, and four.

Advanced Sliding between Strings. Have students slide their fingers between any two adjacent strings to and from higher fingerboard positions. Upper string students should swing their left elbows toward the centers of their bodies as they shift to higher positions; cello and double bass students should use their left thumbs to bar across the strings when playing in higher positions. The thumb is used to play pitches in extremely high registers. These registers do not typically appear in high school orchestral literature.

Finding Harmonics. Instruct students to lightly slide one finger up and down the length of one string. Have students find at least five harmonics on any one string. Students should play the harmonics separately and then slur from one harmonic to the next.

Slides in One Bow. Request students first to shift between any two pitches you select while slurring the two pitches. As students' skill develops, have them shift more than one time between the pitches in one bow (e.g., shifting between the pitches three times during one bow stroke).

Tremolo Shifts. Have students bow tremolo while shifting to and from pitches. This strategy helps students refine the independence of hands that is necessary for more advanced shifting skills.

Double Bass Dots. Place black adhesive dots on the player's side of the instrument neck to indicate the location of higher positions.

Wavy Bows. Have students practice increasing and decreasing weight (pressure) throughout the bow stroke. Then have them practice shifting motions during the release of weight. In this strategy, students will develop the skill to lighten the weight on the bow during shifts.

PEDAGOGY FOR REFINING VIBRATO

Review the vibrato teaching strategies described in Chapter 4. Once students can demonstrate a slow, wide, controlled vibrato, use the following teaching strategies to refine their vibrato motions.

Checkpoints, Checkpoints. Use the checkpoints listed in the following table to evaluate the basic vibrato skills of your students.

Skill	Checkpoint
Violin/Viola *Hand* (*Wrist*) Vibrato	The motion is generated by the hand waving from the wrist joint. The first knuckle of the vibrating finger flexes. There is only minimal arm motion. Only one vibrating finger is on the string at a time. The side of the hand slides up and down, either touching the side of the neck or positioned slightly away. The vibrato motion is even. There is an audible change in pitch, with an interval formed by the vibrato pitch and a pitch slightly below.
Violin/Viola *Arm* Vibrato	The motion is produced by moving the arm, wrist, and hand back and forth as a unit. The wrist is straight but relaxed, forming a straight line between the elbow and base hand knuckles. Only one vibrating finger is on the string at a time. The side of the hand slides up and down while touching the side of the neck, or the hand is positioned slightly away from the neck when the hand is vibrating. The motion is even. There is an audible change in pitch, with an interval involving the vibrato pitch and slightly below the pitch.
Cello/Bass Vibrato	The motion is produced by pivoting (rotating) the lower arm. The elbow does not move up and down. Only one vibrating finger is on the string, except for third finger, which may touch to assist the fourth finger when vibrating. There is an audible change in pitch with an interval formed by the vibrato pitch and a pitch slightly below.

Counting the Oscillations—Counting the What? As students are vibrating, they can count aloud the number of vibrato oscillations in one bow stroke. Consider sounding the pitch, rolling below the pitch, and then rolling back to the pitch as one oscillation. Once students' skills begin to develop, increase the number of oscillations per bow stroke.

Varying the Speed. Gradually have students speed up the tempo of their vibrato motion. Use a metronome, foot tap, or both to help coordinate students' motions in class.

Varying the Width. Give students opportunities to vary the width of their vibrato interval. Begin with wider intervals and then narrow them.

Fixin' the Nanny Goat. If you find students' vibrato motions are too fast, or the vibrato interval is too small, instruct them to (1) add more arm motion to widen the vibrato and (2) slow down the speed of the vibrato motion.

Attack Stroke Vibrato. Have students begin each vibrato motion with a bow accent. Pulling the bow faster to produce more sound or an accent often helps speed up a vibrato motion that is consistently too slow and wide.

Parallel Motion. Demonstrate to students that the desired vibrato motion for any of the four string instruments is parallel to the side of the finger, not across the fingerboard.

Alternating Vibrato Types. Once upper string students have mastered one of the basic types of vibrato (arm or hand/wrist), have them begin to learn the other type. Then have students practice scales, alternating vibrato types as they change notes in the scale.

Vibrato Feelings. Place your hand on the vibrating finger, hand, or arm of the student. Move their finger, hand, or arm to produce the correct motion if there is something wrong with their motion. Pair up students to feel and correct each other's motions. Also, you may have students feel the correct motion you make when vibrating.

PEDAGOGY FOR DEVELOPING ADVANCED AURAL SKILLS IN THE SCHOOL ORCHESTRA

It is critical to continue developing students' aural skills introduced in the beginning and intermediate string classes. Advanced aural skills include developing students' abilities to do the following:

1. match pitch patterns found in more advanced scales, such as A, E, E-flat major, and c minor
2. play more advanced melodies by ear
3. perform and understand secondary chords
4. select chords by ear to accompany scales
5. select chords by ear to accompany melodies
6. demonstrate advanced instrument tuning

Also refer to Chapter 8 for additional ideas for developing students' aural skills.

Advanced Pitch Matching

Introduce pitch matching in more advanced scales (A, E, E-flat major, and c minor) by using the intermediate pitch-matching teaching strategies suggested in Chapter 4 (e.g., Four-Note Echoes, Matching Arpeggios, Finding Octaves, Matching Leaps, Matching Octaves, and Six-Note Echoes). Also, additional strategies may be incorporated such as Invitational Matching and One-Time Matching.

Invitational Matching. Play a short fragment to be matched and then call on a student to attempt to match the fragment. If the student is successful, the student gets to make up a fragment, play it, and call on another student to match. If the student called on is not successful, play the fragment again and call on another student to try to match it.

One-Time Matching. Same as Invitational Matching, but play the fragment only once for students. Do not play the fragment again if the student called on cannot match it correctly. Simply call on another student to try matching the fragment.

Play More Advanced Melodies by Ear

Once students can play simple melodies by ear in easier keys, such as G, D, and C major, challenge students to play them in more advanced keys, such as A and E-flat major. Select the first pitch for the students so that a melody is transposed to a more advanced key (e.g., starting "Jingle Bells" on the note G, which puts the melody in E-flat major). Additional teaching strategies that are fun include the following:

Stacked Melodies. Have one section of the orchestra play a melody in one key and another section of the orchestra play it in a different key.

Dueling Strings. Select individual students or groups of students to play the same melody in different keys at the same time, attempting to throw each other off. The player or group of players that maintains their key to the end of the melody wins!

Perform and Understand Ensemble Secondary Triads

Review with students how to divide up primary triads and perform them in the orchestra. Use the teaching strategies suggested in Chapter 4. Once students are comfortable understanding and performing chord progressions using primary chords, begin adding ii, vi, and vii chords. In addition, begin playing simple chord progressions on the keyboard and have the orchestra imitate them by ear.

Select Chords by Ear to Accompany Scales

Now students are ready to select and perform chords that accompany a scale.

Scales and Tonics. Have one section of the orchestra play a scale while the rest of the orchestra sustains the root or tonic chord of the scale.

Scales with Roots. Request one section of the orchestra to play a scale and the rest of the orchestra to play the roots of primary chords to accompany the scale.

Scales with Chords. Have one section of the orchestra play a scale and the rest of the orchestra divide up chord pitches and play primary triads to accompany the scale. Have students experiment by playing chords in inversions. As students' abilities develop, have them begin selecting and adding secondary chords to accompany scales

Select Chords by Ear to Accompany Melodies

Once students understand how primary and secondary chords can be used to accompany scales, they are ready to apply that skill to accompany melodies.

Teacher-Led Accompanied Melodies. Select one section of the orchestra to play a familiar melody, such as "Jingle Bells" or "Go Tell Aunt Rhody." Have the rest of the orchestra accompany by playing chords that fit under the melody indicated by your hand signals (see Chapter 4, Finger Signals).

Student-Led Accompanied Melodies. Have students determine by ear which primary chords best fit under a melody. Select one student to lead the orchestra using hand signals to accompany one section playing the melody. Also, you may write chord symbols on a chalkboard and have a student point to the appropriate chord, determined by ear, while the orchestra is playing the chords to accompany the melody.

ADVANCED INSTRUMENT TUNING

Continue reviewing the two intermediate instrument tuning strategies described in Chapter 4. Once these are mastered, introduce an additional tuning routine. Any of the tuning routines may be used. Some teachers like to vary their routines so that students' attention to tuning will remain focused.

Sample Tuning Routine 3

- Model A is sounded by teacher, student, or electronically.
- Basses tune their harmonic A on the D string to the model A.
- Basses tune all strings using harmonics.
- Violins, violas, and cellos tune A strings.
- Violins play A strings while violas and cellos tune D strings to violins.
- Violas and cellos play A strings while violins tune D strings.
- Violins play D strings while violas and cellos tune G strings to violins' D string.
- Violas and cellos play D strings while violins' tune G strings.
- Violins play G strings while violas and cellos tune C strings to violins' G strings.
- Violas and cellos play A strings while violins tune E strings.

PROBLEM SOLVING: ADVANCED STUDENTS'
COMMON PLAYING PROBLEMS AND SOLUTIONS

The following table provides examples of some of the most common playing problems advanced students experience for all instruments. Titles of various teaching strategies described in this chapter are suggested.

Problem	Solution
Consistent decrescendo on down bow	Equal Sound Throughout
Using too much (too fast) bow	Timed Bowing
	Changing Speeds with Clicks
Louré (portato) bowing that is too stopped and accented	Hooked Staccato vs. Louré
	Scaling Styles
Ponticello too harsh/no pitch	Ponticello vs. Sul Tasto
Tremolo uneven	Hand Waving Tremolo
No accent on collé stroke	Pizzicato Collé Frog Collé
String crossing motion too large in fast passages	Metronome Crossings
Spiccato too rough	Add-a-Lift
	Alternating On to Off
Spiccato motion tense	Alternating On to Off
	Heard But Not Seen
	On the String First
Spiccato uneven	Foot and Metronome Bounces
	Downs and Ups and Ups and Downs
Shifting tense	Finding Harmonics
	Tremolo Shifts
Too much sliding sound during slurred shifts	Wavy Bows
Basic vibrato motion incorrect	Checkpoints, Checkpoints
	Parallel Motion
Vibrato width too fast	Varying the Speed
	Fixin' the Nanny Goat
Vibrato too wide or narrow	Counting the Oscillations— Counting the What?
	Attack Stroke Vibrato
Vibrato not expressive	Vibrato Feelings
Vibrato speed and width always same	Alternating Vibrato Types
	Vibrato Feelings

6

PLANNING THE SCHOOL
ORCHESTRA REHEARSAL

As directors of string ensembles and orchestras, we spend a lot of time in the classroom and the orchestra rehearsal room preparing students for programs, contests, and the like. These situations, for the most part, involve group instruction. Since the rehearsal situation is the event with which we prepare students, and the situation in which students are primarily contacted by us, it is vitally important that we prepare for each rehearsal.

Several pre-rehearsal steps must be completed to ensure success in the rehearsal room. In addition to ensuring that the room is an appropriate size, that it has ample lighting and proper acoustics, that there are enough chairs, stands, and parts for each student, and that instruments and other equipment are in excellent working order, you must mentally plan for each rehearsal. This will involve the establishment of goals and objectives and day-to-day lesson planning using those goals and objectives.

YOUR GOALS AND OBJECTIVES

You will be working with a variety of students generally placed in groups according to either grade or ability level and sometimes a combination of both. It is not uncommon to think of your orchestra groups as first year, second year, third year, and so on; beginning, intermediate, and advanced; or elementary, middle school/junior high, and high school; or some combination of these categories. Whatever the label, you need to determine the goals you want each group of students to accomplish. The following are some factors to consider when determining your goals:

1. Length of time per class and number of days a week you are able to meet with your students.

2. Your school system. Will you be teaching in an arts school or in a specially funded program? Are there community leaders and parents who can assist you with your program? What is the performance tradition of the program? Will your students perform regularly? Do they tour? If so, do they tour inside the region, the state, the country, or internationally?

3. Students' opportunities to take private or group lessons outside of your school. (Note: Some schools offer private lessons or small group lesson training as part of the school curriculum.)

4. Opportunities to perform in groups (chamber music, youth orchestras, community ensembles, etc.) outside of your school program.

5. Motivational level of the students with whom you will be working in relation to the environment in which they live. (A university environment, concerts both from groups within your area and from concert series of touring artists, special funding programs such as artist-in-residence programs, and volunteers from the school district may all affect students' motivational level.)

Let's look at each one of these factors and see how they will affect your goals and objectives.

Your Class Length and Your School Orchestra's Tradition

It is obvious that the more time you spend with your students, the more you can accomplish with them. Curriculums vary widely across the United States. In a study of string programs across the nation, Gillespie and Hamann (1998) found that elementary and beginning programs generally meet two or three days a week from twenty to forty minutes per class, with thirty minutes of meeting time as the most common. Middle, junior high, and high school programs tend to meet five days a week. Generally, middle and junior high school meeting times average forty-five minutes in length, while high school programs meet for fifty minutes.

If the school in which you will be teaching is an arts school, magnet school, or part of a specially funded program, you may get additional support for your program. This support can come in the form of aides or assistants, extra instruments, extra rehearsal times allotted for concerts and other special events, curriculums that provide training in chamber music, strolling strings, and mariachi groups, arts infusion events, and other support, including scholarships and special funding opportunities. Arts or magnet schools, or programs that have strong orchestral traditions, generally breed pride among the students in that program. Such students may be expected to practice more frequently and become excellent "orchestra citizens." Strong programs attract community leaders and parents who are often very willing to offer assistance for your program. This assistance can come in the form of funding to help the orchestra go on national or international tours, or it can come in the form of support for your program at school board meetings, booster club meetings, or perhaps town council or community meetings.

Private Lessons and Outside Performance Opportunities

Private lesson study has always been considered beneficial to string students and to the orchestral programs in which students participate. In a study examining differences between middle, junior high, and high school string students who studied privately and those who did not, Hamann and Frost (2000) found the following characteristics among string students who studied privately:

1. More often planned to attend college and play their instrument in a college orchestra.

2. Enjoyed practicing, practiced longer and more frequently, established goals to achieve during their practice sessions, and had established practice times reserved each day.

3. Felt anxiety, depression, or guilt when they were not able to practice, and would practice regardless of the amount of homework that needed to be completed.

4. Found that practice was emotionally satisfying, felt good after practicing, were physically exhausted after a session, tended to practice after they were physically spent, but were more careful to monitor for pain during practice.

5. Reported a need to practice for either seating or grading exams, or to avoid embarrassment, or to gain approval from peers or a teacher.

6. Enjoyed practicing when they had something challenging or fun to play or could sense improvement in their playing. Students not studying privately liked to practice for enjoyment, to relax and relieve stress, or to help them escape.

String students who have the opportunity to study privately appear to derive many benefits from their study. While some schools offer private lessons or small group lesson training as part of the school curriculum, many do not. But if your school offers private lessons, or if significant numbers of students in your program are studying privately, you can expect benefits to your program. Private study encourages more concentrated practice and appears to instill a sense of direction and goal orientation in students. These factors certainly can be positive contributors to your orchestral program and need to be considered when establishing your rehearsal and program goals.

Another factor to consider is whether your students play in other ensembles or groups. Do your students have opportunities to perform in youth or community orchestras, chamber music groups, denominational ensembles, or other such offerings? If so, the additional training and experience your students are obtaining from these settings can enhance your program.

When considering your orchestra group's goals and objectives, it helps to know as much about your students as possible. Your students' experiences, opportunities, and exposure to various events can allow you to consider goals and objectives that may be at higher levels than basic ones. First, however, it is important for you to identify basic goals for students in each of your groups.

GUIDELINES FOR ORGANIZING THE REHEARSAL

First-Year Classes: Basic Goals and Objectives

1. Have acceptable bow hand shape, instrument position, and body posture without tension.
2. Perform the détaché and martelé strokes: bow parallel to bridge and acceptable tone production.
3. Perform basic string crossings.
4. Have correct left-hand shape including correct finger placement in first position with correct finger patterns.
5. Match and manipulate pitches both vocally and on the instrument.
6. Have a basic knowledge of time signatures of 4/4, 3/4, 2/4, and 6/8.
7. Have a basic knowledge of rhythm patterns (note and rest values) using quarter notes, quarter rests, half notes, half rests, whole notes, dotted half notes, eighth notes, and eighth rests, as well as ties and two-, three-, and four-note slurs.
8. Understand the first position notes in the keys of D, G, and C.
9. Name notes in major keys: D, G, C, F.
10. Play violin and viola finger patterns, cello extensions, and bass shifting required for D, G, C, F-major scales. (Other scales such as B-flat major, A major, and g minor may be introduced if classes meet more than twice per week. These keys are included in Chapter 4.)
11. Be able to play pizzicato with a good sound.
12. Be able to use full bows and play with a resonant sound.
13. Be able to play with a slower bow stroke, closer to the bridge for an intense tone.
14. Be able to slur.
15. Be able to play with a hooked bowing.
16. Be able to play some rounds and harmonized orchestra tunes that utilize things learned at Grade 1.
17. Develop basic improvisatory skill.
18. Imitate raising and lowering a pitch by ear.
19. Imitate simple four-note pitch patterns by ear.
20. Imitate simple rhythms involving whole, dotted half, half, quarter, and eighth notes and rests.
21. Imitate simple major and minor scales by ear.
22. Play at the dynamic levels of piano, mezzo forte, and forte.

Second-Year Classes: Basic Goals and Objectives

1. Be able to tune instrument.
2. Perform rhythmic patterns of dotted quarter, eighth; quarter, eighth, eighth; or eighth, eighth, quarter.

3. Perform bow styles and bowings of staccato, accent, hooked bowing, spiccato, long slurs, slurred string crossings, simple double stops, and détaché.

4. Name notes in the d natural minor scale.

5. Play violin and viola finger patterns, cello extensions, and bass shifting for the d natural minor scale.

6. Perform in the keys of F, B-flat, E-flat, and A and play two-octave scales and arpeggios in these keys. (These keys may be introduced if classes meet more than twice per week. The keys are included in Chapter 4.)

7. Know cello extensions and extended finger patterns for violin and viola.

8. Shift (cellos—second position, and basses—second position).

9. Perform in half position (string basses).

10. Accurately sight-read musical examples in the major keys of D, G, C, F, and d natural minor incorporating rhythmic note and rest values including 2/4, 3/4, 4/4, whole notes and rests, dotted half notes and rests, half notes and rests, quarter notes and rests, dotted quarter notes and rests, and eighth notes and rests.

11. Play faster with facility.

12. Begin refinement of basic improvisatory skills.

Third- and Fourth-Year Classes: Basic Goals and Objectives

1. Play in seven keys—up to three flats and three sharps.

2. Perform with developed martelé, spiccato, sautillé, and détaché strokes.

3. Perform double stops.

4. Play two-octave scales and arpeggios up to three flats and three sharps.

5. Play basic rhythmic patterns needed to perform most junior high orchestra music.

6. Play with facility and handle short, technically difficult passages.

7. Be able to follow a conductor.

8. Understand phrasing, dynamics, and the four basic period and style characteristics and how to play them.

9. Develop intermediate improvisatory skills.

10. Be able to perform expressively within an ensemble with an awareness to intonation, blend, balance, timbre, musical independence, and tone quality.

11. Begin the development of vibrato.

12. Be able to shift from first through fifth positions.

13. Develop a knowledge of all notes within first through fifth position.

The High School Orchestra: Basic Goals and Objectives

1. Perform all major and minor scales two octaves.
2. Perform marcato and ricochet strokes and refine détaché, martelé, spiccato, staccato, and sautillé strokes.
3. Perform sul tasto, sul ponticello, and tremolo strokes.
4. Perform right- and left-hand pizzicato.
5. Have a refined vibrato.
6. Perform with refined tone quality and control with correct intonation.
7. Perform with refined vibrato and refined shifting techniques.
8. Perform in upper positions.
9. Develop the understanding, skills, and techniques to perform music appropriate for the high school orchestra.
10. Refine improvisatory skills.

DIFFERENCES AND COMMONALITIES IN TEACHING WIND, BRASS, AND STRING INSTRUMENTS

You may ask, why include a section on differences and commonalities in teaching wind, brass, and string instruments in a string methods book? The most obvious answer is that as orchestra directors, we hope to be conducting both string orchestras and full orchestras. A not-so-obvious answer is predicated on the research findings of Gillespie and Hamann (1998), who found that approximately one-third of all school orchestra directors in the United States did not indicate their major instrument to be a bowed string instrument. Thus, many orchestra directors were trained to be primarily band directors, choral directors, and so on. These individuals now find themselves in front of an orchestra. A discussion of differences and commonalities in teaching wind, brass, and string instruments should now seem not only appropriate but also necessary.

One of the wonderful things about teaching strings is that most of your student-directed technical focus will be on observable external elements. Bow hand shapes, left-hand positions, finger shapes, instrument holds, and so on are readily noticeable. The same is true for teaching percussion instruments. Wind and brass playing functions such as tonguing, formation of an embouchure, and so on are not as easily viewed and, among some music instructors, are more difficult to teach because of it. Thus many of the techniques needed to perform a stringed or percussive instrument can be viewed and corrected externally, while similar techniques on wind and brass instruments are viewed as more internally generated, meaning that they are not readily viewed or corrected by sight and must rely on other teaching approaches for presentation and observation.

Sound Generation and Tone Quality

Sound generation and tone quality are similar on strings, brass, woodwinds, and percussion in that they all require a good model concept to emulate, and all require excellent aural perception skills in the performance of this concept. Sound generation and tone quality are also affected on all instruments by the quality of the instrument being played. In general, the better the instrument an individual plays, the better the sound his sound will be. All instruments' sound generation qualities are additionally affected by the way the instruments are held. Proper instrument/bow/mallet hold is essential to ensure good sound generation and tone quality. Given these commonalities among the instruments, we can now discuss the differences.

Sound on bowed string instruments is basically produced by the bow. The combination of bow speed and bow pressure, along with bow placement on the string, all affect the sound generation and the type of tone produced on bowed string instruments. In addition, the left hand has a role in sound generation: when a finger is firmly or solidly centered on the fingerboard with correct placement for the note desired, the tone quality of that pitch will be greatly enhanced and will resonate when combined with proper bowing techniques. When a finger is not firmly or solidly centered, and the finger placement is not exactly correct for the pitch being desired, the sound will not be focused and will not resonate even when correct bowing techniques are used.

Sound generation and tone quality on woodwinds are greatly affected by the quality of the reed as well as the quality of the embouchure. Embouchure and its placement also affect the tone on brass instruments. Breath support and air flow are critical to sound generation on the woodwind and brass instruments, while proper mallet and stick hold, striking, scraping, and placement are essential for quality percussion sound. On instruments with open holes, such as clarinets and some types of flutes, the quality of the sound will be affected if the holes are not properly covered. Valves not depressed properly, slides not positioned correctly, or hands not properly placed in a horn can also negatively affect the sound or tone quality on wind and brass instruments.

In summary, quality sound generation and tone quality on strings, brass, woodwinds, and percussion all require a good model concept, excellent aural perception skills, quality instruments and proper instrument/bow/mallet hold. In addition to these principles, the sound generation in bowed strings is produced by the combination of bow speed, bow pressure, and bow placement along with correct left-hand finger placement. Sound generation for woodwinds and brass is affected by the quality of the reed and embouchure along with breath support and air flow and finger placement, valve or slide technique, or in the case of percussion, proper mallet or sticking procedure.

Intonation

Once students understand, through aural, visual, and verbal identification, the concept of intonation and the system of whole and half steps that are needed to perform the vast majority of literature written for the instruments, the task of transferring that knowledge to various instruments can begin. Some common principles between intonation on brass, woodwind, and string instruments are as follows:

1. Proper instrument hold facilitates proper intonation.
2. Audiation and aural perception plus awareness are necessary to produce correct intonation.
3. Good tone quality enhances accurate intonation.
4. An internal model of accurate intonation must be present for students to play in tune.

Appropriate intonation on stringed instruments involves proper finger placement on a string and is no more complicated than placing a finger at an appropriate point on the fingerboard. The difficulty is in consistently reproducing this act and in rapid succession, given a multiple of different pitches. Kinesthetic memory, along with aural memory and assessment, is needed to help "train the hand and the ear." Proper instrument and left-hand shape are essential for this process to be successful. Additionally, the student must realize when any given pitch is not in tune and then must recognize what action needs to be taken to produce the correct pitch. This generally involves movement of the hand or a finger either toward or away from the bridge. Both kinesthetic and aural skills along with intonation assessment skills and procedures must be acquired by each student to produce accurate intonation on a stringed instrument. These principles are the key to good intonation, and it is your task to help students acquire these skills. Activities that reinforce these principles, such as singing a pitch and having students match that pitch, having one student adjust the finger placement of another student through verbal or physical directives/movement, repetition of "dropping on a pitch," and so on aid students in their progression to acquiring proper intonation.

For brass and woodwind players, not all elements affecting intonation are as easily viewed as they are for string players. Appropriate valve or key choice and use of alternate fingerings, placement of the hand in the bell of the horn, slide placement on trombone, or covering holes appropriately on instruments such as an open-holed flute or clarinet, breath control and embouchure/embouchure control are not easily viewed externally and may be more challenging to alter and correct.

In summary, developing correct intonation on brass, woodwind, and string instruments involves reinforcement of instrument hold and hand position, audiation ability, and a good aural model of appropriate intonation and good tone quality. Specifically, correct intonation on stringed instruments involves proper fingering to help develop kinesthetic memory as well as aural memory. These two elements, combined with accurate assessment and appropriate corrective procedures, will help produce reliable intonation on stringed instruments. Intonation on brass and woodwind involves hand or slide placement, finger placement (covering holes on certain instruments), appropriate valve or key choice, and correct embouchure and breath control.

Shifting and Range

While shifting and range generally encompass the concept of a wide spectrum of pitches, they are terms that are not *both* commonly used by string or brass and woodwind players. The pedagogical term *shift* is used most often by string players, while the pedagogical term *range* is more commonly used by brass and woodwind players.

In pedagogical terms, a shift on a stringed instrument involves movement of the left hand from one position (first, second, third, etc.) to another position. One objective of a shift is to get to a point, on any given string, at which notes of a higher or lower pitch can be played. For example, if one is playing a one-octave D-major scale on the double bass beginning on the D string, there would need to be a shift at some point to reach the octave C-sharp and D. Another objective of a shift is to maintain a certain timbre. If one is playing a one-octave G-major scale on the cello and wanted to maintain the quality of sound produced by the G string, then the scale could all be played on the G string. That would involve two shifts. Two basic objectives of shifting are to reach notes that are not accessible in any given position and to maintain a particular timbre.

Range in mathematics means spread or dispersion. In music, range refers to the distance an individual can play, on a given instrument, from the lowest to the highest pitch. Quality and strength of embouchure, breath support, quality of reeds, quality of instrument, experience, practice, and so on are all factors that contribute to one's range capabilities on a given instrument. Since stringed instrument range is not restricted by such factors, range tends to be a term that is used most generally with brass and woodwind instruments. Beginning brass and woodwind players face certain range problems, including the "break" on the clarinet, low Cs on the flute, or high Cs on the trumpet. Thus, range must be considered when selecting full orchestra music.

In summary, shifting involves movement of the left hand from one position to another with the objective of either playing notes that are not accessible in a position or to maintain a particular timbre. Range is affected by various factors including the quality and strength of an embouchure, breath support, quality of reeds, or quality of an instrument. The concepts of shifting and range are both important pedagogical factors to consider in the teaching and understanding of string, brass, and woodwind instruments and in the selection of orchestral literature for your groups.

Articulation

Perhaps one of the more important concepts in string, brass, and woodwind teaching is that of articulation. While the tongue is used in brass and woodwind articulation, the bow is used for the same purpose in string playing. Seemingly similar markings can result in different articulations, depending on whether it is being played by a string or brass/woodwind player. For example, a group of notes with a slur marking and a dot under each note is perceived as a legato articulation by brass and woodwind players, and they would play such a passage with a smooth, connected sound. For the string player, this is an indication of slurred staccato, indicating a series of successive martelé-like strokes or staccato articulation being played in one bow direction. Thus, it is extremely important that the principles behind articulation for all instruments be studied and understood to effectively communicate these concepts.

In summary, string playing articulations are produced by bow placement and by the attack and release. String articulation is also influenced by the number of notes played per bow. String playing articulation preparation is visible, even though muscles in the fingers, arms, and shoulders are used to help prepare each bow articulation; the basic motion and approach are seen externally.

In brass and woodwind playing, articulation is created by the stopping and starting of the air stream or flow by the tongue. The placement of the tongue in the mouth affects the articulation, as does the vowel syllable being used when playing. A trumpet player using the syllable "dah" will get a different articulation than the same player using the syllable "tee." The orchestra director needs to be aware that different syllables create different articulations among the brass and wind players, just as bow placement on or off the string and the type of attack and release will produce different articulations among string players.

Transposition

To be a successful full orchestra conductor, it is important that your knowledge of the wind and brass instruments includes familiarity with transpositions. In addition to the usual transpositions, many full orchestra works require a variety of transpositions. The following transposition chart provides the basic information you should know and includes the written pitch and the sounding pitch.

Section	Instrument	Actual Sound
Woodwinds	Piccolo in C	Octave higher than written
	Flute in C	As written
	Oboe in C	As written
	Oboe d'amore in A	Minor third lower than written
	English horn	Perfect fifth lower than written
	Clarinet in B flat	Major second lower than written
	Clarinet in A	Minor third lower than written
	E-flat soprano	Minor third higher than written
	E-flat alto	Major sixth lower than written
	B-flat bass	Major ninth lower than written
	B-flat contra bass	Seventeenth lower than written
	Bassoon	As written
	Contra bassoon	Octave lower than written
	E-flat soprano saxophone	Minor third higher than written
	C soprano saxophone	As written
	B-flat soprano saxophone	Major second lower than written
	E-flat alto saxophone	Major sixth lower than written

(continued)

Section	Instrument	Actual Sound
Woodwinds (*continued*)	B-flat tenor saxophone	Major ninth lower than written
	E-flat baritone saxophone	Octave plus major sixth lower than written
	B-flat bass saxophone	Octave plus major ninth lower than written
Brass	Horn in	
	B flat—basso	Major ninth lower than written
	C	Octave lower than written
	D	Minor seventh lower than written
	E flat	Major sixth lower than written
	E	Minor sixth lower than written
	F	Perfect fifth lower than written
	G	Perfect fourth lower than written
	A flat	Major third lower than written
	A	Minor third lower than written
	B flat—alto	Major second lower than written
	Trumpet in	
	B flat	Major second lower than written
	A	Minor third lower than written
	D	Major second higher than written
	E flat	Minor third higher than written
	E	Major third higher than written
	F	Perfect fourth higher than written
	C	As written
	G	Perfect fourth lower than written
	Fluegelhorn in B flat	Major second lower than written
	Trombone	Bass or C clef: as written
	Trombone (treble clef)	Major ninth lower than written
	Bass trombone	As written
	Bass trombone (treble clef)	Major ninth lower than written
	Tuba	As written
Percussion	Timpani	As written
	Xylophone	Octave higher than written
	Glockenspiel	One or two octaves higher than written
	Bells	Octave higher than written
	Vibraphone	As written
	Tubular bells (chimes)	As written
Strings	Violin	As written
	Viola	As written
	Cello	As written
	Double bass	Octave lower than written
Other	Harp	As written
	Piano	As written
	Celesta	Octave higher than written

Summary

Many of the differences and commonalities in teaching wind, brass, and string instruments are a result of the instruments themselves. Specifically, technical focus on string instruments is observable externally, and while some technical components of brass and wind playing can be observed externally, many of them involve such things as tonguing, which cannot be viewed this way.

Regardless of the instrument, all technical approaches require the student to have an excellent visual and aural model. The visual model is one by which the student can imagine the feel of playing an instrument and also imagine the way she would look when playing this instrument. The aural model is one in which the student can hear the ideal sound he would be producing while playing the instrument.

These models, when "brought into the class," are to be used in the self-evaluation process when students are actually playing an instrument. Through aural, visual, and verbal identification and assessment strategies, internal student models are used to self-evaluate the various facets of performance technique on any given instrument. Thus, the successful orchestra director will be aware of both the differences and commonalities in teaching wind, brass, and string instruments.

KEYS TO EFFICIENT AND EFFECTIVE DEVELOPMENT OF PLAYING TECHNIQUE IN THE STRING CLASS

While you must concern yourself with both the wind and the string instruments, as a string teacher, the majority of your time will be spent developing efficient and effective technique among your string students. The following twenty-one keys to the development of playing technique in the string class may be useful to you in developing your teaching strategies:

1. Determine the overall technique vision for your classes. For example, your technical vision for your elementary group (first and second year) may be to develop a solid playing foundation, for your middle/junior high group (third and fourth year) to refine and extend their skills, and for your senior high group, to develop advanced skills and expressiveness.

2. Use modeling in your teaching. It is an excellent practice to teach with an instrument in your hands, showing them, through demonstration, what you want. Modeling provides for a nonverbal or at least a limited verbal teaching event, and it is effective and efficient and tends to help keep students on task.

3. Use nonverbal instruction whenever possible. Limit your verbal teaching whenever possible. Nonverbal instruction is effective and efficient and provides an alternative to verbal directives that tend to keep the student on task.

4. Rote to note can often be effective when there is a need to eliminate the process of note reading in order to learn a passage in which a sequence of skills are presented and then followed by music use.

5. Be aware of your proximity in relation to your students. Move about the classroom. Don't get fixed in one position. When you move about the classroom, you can hear and see things you may not have noticed by staying in one location.

6. Use touch to help students "feel" or refine a skill. Appropriate teacher touch can help many students experience the tactile sensation that is needed to perform certain technical elements of playing. (Note: It is important to ask the student whether it is permissible to touch her before actually touching. Some students may not want to be touched, and you must respect that request.)

7. Dissect and combine skills. Dissect complex playing skills into prerequisite skills, then combine the skills to produce complex skills (e.g., teaching spiccato "on the string" first).

8. Use multiple teaching strategies to present the same playing skill. Each of your students is unique and will learn in different ways. The more ways you can present the same concept, the better the chances are that your students will learn the concept from one of your many teaching strategies.

9. Always review. In order to reinforce skills presented previously, a review is often needed to ascertain whether additional time is needed to maintain or review that skill. Once a review has been conducted, you can then proceed to build upon that concept with the reassurance that you have established a reliable technical foundation for additional development.

10. Present yourself as a leader. Your students look to you for guidance and assistance. You need to accept and convey the role of a leader. Leadership is seen by students through your body balance and lengthening, ease of movement, elevated posture, eye contact (constant, to all areas), vocal projection, confidence, musicianship, preparation (lesson plans), variable voice pitch/dynamics, and variable facial expressions. Remember, if you don't lead the class, someone else will!

11. Use humor in your teaching. Humor helps students learn, and it shows them that you are willing to laugh at yourself and with your students.

12. Develop a routine. Many aspects of rehearsals remain essentially the same from rehearsal to rehearsal. Develop a rehearsal structure that identifies these patterns of activity and develop your rehearsal routine. Rehearsal routines save instructional time and promote efficiency. Examples of possible rehearsal routines include an organized tuning process or a warm-up procedure.

13. Be aware of your pacing. Pacing is the speed of instruction or the rate at which information is presented. You need to control the pacing

within your rehearsal, being aware of your tempo of delivery in relation to student needs and cognition. You need to be flexible and yet plan your pacing by design. Plan for your activities and think about the pace at which you will present your ideas.

14. Perfect your classroom management—your ability to control the behavior of groups of students and to get students' attention. Effective and efficient rehearsals cannot be achieved unless you are in control of your group.

15. Select repertoire for technical development. Use music to reinforce technical concepts. For example, you may wish to select a musical example to develop a rhythmical concept. You can first teach the concept by rote, then include the concept in the musical example, having the students play it again, and finally have the students demonstrate the concept by playing the passage within the content of the musical line.

16. Carefully develop students' playing skills. Develop student technique to allow *careful* building of playing skills. When developing performance skills, go at a rate that keeps the students challenged but not overwhelmed.

17. Use students as teachers. Develop student team teaching groups and have your students teach each other in class.

18. Identify student leaders. Engage student leaders to work with the class while the teacher works with individual students. This frees the teacher to move throughout the class. For example, section leaders can work on bowings and so on while the teacher works on a particular problem with another section.

19. Recognize positive behavior and achievement. Don't be hesitant to praise your students when they are doing well.

20. Use self-evaluation procedures. Using audiotape, videotape, timeline analysis, sociograms, checklists, and so on to evaluate your rehearsal helps both you and your students in the learning process.

21. Be aware of students' natural learning styles. For example, students learn through visual, aural, and tactile means. Some students are better concrete learners than abstract learners are. You need to identify the learning styles of your students and adjust for these different styles using approaches that present sequential, global, analytical, discovery, or tactile learning. Your teaching needs to "show, explain, and feel."

GUIDELINES FOR CHOOSING MUSIC

Part of the process for choosing music begins with the goals you have selected for each of your groups for the year. You must decide which musical selections will best help you and your groups accomplish those goals. Given that you may be working with both string and full orchestra from the elementary through the high school level, think about the following technical considerations. Determine the key or keys of your works in relation to the grade level ability of each group. Elementary full orchestra keys need to accommodate young, developing wind players as well as young, developing string players. Keys such as F, C, and B-flat are commonly used in elementary full orchestra situations, while keys such as D, A, and G are more commonly used for elementary string orchestra selections. Decide whether the works under consideration are best for each of your groups' unique instrumentation settings.

For your string orchestras, consider the strength and numbers of instruments in each section, and choose music that not only will challenge and help each individual grow, but also will sound the best with the group. Consider also the independence of each section part. You may wish to choose works that are doubled or have less dominant musical lines for sections that are weak.

For your full orchestras, evaluate the instrumentation needs of each work. Then determine whether you have or can get the proper instrumentation for the performance of each work considered. Also, consider whether you can arrange a work so that your group can effectively and musically perform it.

Think about range restrictions for the brass and woodwinds, shifting or position work for the strings, articulation requirements such as double or triple tonguing for the brass, or special bowing requirements, rhythmic complexities, line independence, and dynamic range in regard to range and register in both brass and winds. In general, consider all technical and musical aspects of each work when choosing music. The length of a work should also be thought about in relation to your students' ability to concentrate. Some works may be technically easy for a group and yet may require musical sensitivity and maturity beyond the reach of a group.

In addition to technical challenges, you must consider the implications for student learning and development when choosing your music. When making your musical selections, consider the following:

1. the goals and objectives you hope each group will accomplish through the music you have chosen to play
2. the style of music (classical, pop, show tunes, etc.) and the periods (Baroque, Classical, Romantic, etc.) to which you want each group to be exposed
3. the ability level of the group in relation to the works selected

Selecting Music Based on the Goals and Objectives of Your Groups

Each of your groups, whether they are just beginning their string study or have reached higher levels of ability, need to be guided. You are the guide who decides what each group will work on next, what techniques and skills they will learn. The basic goals and objectives outlined earlier provide useful guidelines for helping you lead your students through a meaningful course of study from year to year. It is with these goals and objectives in mind, along with knowledge of your students' skill levels, that you can begin to select music for your pupils. Through the music you choose, and a purposeful and well-conceived course of study, you teach your students the techniques and skills they need to advance and develop, and the musical knowledge and sensitivity they need to become lifelong performers and connoisseurs of music.

When you select each group's music, an important consideration is to weigh what each work will contribute to student learning as directed through your course of study. Think about daily lesson plans you would use to present and teach each work, and then decide whether your students could accomplish the goals and objectives you set forth for them. If the answer is yes, then the work you are reviewing is certainly an appropriate piece for consideration.

Selecting Music Based on Style and Periods

Perhaps one of the more difficult music selection decisions you will make is the style of music your groups will play. In addition to the goals and objectives that could be attained through the study of a particular work, your students' musical style preferences, as well as your own style preferences, will also influence your music selection considerations. Additionally, if the music you are choosing is to be performed at a concert, you need to consider your audiences' musical style preferences and the nature or the underlying theme (if there is one) of the performance or concert itself.

Hamann and Frost (2000) found that while external pressures and rewards (grades, trips, parental encouragement) did provide some incentive for practice, most students practiced simply because they liked playing their instruments, and they practiced when they perceived their music to be fun. It is important, then, that part of your music selection be based on student interests. However, this does not mean that you abdicate your responsibility to help each student in each group expand and enrich his enjoyment of a variety of music and styles. Share the music selection agenda. Discover your students' musical tastes and their preferences, and select works that fulfill their needs as well as your needs as the orchestra director. Thus, your music selection could include multicultural music, jazz, and pop, as well as classical works.

Although some of your musical selections may not be classical works, many of them will be classical compositions. Part of the rationale for choosing classical compositions is that they are excellent works from which a variety of techniques and skills can be presented and learned. Music from each period, whether Baroque, Classical, Romantic, and so on, offers new challenge and provides potentially exciting learning opportunities for your students. For example, if one of your educational goals is to have students develop facility in playing rapid, energetic, detached bow strokes, then you may wish to select music from the Baroque period. Music from the Baroque period, especially the faster movements, which contain nonslurred moving notes, is excellent for teaching the staccato stroke as you encourage your students to duplicate the resonant sound characteristics of the Baroque stringed instruments. If you were teaching an off-the-string bowing style, such as spiccato, you would want to select a work from the Classical period, especially a work containing eighth notes (generally played off the string) in nonslurred passages of faster movements or in accompanying figures, repeated notes, or scalelike passages.

Your musical selection process thus includes analysis of your goals and objectives as well as stylistic considerations. Your classical music selection process will also be influenced by period performance practice considerations in relation to the goals and objectives you establish for each group.

Selecting Music Based on Your Groups' Ability Levels

Students like to practice if they are challenged and if they sense improvement in their playing, according to Hamann and Frost (2000). Another key to selecting music is to choose music that is challenging for all of your students and yet not so out of reach for them that they cannot advance their skills and improve. One approach often advocated is to balance music selection between easy and challenging works. If we assume that three works are to be selected for study with a final goal of a performance, one composition should be selected that the group can read well. This work should require minimal rehearsal time to reach performance level and yet should be musically rewarding and interesting enough to maintain interest until it is performed. Another piece should be more difficult and at the group's level. Preparation of this composition will require considerably more effort on the part of both you and your students. However, the work should be able to be performed at the highest level of performance readiness, given appropriate rehearsal effort and time. The third piece should be somewhat above the ability level of the group. The purpose of such a work is to push the envelope of learning past comfortable student ability levels to pedagogical heights that, even after considerable time and effort, may not fully be reached.

In summary, when selecting music for your group, you need to consider the goals and objectives you have selected for your groups. The techniques and skills you want your students to learn are presented through the music you select for them regardless of the style of music or the period in which it was written. The selection of music for each group will determine the success of each rehearsal. Music that is not challenging either technically or musically will not allow for individual and group growth, nor will music that is too challenging provide the needed framework for you to develop your groups' potential. The music you choose must both challenge and reward your students. In turn your students will, through their self-motivated practice procedure, acquire the goals and objectives you have outlined for them.

Music selection is one of the most important aspects of establishing successful rehearsals. It is imperative that careful and thoughtful consideration be given to this important task.

PREPARING A SCORE

Once you have chosen the music for your groups, you must prepare your score. Your considerations include two basic components—musical and technical—

which you already used when you selected the music. The style, period, and technical difficulty of the works were part of your analysis in the decision process. Analyzing technical and musical elements within your scores continues as you prepare each work for rehearsal.

While there is no set order for preparing a score, several suggestions, routines, and procedures will assist you in your task. One procedure, which you have already completed, was a review of the score with an eye toward the technical aspects of the work as well as the musical qualities. You have already noted the general rhythmic structure and complexity of the piece, key and meter/tempo and/or key and meter/tempo changes, overall form of the work, technical demands, including range and skill demands, and in general, the demands of the work in relation to the ability of your group. You are well under way to preparing the score for your first rehearsal.

A pencil and perhaps a pad of paper, along with highlighting markers and a metronome, can be helpful now. One of your first tasks is to number your score measures. If you have no student assistants or would rather not ask your students to do so, you need to number the student parts as well.

Becoming More Familiar with the Score

One level of score analysis generally recommended is to audiate, hum, or sing all of the parts in the score with particular attention to the flow of the melodic lines. If possible, a metronome should be set at the recommended tempo and the process begun. If a slower tempo is initially needed to accomplish this task, you should eventually audiate, hum, or sing all of the parts at tempo before the first rehearsal. As you sing each part, you should further note the overall structure of the work, the melody and countermelody, and the style of the work. Once you are able to sing each part, you should follow the melody throughout the work. Some conductors mark different lines using colored highlighters. If you choose to use highlighters, use one color to denote melodies and a different color to indicate countermelodies.

As you become familiar with the melodic and harmonic structure of the composition, noting whether it is major, minor, modal, chromatic, twelve-tone, atonal, polytonal, and so on, you will begin to understand how each part fits into the overall structure of the composition. As you become familiar with each individual part, you will begin to note potentially challenging melodic passages, rhythms, key or meter changes, finger patterns, and the like. Note such findings on your notepad. Indicate any perceived problems students may encounter during the rehearsal, and offer some suggestions for helping them overcome those difficulties. A more in-depth discussion of these techniques will be conducted in Chapter 7. You should also note or highlight musical terms in the score. If you do not know a term, this is the time you should look it up and write down its meaning. You should also highlight key, meter, and tempo changes, noting ritardandos and accelerandos, fermatas, grand pauses, breath marks, cues, dynamic changes, and various accents and articulation markings.

Playing through each of the parts in the score is another way of becoming familiar with it. First, the individual lines can be played on your principal instrument. This can help you develop a sense of line. Next, you should play through each of the parts using the instrument for which it was written. Now you can better understand what problems your students may encounter when playing the parts. These can be noted in your rehearsal log and used for future practice sessions.

Another practice often recommended in score preparation is to complete a harmonic analysis of the work. Harmonic analysis can be completed in different ways, but the basic idea is to become familiar with the tonal structure of the piece. The result of your analysis should reveal tonal structure, form, identification of development and recapitulation, and other such musical features. Along with your harmonic analysis, you should seek out information concerning the musical style of the work and the composer. This can aid your understanding of the composition and will help your students in their study of the work.

Checking the Parts against the Score

At some point in your score preparation, you need to check the parts against the score. While the publishing industry tries to ensure that correct notes, rhythms, accidentals, key signatures, bowings, fingerings, and so on appear in all parts, mistakes do occur. Part of score preparation is simply reviewing each instrumental part and comparing it with the score to ensure that they are identical. Discrepancies or incorrect notes and rhythms must be corrected before parts are distributed. Generally a copying error is more prevalent in a part than in a score. Often the score is viewed as correct when discrepancies are found. However, a score may also have errors, and the intelligent orchestral conductor will question both documents before a decision on the appropriate correction is made.

Bowings and Fingerings

Editors or composers frequently provide bowings and fingerings in orchestral scores. This is particularly true of beginning to intermediate level music (Grades 1 to 4). Part of your responsibility as an orchestra conductor is not only to check to determine whether the bowings and fingerings are similar within the parts and score, but also to determine whether the bowings and fingerings provided are appropriate. When bowing or fingerings are not provided but are needed, it is your responsibility to determine what the appropriate markings should be. It is extremely important to establish appropriate bowings and fingerings before the music is distributed. Bowings or fingerings are difficult to change once students have practiced or learned them differently than you desire. Score preparation therefore includes careful evaluation of bowings and fingerings before rehearsal begins.

Part of your consideration for establishing fingerings is technical. For example, a rapid, repetitive passage that crosses strings frequently may be fingered so that, with some shifting, the passage can be easily played on one string. Other such considerations include fingering passages so they can be more easily played in different positions. Fingering passages in different positions can change the character of the sound, which may be desirable when certain timbre considerations are desired. Conversely, timbre and color considerations may not be as important as compared with clarity issues, and fingerings can reflect this shift in emphasis.

Bowing choices are also based on technical and musical considerations. For example, down bows are considered to be stronger strokes than up bows. Thus, down bows are indicated for accented notes. A series of accented notes may be performed with a series of down bows. In beginning string literature, considerable effort is given to having the strong beats within a measure played with a down bow. In 4/4 time then, a down bow would be used to play a note on the first beat of a measure, while an up bow would be used to play the fourth beat of the measure. Some of your bowing decisions may be based more on technical aspects of playing rather than musical considerations. Cello and double bass players do not like to play in the upper half of the bow for extended periods of time, as it is extremely demanding and exhausting to do so. Conversely, violins and violas find playing in the upper half of the bow as easy as or easier than playing near the frog. Additionally, some passages may be easier to play when a hooked bowing is used, as opposed to using separate bow strokes. As you review each string part, you need to decide what bow strokes each section will use. Of course, an overriding consideration for bow stroke choice is often unity of sound, not only within each section but also between sections. Uniformity of sound is often achieved through uniformity of bow stroke.

In summary, your choice of fingerings and bowings should be guided by both technical and musical considerations. Musical considerations include the period and style of the work being performed. Timbre and tone color, natural and marked accents, dynamics, the shape of a phrase, unity of sound, and a host of other musical phenomena are all to be considered when choosing appropriate fingerings and bowings. Technical considerations, such as string crossings, clarity of sound, ease of playing, and accuracy of passages, will also be affected by your choice of fingerings and bowings. Your choice of fingerings and bowings will affect the performance outcomes of your groups. You must consider and prepare fingerings and bowings before music is distributed.

Final Steps to Score Preparation

You have chosen your musical compositions; your measures are numbered; your harmonic and melodic analyses are completed; you have pages of potential problem measures identified with possible solutions noted; melodic lines, cues, dynamics, and the like have all been identified and highlighted; terms have been defined; and articulations, bowings, and fingerings have been considered. Now you need to think about your presentation of this work. One of the first considerations of any conductor tends to be the physical act of conducting the piece. For less experienced conductors, this portion of the preparation will require considerably more time and effort than it will for experienced conductors. Inexperienced or experienced, your goal is the same. One way to convey intent when working with large musical groups is through the medium of conducting. As you have learned or are learning through your various conducting classes and experiences, a host of things must be considered and practiced to effectively communicate through this medium. Establishing and maintaining tempi, phrasing, articulation, dynamic indications, cueing, indicating crescendos, diminuendos, ritardandos, accelerandos, tempi changes, holds, pauses, and so on are some of the tasks you will be expected to expedite on the podium.

Your conducting practice should always be undertaken with a metronome within reach. It is essential that you establish the correct tempo in your mind and maintain that tempo until or unless other musical indications dictate otherwise. You need to continually rehearse your score until you can appropriately convey entrances, cutoffs, tempi, expression, phrasing, dynamics, and all other musical considerations you have determined to be essential to the successful performance of each work. The following selected strategies for rehearsing your orchestra should help guide you in preparing for the rehearsal as well as conducting the rehearsal itself.

Preparing for and Conducting Rehearsals

General Guidelines

1. Rehearse as you would practice a solo on your principal instrument (e.g., isolate sections using brackets, starting with the most difficult sections).
2. Audiotape or videotape rehearsal.
3. Have students memorize difficult passages.
4. Modeling—teacher or student models passage on string instrument, sings the passage, plays the passage on the piano, or plays the passage back to the students as they perform it.
5. Determine priority order for your rehearsal: notes, intonation, tone, rhythm, style, expressiveness. Priorities change from first rehearsal to concert.

Sound Production

1. Analyze bow placement (before passage begins, during passage, and at end of passage), use a miles per hour analogy for establishing bow speed, use clothespins clipped onto the bow to isolate different parts of the bow, teach students to be able to play in all parts of the bow, and help them remember on what part of the bow the passage should be played.
2. Analyze bow speed of students to prevent them from getting trapped in the wrong part of the bow. Use a miles per hour analogy to describe proper bow speed—at times it may need to be faster and at times slower.

3. Listen to the orchestra from behind or from the back of the auditorium.

4. Move the orchestra to stage edge to increase overall sound.

5. Turn basses out to audience (almost parallel to stage edge) for sound projection.

6. Use faster bow speeds to create resonant and free string sound throughout the lower string instruments. Lower string instruments use somewhat slower bow speeds than upper strings.

7. Alter bowings to fit the group. Sound lanes—divide up distance between the bridge and fingerboard for the best place for the best sound.

8. The orchestra should be able to produce different tone colors by changing relationships between bow speed, weight, and sounding (contact) point.

Technique

1. Break passage down to prerequisite technique—dissect and recombine skills (e.g., break down to open strings, vibrato motions, spiccato motions).

2. Pizzicato difficult left-hand passage.

3. Practice spiccato passages on the string for left-hand security.

4. Shifting—find intermediate note, practice shift to intermediate note, practice plunking down note in higher position from intermediate note, shift sounding intermediate note, then practice shift without sounding intermediate note.

5. Cello extensions—between first and second fingers, pizzicato then arco, go behind the cellos to watch thumbs, practice face extensions.

Tempo

1. Variation—slow to fast to coordinate bowing and left-hand technique.

2. Rushing—place false bow speed accents on principal beats, tap foot, move body, use faster bows to slow down playing.

3. One instrument section acts as metronome playing open strings only on principal beats.

Rhythm

1. Teach, evaluate, and reinforce with pizzicato. Reward students by allowing them to play with the bow. The teaching sequence becomes playing with pizzicato, bowing without slurs, then playing as printed.

2. One section counts beats out loud while another pizzicatos its rhythm.

3. Have one section bow its rhythmic passage while the rest of the orchestra pizzicatos their parts.

4. Have students move or sway while playing to keep a steady beat.

Dynamics

1. Softer—one student plays at soft dynamic; other students join but cannot play any louder than first student.
2. Softer—instruct students to use less bow or slower bow.
3. Louder—instruct students to use a heavy bow, faster bow, or weighty bow.
4. Deliberately allow students to play soft passage loudly for fun and then at proper dynamic level.

Balance

1. Only one student plays melody. Other instrument sections must accompany the solo student at the appropriate dynamic level.
2. Be sure to teach students which musical line must be heard.
3. General principles: Inner parts need to play louder, lower strings need to play louder, repeated notes are not as important, sustained notes are not as important as moving notes, moving part is generally more important.

Intonation

1. Sustain and tune problem pitches.
2. Add one in-tune player at a time.
3. Tune chord progressions, sustaining one chord tone at a time: root, third, fifth.
4. Tune between sections of the orchestra.
5. Play problem intonation pitches very softly and tune; this forces players to listen.
6. Sustain pitch on downbeat of each measure or only on principal beats.
7. Take out vibrato to tune pitches.
8. Bow pizzicato pitches to hear and correct intonation problems.
9. Have students demonstrate the finger pattern on each string in the key of the piece being rehearsed.
10. Rehearse problem passages slowly to give yourself and the students a chance to adjust pitches.
11. Be especially careful to check the intonation of notes at the end of phrases.
12. Realize that string students and orchestras can play in tune—do not lower your intonation standard. Students will play in tune as they are demanded.

Musicality

1. Phrasing—shape through bow speed, weight, lanes.
2. Showing through singing and modeling.
3. Marked phrase shapes in music using curved, dotted lines.

One guiding principle to remember for any rehearsal is the following: An orchestra will perform only as well as it has been rehearsed.

LESSON PLANS

With the score prepared, you now begin to develop your plan to present information to your students. While we will talk about specific lesson plans a bit later in this chapter, a basic understanding of lesson plan construction should be visited at this time.

When developing a lesson plan, keep the following guidelines in mind:

1. *Determine the objective(s)* of your lesson and state those objectives in terms of what the students will learn. Each of your lesson objectives helps fulfill goals and objectives from your curriculum guide. Each group will have different goals and objectives for the year. Your lesson plan makes these learning goals and objectives a reality for your students.

2. With your objectives firmly in mind, *research the topic as you defined it by the objective.* Based on your experiences, experiences of others gained through conversations, lectures, or interviews, or information you have gathered from written or observed materials, determine what you know about this topic. How have others dealt with the topic you are about to present? Ask yourself, how can I share information I have learned about this topic with my students?

3. Now that you have your topic information, *decide how you are going to deliver this information.* What methods can you use to result in a meaningful learning experience for your students? Consider the ways people learn: by doing, discussing, listening, and observing (visual, auditory, kinesthetic/tactile learners). Also consider the various levels at which student learning occurs: consult the three taxonomies for the cognitive, affective, and psychomotor domain learning hierarchies.

4. *Develop a usable lesson plan format.* Your lesson plan should be easy to follow, with the objectives and materials you need clearly stated. Be sure your plan is easy to follow at a glance. Avoid paragraphs.

5. *Decide how you will organize your lesson.* Answering the following questions will help you organize your lesson. What topics do you have to review to have a successful lesson? What new information are you presenting? How will you present this information? What function will your warm-up play in the introduction of this material? Will you organize your presentation so that you go from known to unknown, general to specific, or specific to general?

6. *Choose your support material.* We are fortunate to have many outstanding pedagogues in the string world. Phyllis Young (*Playing the String Game* and *The String Play*), Paul Rolland (*The Teaching of Action in String Playing*), Kato Havas (*A New Approach to Violin Playing*), and Shinichi Suzuki (*Nurtured by Love*) are just a few of the individuals who have introduced us to fresh, creative, and exciting approaches to use in our classrooms. In addition to the traditional handout, technological media pre-

sentation equipment such as overhead projectors, liquid crystal displays, audiovisual displays, CD-ROMs, and audiovisual digital recording devices add to the growing list of available materials. Technological equipment combined with those materials suggested by string pedagogues, along with your own creative imagination, can provide a plethora of exciting support materials for your lesson. On the whole, it is better to have too much support material than not enough. On the one hand, if you see that your students are understanding the point you are presenting, you do not have to use everything you brought into the lesson. On the other hand, if you have limited (one or two) support materials or ideas and the students do not understand your point, the lesson will come to a grinding halt. The purpose of support materials is to help you deliver your information in as many ways as possible so that each student is provided the optimum opportunity to learn the lesson materials.

7. *Prepare a definite beginning and ending to your lesson.* First, you must decide how you will get your students' attention. What hook will you use to get your students interested in your lesson? What kind of support materials will help you introduce your topic? Second, once you have introduced your topics, tell your students what they will learn in the lesson and how they will learn it. As you go through your various learning strategies and students acquire the information, tell them what they just learned. Do not be afraid to repeat this information over and over to them within the course of the lesson. Finally, summarize or provide a short overview of what was covered during the class. The conclusion may stick with the students longer than any other part of the lesson, so allow ample time to bring your lesson to a definite closure. In addition to a summary of what was learned in the class, your closure can also preview the next lesson and inform them of the homework you expect them to perform by the next session.

8. Plan for and prepare assessment strategies and procedures to be used as part of the lesson plan. These assessment strategies and procedures will help you ensure that students are learning the materials and will also help motivate students.

9. *Prepare the final written plan.* Have a way of highlighting main parts of your lesson and setting off examples, materials, and other key items in the lesson plan.

10. *Practice!* Work on delivering your lesson. Practice using your support materials, conducting, or whatever is needed for your lesson plan. You must be aware of what you are doing and how you are performing at any given moment. You must analyze what students are doing and how they are performing at any given moment. Beyond this, you must be thinking what is ahead in your lesson. Thus, you need to be familiar enough with your lesson plan and presentation so that you will be free to notice your students' reactions as well as your delivery style and technique. This is not as simple as it seems, and practice is necessary.

There are many examples of boilerplates that are used in lesson planning. The following lesson plan boilerplate was designed for string classes.

Lesson Plan

Class _____   Date _____

Objective/Topic:

This lesson will aid in the development of the following musical skills:

Right-Hand Skills/Left-Hand Skills

____ Bow Hold/Bow Hand Shape	____ Left-Hand Shape
____ Bow Strokes	____ Extensions
____ Détaché	____ Pivots
____ Attack Strokes	____ Finger Placement
____ Martelé and Staccato	____ Chromatic Alterations
____ Off-the-String Strokes	____ Vibrato
____ Spiccato and Sautillé	____ Shifting
____ Special Effect Bowings	____ Intonation
____ Ricochet	*Instrument Position and*
____ Slurred Staccato	*Body Posture*
____ Chords	____ Body Posture
____ Sul Tasto	____ Instrument Hold
____ Sul Ponticello	
____ Tremolo	*General Musical Skills*
____ Collé	____ Phrasing
	____ Rhythmic Reading
____ Bowings (Direction/ Change)	____ Sight Reading
____ String Crossing/ Arm Levels	____ Improvisation
____ Tone Color/Tone Production	____ Dynamics
	____ Ensemble
	____ Blend
	____ Balance

Additional Skills:

Materials:

Procedure:

Student Assessment Strategies:

Results/Evaluation:

Summary of Overall Lesson Planning

Students should be able to interact with the teacher and other class members while enhancing their creative potentials and developing cognitive, psychomotor, and aesthetic skills. In order to tap these skills in each student, appropriate delivery systems must be used that present materials using the audio, visual, and kinesthetic modes. Whether you use computer-generated sounds and images, props from home that can be touched or imaged in students' minds, or a variety of recording or playback equipment, your classroom lessons must be designed to reach each student in your orchestra.

All of these elements must be present to produce effective classroom teaching. In addition to the type of information you are presenting and the delivery systems you might be using to help you teach that information, you should also focus on the manner in which you present your materials. A teacher's delivery system can enhance the learning atmosphere and environment, and help individualize and personalize the learning process for each student.

The manner in which the teacher carries herself, the ability of the instructor to read student feedback through body language, eye and facial expression, the movement of the teacher about the room, his nonverbal cues, and vocal delivery and expression are important in ensuring that the content of the lesson is presented in a personalized, stimulating, and motivational manner—one that spurs student interest, is directed to individual learning styles, and generates student motivation.

EVALUATION OF TEACHING

It is difficult for us to imagine that any of us would want to be less than the best string teacher we possibly can be, and yet, without constant and consistent evaluation, continued growth and development are not possible. Several teacher evaluation instruments are available for use in accomplishing this purpose. The Survey of Teaching Effectiveness (STE) is an excellent teacher evaluation measure. The STE evaluates an individual's lesson delivery skills as well as her lesson planning and presentation. Whether another teacher uses it to evaluate you or you complete it yourself while watching a videotaped recording of your teaching lesson, the STE provides excellent feedback and information that is readily usable for improvement of your teaching episodes. The STE can also be useful in your lesson planning, as it can function as a guideline for preparation and planning. If all components on the STE are performed in a highly effective manner, you can be assured that your teaching skills are refined and that you are an effective and influential string teacher.

Survey of Teaching Effectiveness (STE)*

I. Lesson Delivery Skills (weighted 40 percent)

Posture	Poor				Excellent
A. *Head and Body*:	1	2	3	4	5

　　　　"Excellent" = Head lifted and centered; body lifted, relaxed,
　　　　　　　and poised
　　　　"Poor" = Head forward or to one side; body rigid or slouched

	Poor				Excellent
B. *Arms and Hands*:	1	2	3	4	5

"Excellent" = Normally relaxed with flowing gestures
"Poor" = Hand(s) in pocket(s), fidgeting/wringing or clenched;
    arms crossed front or back

	Poor				Excellent
C. *Legs*:	1	2	3	4	5

"Excellent" = Balanced; weight equally distributed
"Poor" = Crossed; locked knees; swaying; leaning on one leg

	Poor				Excellent
Eye Contact	1	2	3	4	5

"Excellent" = Movement about room with individual eye contact
"Poor" = Locked; staring; looking over heads or at floor

	Poor				Excellent
Gestures					
A. *Hands and Arms*:	1	2	3	4	5

"Excellent" = Natural, flowing; appropriate for spoken content
"Poor" = Absence of gestures; mechanical; inappropriate,
    and/or contrived

	Poor				Excellent
B. *Upper and Lower Body*:	1	2	3	4	5

"Excellent" = Change of stance, varying proximity to group/
    individuals; upper body directional change
"Poor" = Absence of movement; nervous pacing

	Poor				Excellent
Facial Expression	1	2	3	4	5

"Excellent" = Naturally varying; uncontrived changes of eyes,
    mouth, and facial muscles
"Poor" = Absence of variation; exaggerated and/or contrived
    facial movement

	Poor				Excellent
Vocal Inflection					
A. *Dynamics*:	1	2	3	4	5

"Excellent" = Comfortably and easily understood; naturally
    varying with appropriate accents and emphasis
"Poor" = Too soft to hear; uncomfortably loud; forced from the
    throat; static

	Poor				Excellent
B. *Tempo and Phrasing*:	1	2	3	4	5

"Excellent" = Comprehensible pace with moderate variations
    and appropriate pauses for emphasis
"Poor" = Too fast for comprehension; too slow for interest;
    fixed tempo with lack of pauses

	Poor				Excellent
C. *Pitch*:	1	2	3	4	5

"Excellent" = Natural variations for emphasis; voice is pitched
for teacher/student listening comfort and
ease (i.e., predominantly in lower third of
range)

"Poor" = No variation; contrived; speaking predominantly in
upper two-thirds of range

	Poor				Excellent
D. *Diction*:	1	2	3	4	5

"Excellent" = Clearly articulated vowels and consonants;
projected and resonating; easy to understand

"Poor" = Placed in back of throat, swallowing words; lack of
resonance; lazy tongue and lips

II. Planning and Presentation of Lesson (weighted 60 percent)

Evidence of Lesson Planning

	Poor				Excellent
A. *Content*:					
1a. *Materials—Appropriate Music*:	1	2	3	4	5

"Excellent" = Music appropriate for the age and ability of
the students

"Poor" = Music not appropriate for students

	Poor				Excellent
1b. *Materials—Music and Concept*:	1	2	3	4	5

"Excellent" = Music exemplary of the concept being developed

"Poor" = Music unrelated to concept; poor example

	Poor				Excellent
1c. *Materials—Supportive*:	1	2	3	4	5

"Excellent" = Used appropriate supportive materials (i.e.,
charts, recordings, videotaped presentations,
computers, pictures)

"Poor" = Materials unrelated to concept; poor materials

	Poor				Excellent
2. *Objectives*:	1	2	3	4	5

"Excellent" = Determined appropriate objectives; students
were made aware of objectives

"Poor" = Objectives were not appropriate; students were
unaware of lesson objective focus

	Poor				Excellent
B. *Organization*:					
1a. *Activities—Type*:	1	2	3	4	5

"Excellent" = Type of activities were appropriate for
students' age and skill, and/or for number
of students in the setting

"Poor" = Inappropriate activities for students' abilities, age,
or for the number of students in the setting

	Poor			Excellent

1b. *Activities—Number*:   1   2   3   4   5

"Excellent" = Number of activities were appropriate for
students' age, skill, and for the length of the
class; each activity was of appropriate length

"Poor" = Inappropriate number of activities for students, situation, and setting; inappropriate length of activities

	Poor			Excellent

1c. *Activities—Sequencing*:   1   2   3   4   5

"Excellent" = Activities were sequenced logically

"Poor" = Lack of order and/or flow of activities; activities
missing in learning sequence

Subject Matter Competence   Poor   Excellent

A. *Information and Demonstrations*:   1   2   3   4   5

"Excellent" = Presented correct information; accurate
demonstrations

"Poor" = Presented incorrect, contradictory, or misleading
information; did not or could not accurately
demonstrate (i.e., clapped or sang incorrect rhythms);
did not demonstrate or provide information

	Poor			Excellent

B. *Musical Model*:   1   2   3   4   5

"Excellent" = Expressive and accurate (i.e., attention to phrasing)

"Poor" = Nonexpressive, incorrect, or inappropriate modeling;
no modeling evidenced

	Poor			Excellent

C. *Conducting*:   1   2   3   4   5

"Excellent" = Appropriate gestures for the group and the situation

"Poor" = Inappropriate gestures or not evidenced

Pacing   Poor   Excellent

A. *Logistics*:   1   2   3   4   5

"Excellent" = Organized, orderly; evidence of student learned
logistics (i.e., students get instruments or books
quickly, efficiently, quietly, and return to their
seats and continue to prepare and ready themselves for the rehearsal/class)

"Poor" = Chaos; students have no planned routine(s) that
enable them to prepare for rehearsal/class

	Poor			Excellent

B. *"On-Task"*:   1   2   3   4   5

"Excellent" = Class began and ended promptly, wasted time minimal, time effectively utilized; definite closure to lesson

"Poor" = Class began late, students released late, and students
hurriedly put away instruments/equipment/materials;
time not utilized effectively; class ended without closure

	Poor				Excellent
C. *Flow*:	1	2	3	4	5

"Excellent" = Appropriate balance between teacher direc-
tives/explanations and student participation;
one activity led to another without interruptions
or breaks

"Poor" = Teacher talked too much; too much time spent going
from one activity to another; long, disruptive breaks
between and within activities

	Poor				Excellent
D. *Responsiveness to Group*:	1	2	3	4	5

"Excellent" = Teacher responded appropriately to group and
individual musical/technical needs and problems

"Poor" = Teacher was unaware of, did not respond, or
responded inappropriately to group or individual
musical/technical needs and problems

Sequencing Pattern/Rehersal Cycle	Poor				Excellent
A. *Directive*:	1	2	3	4	5

"Excellent" = Specific directive identifying task to be
accomplished

"Poor" = Nonspecific directive with no specific task to be
accomplished

	Poor				Excellent
B. *Feedback*:	1	2	3	4	5

"Excellent" = Specific positive or negative feedback provided;
utilized student ideas and comments when/where
applicable

"Poor" = No feedback or nonspecific feedback provided

Teaching Style

	Poor				Excellent
A. *Charisma, Energy, Confidence, Enthusiasm*:	1	2	3	4	5

"Excellent" = Secure, animated; captured student attention and
interest

"Poor" = Sluggish, lethargic, insecure; students were bored or
disinterested

	Poor				Excellent
B. *Interest Shown in Students/Topic*:	1	2	3	4	5

"Excellent" = Sincere; interest evident in student welfare and
in topic presented

"Poor" = Lacked sincerity; interest in student or topic not
evident; "only went through the motions"

C. *Supports and Encourages*   Poor   Excellent
   Students' Efforts: 1   2   3   4   5
   "Excellent" = Sincere praise provided; emphasized positive
              aspects of student efforts; constructive
              suggestions and comments provided
   "Poor" = Sarcastic; belittled students and students' efforts;
           emphasized negative aspects of student efforts;
           contrived praise

Evaluation Totals

Part I
   Posture   _____ ÷ 3 = _____
   Eye Contact   _____ ÷ 1 = _____
   Gestures   _____ ÷ 2 = _____
   Facial Expression _____ ÷ 1 = _____
   Vocal Inflection   _____ ÷ 4 = _____

Total of Part I   _____ × 2 × 0.40 = _____

Part II
   Evidence of Lesson Planning _____ ÷ 7 = _____
   Subject Matter Competence   _____ ÷ 3 = _____
   Pacing   _____ ÷ 4 = _____
   Sequencing Pattern   _____ ÷ 2 = _____
   Teaching Style   _____ ÷ 3 = _____

Total of Part II _____ × 2 × 0.60 = _____

Total Score
   Total of Part I _____ + Total of Part II _____ = _____

Total Score Range: 10 (Ineffective) to 50 (Extremely Effective)

"Empirical validity for the STE was established to be $rs = 0.89$. Adjudicators were directed to rank video-taped teaching episodes of students from 'best' to 'least best.' Approximately three weeks later, the same adjudicators were again directed to assess the video-taped teaching episodes using the STE. Scores for each of the teaching episodes were then ranked and compared to the ranking produced previously" (Hamann, Lineburgh, and Paul 1996, 11). Fant (1996) correlated ratings of adjudicators who used both the Rehearsal Effectiveness Scale by Bergee (1992) with those from the STE. Fant found a correlation of $r = 0.89$ between scores on the two measures.

Reliability of the STE was established in a test-retest procedure. Reliability for the STE was found to be $r = 0.83$. Intercorrelations between the categorical scores and Total Score of the STE were computed ($N = 159$). Intercorrelations between the categories on the STE were found to range from $r = 0.61$ to $r = 0.95$ (Hamann, Lineburgh, and Paul 1996, 11).

THE NATIONAL STANDARDS

We are very fortunate to be teaching at a time when two of our national organizations have presented standards. These standards can be used to help us prepare comprehensive lesson plans and to help us develop as teachers.

In 1998 and 1999, conferences and meetings were held by members of the American String Teachers Association. As a result of these proceedings, recommendations were forwarded establishing criteria that would serve as standards for orchestra directors. These are the standards that all orchestra directors are recommended to possess to help ensure success in the profession, and they are set forth in the following outline.*

I. As a Musician

     1. demonstrates a high level of musicianship in performance

     2. performs at an intermediate to advanced level on at least one string instrument

     3. demonstrates at least basic to intermediate performance concepts on one string instrument and understands advanced and artistic concepts on other string instruments

     4. demonstrates ability to play by ear and improvise

     5. demonstrates a basic knowledge of performing and teaching the woodwind, brass, and percussion instruments at least at a basic level, with an understanding of intermediate to advanced concepts

     6. demonstrates orchestral conducting skills

     7. demonstrates keyboard skills of at least a basic to intermediate level and accompanies melodies using at least I–IV–V chords

     8. demonstrates aural discrimination skills

     9. demonstrates the understanding of prevention of performance injuries

     10. demonstrates the knowledge of a wide range of music repertoire for teaching diverse styles, genres, cultures, and historical periods

II. As an Educator

     1. understands and applies pedagogy for violin, viola, cello, and bass

     2. demonstrates effective rehearsal techniques for string and full orchestra

     3. demonstrates the knowledge of a variety of string and orchestral instruction materials at all levels

4. demonstrates the knowledge of repertoire for student performance, including solo literature, orchestra music, and chamber music

5. demonstrates skill in arranging music for school orchestras

6. demonstrates strategies for integrating music with other disciplines

7. understands different student learning styles, levels of maturation, and special needs and adapts instruction accordingly

8. demonstrates knowledge of comprehensive, sequential K–12 music curricula, including string and orchestra, with appropriate goals and expectations for all levels of proficiencies

9. demonstrates understanding of the principles of a variety of homogeneous and heterogeneous pedagogical approaches for teaching string classes (e.g., Suzuki, Rolland, Bornoff)

10. exhibits effective classroom management skills and strategies

11. demonstrates understanding of how to teach students of diverse ages, socioeconomic, ethnic, and geographic backgrounds

12. demonstrates effective methods of assessing and evaluating student achievement

13. knows about instrument rental and purchasing

14. knows current technology for instruction, research, and musical applications

15. knows of current music and general education policies, including current scheduling practices for successful string and orchestra programs

16. demonstrates ability to gather pertinent orchestra program data

17. understands the importance of maintaining a balance between personal and career interests

18. demonstrates ability to develop budgets for equipment and supplies

19. demonstrates understanding of effective advocacy strategies for comprehensive music programs that include string/orchestra programs

20. demonstrates clear communication in written and oral form

21. demonstrates understanding of the K–12 National Music Education Standards and other state and local standards for music

III. As a Professional

    A. Musician

        1. continues to perform

        2. demonstrates concepts and understandings necessary for student achievement of Grade 12 National Music Education Standards

  3. exhibits effective, ongoing professional self-assessment

  4. continues to pursue opportunities for learning as a musician

B. Professional Affiliations and Related Activities

  1. maintains active involvement in professional associations, such as MENC, ASTA/NSOA, SSA, and CMA

  2. continues to interact with other music educators, observes other programs

  3. demonstrates professional ethics, appearance, behavior, and relationships within the profession, the school, and the greater community

  4. participates in ongoing professional development to improve teaching effectiveness

  5. serves in leadership roles with state and local MEAs, ASTA/NSOA chapters

C. School and Community Relations

  1. develops a healthy rapport with school administrators for nurturing a successful string and orchestra program

  2. understands the value of positive interaction with other members of the music and arts community

  3. establishes and maintains positive relations with school administrators, staff, and fellow teachers through communication and dialogue

  4. articulates the positive aspects of the string/orchestra component of a school music program through writing and speaking

  5. communicates effectively with parent support/booster groups, including clear and grammatically correct communication

  6. advocates effectively for a strong school orchestra program

The second set of standards presented here was created in 1994 by the Music Educators National Conference. The following outline sets forth the standards, identifies how to use the standards in selecting music, provides recommended rehearsal strategies for teaching the standards, and presents common orchestral works along with suggested rehearsal strategies that are focused on teaching the national standards.

I. Introduction

A. What are the music content standards? Singing, performing, improvising, composing, arranging, reading, notating, listening, describing, evaluating, and relating music to history and the other arts

B. Goal of the standards in a rehearsal: teaching performance with understanding

C. Most common problems in teaching the standards: no time and know-how

II. Selecting Music to Teach the Standards in Rehearsals

A. Select repertoire for your rehearsals and concerts that avails itself to teaching the standards. For example:

1. Select a wide range of repertoire, considering composer, historical period, multicultural, other arts, composing/arranging/improvising, historical event, different musical styles, different historical periods, and different countries.

2. Select music written by a composer whose biography is available so that you can correlate his or her life with related historical and artistic developments.

3. If selecting an arrangement, be sure the score of the original is available so that students can compare it with the arrangement.

III. Recommended Rehearsal Strategies for Teaching the Standards

A. Select one or more of the following to do during rehearsal:

1. Discuss the life and contributions of the composer.

2. Provide the words to the melody if it is based on a song. Have students sing the melody and discuss the difference they experience musically when they play it on their instruments.

3. Play recordings of different performances of the work, including one by the students, and evaluate the quality of the performances using one musical aspect at a time: tempo, dynamics, intonation, phrasing, style, expressiveness, balance, and so on.

   a. Variation: Select some students to deliberately play a passage incorrectly, and have other students identify the inaccuracy.

4. Discuss important historical events that occurred during the life of the composer.

5. Discuss important developments in the arts during the life of the composer.

6. Discuss important developments in the arts other than music that occurred during the life of the composer.

7. Discuss developments in academic subjects other than music.

8. Let the students see the score of the work so that they can study the form and structure of the piece, trace the development of melodies, and understand how their instrument's part compares with that of other instruments in the composition.

9. Play, listen, and discuss other works by the composer to understand the unique music created by the composer.

10. Have students transpose the melody or melodies in a work to other keys.

11. Allow students to help determine appropriate tempi, styles, and phrasing for a performance of the work.

12. Compare arrangements with the original. Provide recordings and scores of the original for discussion.

13. Use the national achievement standards to guide your teaching.

14. Teach composing and improvising within limits (e.g., meter, number of measures, key, note values, pitches, style, simple echoes, call and response, etc.) and have students perform.

15. (1) Evaluate how you are already teaching the standards, and (2) begin with five-minute rule: incorporate teaching the strategies in your rehearsals for five minutes.

IV. Sample Common Repertoire with Suggested Rehearsal Strategies for Teaching the Standards

Selection	Teaching Strategy	Standard
American Folk Song Suite (Grade 1) Arranged by Isaac Kendor Music	Define folk song. Provide words to one of the five familiar folk songs included in this suite and have students sing.	Singing alone and with others
	Play examples of folk songs in other cultures (e.g., Slavic folk song "Morning Dance" and the English folk song "London Bridge"). Discuss how each represents the sound of its culture or region.	Performing on instruments, alone and with others, a varied music; understanding music in relation to history and culture
	Discuss how folk songs are transmitted aurally from one generation to the next.	Understanding music in relation to history and culture
	Listen to different accompaniments and arrangements of "America," a melody included in this suite. Describe differences.	Listening to, analyzing, and describing music
	Perform "Go Tell Aunt Rhody" from this suite as a solo melody from Suzuki Book 1.	Performing on instruments, alone and with others, a varied repertoire of music

Selection	Teaching Strategy	Standard
	Select one of the five melodies in the suite and have students write out the melody from their music.	Reading and notating music
	Listen to recordings of folk music from other countries and describe the music (e.g., French national anthem).	Listening to, analyzing, and describing music
	Perform this suite in a concert along with selected folk melodies from other countries.	Performing on instruments, alone and with others, a varied repertoire of music
New World Symphony (Grade 1) Dvorak/Allen Hal Leonard Publishing	Play excerpts of the melody from the original. Compare this arrangement. Discuss differences.	Listening to, analyzing, and describing music
	Play two different recordings of excerpts from the original symphony and have students describe differences in the performances.	Evaluating music and music performance
	Show students the score of the original with the melody highlighted. Show how the melody is treated differently each time through instrumentation, range, and accompaniment.	Reading and notating music Listening to, analyzing, and describing music
	Have students sing the melody as you accompany.	Singing, alone and with others a varied repertoire of music
	Discuss the life of Dvorak, particularly his time in America. Explain why his music in Symphony no. 5 is referred to as the *New World Symphony.* Describe what was going on in history during Dvorak's lifetime (e.g., the transcontinental railroad was completed and the American Civil War took place).	Understanding music in relation to history and culture
	Play other examples of Dvorak's compositions and compare with the sounds in his *New World Symphony.*	Listening to, analyzing, and describing music

(continued)

Selection	Teaching Strategy	Standard
New World Symphony (*continued*)	Describe what was created in other arts and disciplines outside the arts during Dvorak's lifetime (e.g., Lewis Carroll wrote *Alice in Wonderland* and Louisa May Alcott wrote *Little Women*).	Understanding relationships between music, the other arts, and disciplines outside the arts
"Can Can" (Grade 2) Offenbach/Isaac Wynn Music	Define musical theater. Describe how this music was originally composed by Offenbach for musical theater in Paris in 1858. Discuss musical theater in today's times (e.g., Broadway shows, high school musicals, dinner theaters).	Understanding music in relation to history and culture
	Describe some of the important events in American history that occurred during the life of Offenbach (1819–1880), such as the American Civil War, the Gold Rush in California, and the unveiling of the Statue of Liberty.	Understanding music in relation to history and culture
	Describe other important developments in art, drama, and literature that occurred during the life of Offenbach (e.g., Van Gogh creates *The Sunflowers*, Mark Twain writes *Huckleberry Finn*).	Understanding relationships between music, the other arts, and disciplines outside the arts
	Compare other dance music (e.g., ballet, Baroque dance, hoedowns, rock 'n' roll). Discuss similar characteristics of dance music.	Listening to, analyzing, and describing music
	Compare different arrangements of the "Can Can" for student orchestra (e.g., Dackow arrangement). Have students notate some of the differences.	Reading and notating music
	Have students notate the melody and compose different accompaniment.	Composing and arranging a music within specified guidelines
	Perform the music in a legato style. Discuss why it does not sound like the lively performance dance style that Offenbach intended.	Evaluating music and the music performance

Selection	Teaching Strategy	Standard
Danza Nelhybel Kerby Music	Discuss the music of Nelhybel. Play recorded examples. Describe the characteristics of his music. Compare music from other historical periods (e.g., Baroque, Classical) based on a five-note theme: A D C B A.	Listening to, analyzing, describing music
	Have students write out the theme as it appears in their part in the first movement. Compare this compositional technique to twelve-tone-row writing.	Reading and notating music
	Request students to sing their melody.	Singing, alone and with with others, a varied repertoire of music
	Have students compose a melody using only five pitches as Nelhybel did.	Composing and arranging music within specified guidelines
	Danza was first performed in 1971 commissioned for the Manchester College String Festival in Manchester, Indiana. Discuss how compositions are commissioned. Give examples of other famous works that have been commissioned in the other arts (e.g., Picasso commissioned to paint *Guernica*).	Understanding relationships between music, the other arts, and disciplines outside the arts
	Have students play each of the three movements of the work at tempos different from what Nelhybel suggested. Discuss which tempos the students like better and why. Discuss if a composition should be performed only at the tempos specified by the composer.	Evaluating music and performance
Australian Folk Song Suite Ralph Hultgren Kjos Music	Provide students with copies of the score. Select one of the three movements for students to find melody, and then study how the arranger changed the accompaniment to the melody throughout the movement.	Evaluating music and music performance.

(continued)

Selection	Teaching Strategy	Standard
Australian Folk Song Suite (*continued*)	Have students write an accompaniment to a familiar folk melody (e.g., "Mary Had a Little Lamb") using I, IV, and V chords only.	Composing and arranging music within specified guidelines
	Play each of the folk songs this suite is based upon. Sing some American folk songs. How are they similar to and different from those of Australia?	Performing on instruments, alone and with others, a varied repertoire of music; singing, alone and with others, a varied repertoire of music
	Compare the last movement, "Bush Dance," a native song favored by Queensland cattlemen, with songs sung in the late 1800s in America by cowboys (e.g., "Turkey in the Straw"). How are these melodies quite similar?	Evaluating music and music performance
	Discuss the culture of Australia. Discuss why it is similar in many ways to American culture (e.g., both countries have roots in Western Europe).	Understanding music in relation to history and culture
	Australian Folk Suite is based on three Australian folk songs. Challenge students to select three American folk songs they believe best represent America.	Evaluating music and music performance

REFERENCES

Bergee, Martin J. 1992. A scale assessing music student teachers' rehearsal effectiveness. *Journal of Research in Music Education* 40:5–13.

Fant, Greg R. 1996. An investigation of the relationships between undergraduate music education students' early field experience and student teaching performance. Ph.D. diss., University of Arizona.

Gillespie, Robert, and Donald L. Hamann. 1998. The status of orchestra programs in the public schools. *Journal of Research in Music Education* 46:75–86.

Hamann, Donald L., and Robert Frost. 2000. The effect of private lesson study on the practice habits and attitudes toward practicing of middle school and high school string students. *Contributions to Music Education* 27 (2):71–94.

Hamann, Donald L., Nancy Lineburgh, and Stephen J. Paul. April 1996. Teaching effectiveness and social skill development. *Journal of Research in Music Education* 46:87–101.

ADDITIONAL RESOURCES FOR TEACHING THE NATIONAL STANDARDS IN THE SCHOOL ORCHESTRA

Allen, Michael. 1995. The national standards for arts education: Implications of school string programs. *American String Teacher* 45 (3):30–33.

Allen, Michael, Robert Gillespie, and Pamela Hayes. 1996. *Essential elements for strings: Teacher resource kit.* Milwaukee, Wis.: Hal Leonard.

Barber, David. 1986. *Bach, Beethoven, and the boys.* Toronto: Sound and Vision.

———. 1990. *When the fat lady sings.* Toronto: Sound and Vision.

Cole, Brian. 1997. *Stretta music.* Morehead, Minn.: Moorhead Elementary School.

Dabczynski, Andrew. 1995. National standards for arts education: A golden opportunity for string teachers. *American String Teacher* 45 (1):73–76.

Elledge, Chuck, Jane Yarbrough, and Bruce Pearson. 1993. *Music theory and history workbook.* 2 vols. San Diego: Kjos Music.

Grout, Donald. 1980. *A history of Western music.* New York: W. W. Norton.

Grun, Bernard. 1975. *The timetables of history: A horizontal linkage of people and events.* New York: Simon and Schuster.

Hoffer, Charles. 1989. *The understanding of music.* Belmont, Calif.: Wadsworth.

Jennings, Paul. 1990. *The great composers.* Vol. 1. Milwaukee, Wis.: Hal Leonard. Includes cassettes and reproducible student worksheets.

Kjelland, James. 1995. String teacher preparation and the national music standards. *American String Teacher* 45 (4):34–37.

Klevberg, Janet. 1994. *The great composers.* Vol. 2. Milwaukee, Wis.: Hal Leonard. Includes cassettes and reproducible student worksheets.

Machlis, Joseph. 1977. *The enjoyment of music.* New York: W. W. Norton.

McLin, Leon. 1977. *Pulse: A history of music.* San Diego: Kjos Music.

Montgomery, June, and Maurice Hinson. 1995. *Meet the great composers.* Van Nuys, Calif.: Alfred Music. Includes student books, CD, cassette, student activity sheets.

Politoske, Daniel. 1979. *Music.* Englewood Cliffs, N.J.: Prentice-Hall.

Schmid, Will. 1992. Multicultural music education. *Music Educators Journal* 78 (9):41–45.

Straub, Dorothy. 1995. The national standards for arts education: Context and issues. *American String Teacher* 45 (3):24–28.

Straub, Dorothy, Louis Bergonzi, and Ann Witt. 1996. *Strategies for teaching strings and orchestra: Your key to implementing the national standards for music education.* Reston, Va.: Music Educators National Conference.

Volk, Teresa. 1995a. Adding world musics to your string program, part 1: Chinese folk and Thai classical music. *American String Teacher* 45 (3):65–69.

———. 1995b. Adding world musics to your string program, part 2: Arabic music. *American String Teacher* 45 (4):67–70.

Witt, Ann, Dean Angles, Dale Kempter, and James Kjelland. 1991. *Teaching stringed instruments.* Reston, Va.: Music Educators National Conference.

Zunic, Ed. 1997. *A history of Western art music.* Newark, Ohio: Newark High Orchestra.

ADDITIONAL SAMPLE REPERTOIRE FOR USE IN TEACHING THE NATIONAL STANDARDS IN THE SCHOOL ORCHESTRA

Historical Period

Renaissance: *French Renaissance Suite* (Grade 2)—arr. by Dennis Leclaire (Warren Music)
Baroque: *Hornpipe* (Grade 2)—Handel/Meyer (Highland/Etling)

Baroque: *Concerto in G* (Grade 2–3)—Vivaldi/Frackenpohl (Ludwig Music)
Classical: *Symphony no. 73*, fourth movement, "La Chasse" (Grade 3)—Haydn/Dackow (Ludwig Music)
Classical: *Symphony no. 10* (Grade 2–3)—Mozart/Dackow (Ludwig Music)
Romantic: *Ode to Joy* (Grade 1)—Beethoven/Del Borgo (Belwin/Warner Bros.)
Romantic: *Seventh Symphony* (Grade 3)—Beethoven/Donald Olah (MSB)
Contemporary Classical: *Bartok Suite* (Grade 2)—Bartok/Clark (Belwin/Warner Bros.)
Contemporary Pop: *Twist and Shout* (Grade 2)—Russell and Medley/Cerulli (Warner Bros.)

Contemporary/Composing
Student Composing: *Quartet in D Minor* (Grade 3)—Nathan Rudavsky-Brody

Historical Event
Early History of Music in America: *A Shaker Hymn* (Grade 1)—arr. O'Reilly (Highland/Etling)
World War II: Theme from *Shindler's List* (Grade 2)—Williams/Higgins (Hal Leonard)

Related Arts
Opera/Drama: "O Mio Babbino" from the opera *Gianni Schicchi* (Grade 2)—Puccini/Heilman (Helmann Publications)

Improvising/Arranging
Brandenburg Concerto no. 3, second movement (Grade 3)—Bach/Isaac (Highland/Etling)

Multicultural
American: *Early American Suite* (Grade 2–21/2)—Percy Hall (Great Works Publishing)
Ukraine: *Flirtation* (Grade 2)—arr. Dackow (Ludwig Music)
Korea: *Korean Folk Tune* (Grade 2)—arr. Meyer (Highland/Etling)
Venezuela: *Fiesta* (Grade 3)—arr. Conley (Belwin/Warner Bros.)
Brazil: *Fiesta* (Grade 3)—arr. Conley (Belwin/Warner Bros.)
Argentina: *Fiesta* (Grade 3)—arr. Conley (Belwin/Warner Bros.)
Israel: *Songs of Israel* (Grade 2)—arr. Frost (Kendor)
Jewish: *Hanukkah Favorites* (Grade 2)—arr. Niehaus (Kendor)
South America: *Two South American Tangos* (Grade 3)—Villodo and Rodriguez/Isaac (Alfred)

American History/Arranging
The Tennessee Waltz (Grade 2)—arr. Peter Rolland (Rolland String Research Associates)
Golden Slippers (Grade 2)—arr. Peter Rolland (Rolland String Research Associates)

7

REHEARSAL TECHNIQUES

Effective rehearsals begin and end with a myriad of long- and short-range plans. This chapter discusses the essential planning needed for effective rehearsals, with the understanding that the success of any orchestra program is contingent on the director's interpersonal skills, organizational abilities, and musicianship. Covered in this chapter are the guidelines for determining rehearsal strategies, including the planning for the year, preparation before the first rehearsal, tryouts, planning strategy for the first rehearsal, and procedures for carrying it out.

PLANNING FOR THE YEAR

Effective rehearsals begin with organization of the year. Your plan for the year must include the number of concerts that you will be performing with each of your groups, the dates of your concerts, and the time frame in which your programs must be prepared. Once you have determined the number of concerts you will be playing and how much time exists to prepare your groups for them, you can effectively begin your planning. Appropriate music must be chosen for each concert. The guidelines for choosing music are outlined in Chapter 6.

YOUR REHEARSAL ROOM AND EQUIPMENT

Your room and equipment must both be readied for each rehearsal. The environment in which you and your students work must be clean, inviting, and comfortable. While regular maintenance is essential to a healthy rehearsal environment, more extensive preparation may also be needed before the beginning of a new term. Wood or linoleum floors should be waxed and polished, and carpets should be shampooed and vacuumed. Windows should be washed, and walls should be cleaned or painted (or both). The electrical system (lights and outlets) and ventilation system (heating and cooling) should be checked so that they are in proper working order. Lights and outlets should be repaired and replaced, and ventilation systems should be cleaned and checked to ensure adequate air flow and temperature control.

Chairs and stands should be checked to be sure that they are in good condition or have been repaired or replaced. Recording equipment should be serviced as needed, and checked to be sure it is ready for use.

You need to inspect any school-owned instruments and complete any repairs as needed. You also need to ensure that regular maintenance, such as string replacement, bow rehairing, pad replacement, and piano tuning is performed on school instruments. Replenish any supplies, such as value oil, strings, and rosin. Uniforms, if used, need to be cleaned and repaired as necessary. Finally, you need to make sure that instrument storage areas are cleaned and prepared for student use.

TRYOUTS

Regardless of how you want to use the information to place students in your orchestra, you must know how well each of your orchestra members plays. A tryout, or an audition, is one of the most widely used methods to determine student performance level. You need to consider the following. What selections will be performed at the audition? How long will each tryout be? When and where will the tryout or audition be held? How will you evaluate each orchestra member? You should also think about the audition procedure itself. What will you say to each student? How will you make each student as comfortable as possible? How will you handle each particular procedure? What guidelines will you enforce when students play? Finally, you need to think how you wish to use the information you get from your auditions.

What Materials Should I Include in the Audition?

Before you hold auditions, you must decide what you would like to hear your students perform. Since you should already have chosen your music for the year, you already know the works you would like to perform at the first concert. Review each of your selections and choose passages for student preparation and performance. Violins will probably perform different passages than violas, and violas different passages than cellos, and so on. You need to decide whether all of your violinists will audition on violin I parts, or whether they will be given a choice to audition on a violin I or violin II part. You may also wish to have the students prepare a short selection of their own to play for the audition.

Select passages that show each student's ability to play with rhythmic accuracy, excellent intonation, correct bowing, good tone quality, and accurate dynamics. The ability to shift, perform various types of bowing, use vibrato, and play expressively should also be considered when selecting audition materials for strings. If you are auditioning winds and percussion for your full orchestra, you will also need to consider passages that demonstrate students' range, articulation capabilities, register, correct breathing and tonguing, and overall control. Your musical selections should challenge and help students display their ability to play musically, with control, and with technical, rhythmic, and intonation accuracy.

In addition to selecting prepared passages for your students, consider the performance of scales and arpeggios. How many scales and arpeggios would you like your students to play, how many octaves, and at what tempo? What rhythmic structure, both major and minor, what forms of minor, and with what types of bowing or articulation would you like to hear? Should the scales be played by memory? Should a particular fingering pattern be used to play each scale (strings), or should alternate fingering be expected (winds)? Will you require rudiments from your percussion players? If so, which rudiments, at what tempo, and so on? Once you have determined this portion of the audition, you can think about the sight-reading portion of the tryout.

A final component of your audition should be sight reading. Good sight readers are often strong leaders in your orchestra. Individuals who can both prepare a work and sight-read well should be considered for leadership positions in each section of your orchestra.

How Long Should the Audition Be?

You should plan your audition to last between ten minutes and fifteen minutes per student. This will allow each student ample time to display her ability in the areas discussed. You should also consider tape-recording each student's performance. In this way, you can review individual performances should questions arise later.

Plan the length of each section of the audition. If you want to have a ten-minute audition, determine the length of the warm-up, prepared works/excerpts, scale performance, and sight reading. A suggestion could be one-half minute for warm-up, three and a half minutes for prepared excerpts and perhaps a portion of a prepared work selected by the student, one and a half minutes for scales, and two and a half minutes for sight reading. This allows one minute to collect needed information at the beginning of the audition, and one minute to discuss each of your students' performances at the end of the tryout.

In addition to auditioning students on prepared works, scales and arpeggios, and sight reading, you may also wish to consider other evaluation materials, especially if the audition is serving for more than one type of group. The ability to improvise may be of importance to you if you have a jazz strings group. If you have a strolling strings, mariachi, or fiddling group, it may be important for you to determine students' abilities in each of these areas. Thus, audition materials can include a variety of materials, which may increase the time for each tryout. Remember that the purpose of your tryouts is to discover the playing ability of each student. Once this is determined, you can place students in various sections or groups with a higher degree of confidence that you are doing what is best for them and for the group.

When and Where Will Tryouts Be Held?

Ideally, you will be able to hold your auditions two to three weeks before classes begin. If this is possible, you will need to contact each of your students. You can contact them by mail, by telephone, e-mail, or in person. The purpose of contacting your students is to inform them of the time and place of the audition, the length of the tryout, and the music they should be prepared to perform, as well as other materials they should be prepared to play, such as scales, arpeggios, and sight-reading material. Once the students have been informed and have access to the materials they will be responsible to play, you are ready to hold the auditions.

How Will You Evaluate Each Student Audition?

Both you and your students want the most accurate and reliable assessment of audition performances as possible. As the director, you want an evaluation that not only is accurate and reliable, but also reduces the need for subjective, rather than objective, assessment. An audition evaluation form with predetermined categories and criteria can help provide for accurate, reliable, and objective assessment. The items listed in the following audition evaluation form provide criteria that can be considered in an audition situation.

Audition Evaluation Form

Name _____ Date _____

School _____

Address _____ Telephone _____

City _____ Zip code _____

E-mail address _____

Year in school _____ Instrument _____

Group you are auditioning for _____

Private study: _____ Yes: How long? _____   _____ No

Do you plan to attend college? _____ Yes _____ No
                    _____ Undecided

If yes, do you plan to:

    continue in music? _____ Yes _____ No _____ Undecided

    major in music? _____ Yes _____ No _____ Undecided

Rating Scale

5 = Excellent   4 = Very good   3 = Good   2 = Fair   1 = Poor

Category	Rating
Intonation Comment:	

Rhythmic accuracy and tempo
    Comment:

_____

Tone quality
    Comment:

_____

Technique: Strings
    Shifting technique
    Vibrato technique
    Bowing technique
    Fingering technique
    Comments:

_____

Technique: Winds
    Breath control
    Tonguing technique
    Articulation
    Range and control
    Comments:

_____

Percussion: Rudiments
    Sticking
    Clarity
    Accuracy
    Comments:

_____

Scales
    Comment:

_____

Sight reading
    Comment:

_____

Musicianship
    Comment:

_____

General comments: Total score:

_____

In addition to the personal student information, the form contains several categories of musical criteria. Two of the most important musical considerations in any audition are intonation and rhythmic accuracy. Students must be able to play in tune, and they must be able to stay together. Tone quality is often correlated with pitch accuracy. Students with poor tone quality often display weak intonation. Therefore, tone quality should be considered as a viable category for assessment.

The components of string, wind, and percussion technique should offer some ideas for category evaluation criteria. While all of the criteria listed are important, you may want to consider additional criteria. The evaluation of scales, sight reading, and musicianship are individually important and should be considered as separate categories for assessment.

While this audition evaluation form may not be ideal for you, it should offer you ideas from which you can develop your own assessment form. The goal of any form is to allow for accuracy, reliability, and objectivity while permitting your students the chance to display their abilities to the fullest.

The Audition Procedure

Contacting or meeting with your students prior to the audition will help facilitate the actual tryout procedure. When audition time arrives, the student will have had the chance to prepare the music, as well as fill out any forms that need to be completed.

Plan to have students arrive at least ten to fifteen minutes earlier than their scheduled tryout time. Students can use this time to warm up, review materials, and compose themselves before the audition.

As mentioned previously, the audition should be tape-recorded. The tryout procedure should be as consistent for each of your students as possible. A metronome should be used in the audition to ensure consistency and accuracy. You should establish a policy for restarts, tempo infractions, and so on and enforce the policy with all students. A suggested audition procedure is as follows:

1. Greet the student, collect forms, and complete the personal information on the audition sheet. Since some students are more susceptible to anxiety than others, it is important that you create an atmosphere that is as relaxed as possible. By greeting students by name and asking them the questions on the audition sheet, you create a more relaxed atmosphere.

2. Ask your student to warm up and tune. This should be considered part of the audition procedure as you can begin to assess intonation, technique, tone quality, and other criteria at this time.

3. Ask your student to perform prepared excerpts as well as a portion of a prepared work he has selected for the audition. For prepared excerpts, you should select a metronome marking and use the same marking for all students performing like excerpts. The decision to have the student sit or stand should depend on the performance practice of the group for which she is auditioning. If the student would normally sit in the performance group, the student should sit for the audition, and vice versa.

At this point, you can begin evaluating intonation, rhythmic accuracy, tone quality, and so on.

4. Next, you can ask your student to play scales. Usually one major and one minor scale are adequate. Strings should play two-octave scales. Three-octave scales can be considered as well, with the possible exception of the double bass. Winds should be able to play one-octave or, more appropriately, two-octave scales.

5. Sight reading can be the next activity. The beginning and ending sight-reading selection should be clearly marked. A metronome can be used to indicate a suggested tempo. Allow the student one minute to look over, audiate, sight-sing, bow, and finger the part. Since this portion of the audition may be the weakest, you need to make your students feel comfortable with their performance. Highlight your students' strengths and downplay weaknesses, as they may be all too painfully aware of their shortcomings in the area of sight reading.

6. Once your students have completed the audition, let them know how well they did. Give them a brief overview of your assessment in each of the categories. This will allow you time to reconsider your assessments and will let your students know how well they performed. Thank each student before he leaves, and complete your assessment of that student before allowing the next student to enter.

Use of the Audition Information

Once you have auditioned all of your students, you can reassess your selection of music for the year. Ask yourself whether you selected music that was too difficult or too easy for the students. If needed, you may be able to choose and order new or additional works for your groups. You can also use your audition information to seat students in your groups.

One of the favored seating arrangements for strings is to place a weaker player next to a stronger player. Hence the outside players may be stronger players than inside players. For winds and strings, the strongest players are generally given the principal chairs. These individuals need to be both strong performers and possess leadership skills. Often principals are asked to lead sectional rehearsals or provide suggestions for bowing, fingering, articulation, and other such musical considerations.

Many directors rotate players among the various sections throughout the year, generally keeping some type of stand-by-stand balance between weaker and stronger players. Principal players can also be rotated, especially if there are equally talented students for those positions with appropriate leadership skills.

However you choose to use the audition information to place your students, the task of seating students should be completed prior to your first rehearsal. Also, after your auditions you can double-check the appropriateness of your musical selections. You should now know whether you have the right personnel to perform the works you have chosen. Finally, your audition gives you a chance to meet new orchestra members and to revisit orchestra members from previous years.

THE REHEARSAL

The rehearsal is where your lesson plans come to life. All of the planning you have done to this point—your goals and objectives, selection of music, auditions, and so on—leads to effective rehearsals and outcomes.

You have read how to prepare a score and prepare a lesson plan in Chapter 6. Now, you need to structure your lesson plan in terms of an overall rehearsal strategy. While there is always some variation within rehearsals among teachers, teachers tend to agree on the types of materials each rehearsal should contain. An effective rehearsal includes the following:

1. tuning and warm-ups: scales, arpeggios, chorales, and exercises including materials that foster an extension of students' technical, rhythmic, dynamic, and articulation capabilities

2. review of old materials

3. introduction of new materials

4. sight reading

5. announcements and comments

6. end of the rehearsal (performance of a complete work that the group is beginning to play with greater ease)

TUNING

Tuning procedures vary given the age and experience of each group. The following suggestions may help you to develop a tuning procedure most appropriate for your group.

Elementary Groups

Elementary groups generally do not have students playing the double bass. However, if a double bass player is in your elementary group, she should be taught to tune with harmonics as soon as the left-hand position is shown. To tune the D string, given the reference pitch of A = 440, instruct your student to touch the D string with the fourth finger, one-third the length of the string, or third position. This should sound the harmonic A = 220. Once the D string is tuned, tell your student to touch the A string with the first finger, at one-fourth the length of the string. This will produce another A = 220, this time on the A string. Using the A harmonic, produced on the D string with the fourth finger, tune the A string, using the harmonic produced on the A string with the first finger. After the A string is tuned, have your student touch the A string with the fourth finger, one-third the length of the string or third position. This will produce the pitch E. Touch the E string with the first finger one-fourth the length of the string, which will produce a unison E. Tune the E string. Finally, touch the D string (already tuned) one-fourth the length of the string. This will produce the pitch D. Place the fourth finger one-third of the length on the G string. This will produce the pitch D, which can be tuned from the pitch D produced on the already tuned D string.

The concept of tuning takes a lot of time to learn, and constant reinforced practice is needed to develop this skill. While a portion of each class should be used to teach this skill, you must plan your time carefully so you will have time to complete other rehearsal objectives. You should also try to include all students in tuning exercises, even when you are working with individual students. Students can participate by humming a reference pitch or by raising their right hand if they believe a string is sharp, raising the left hand if it is flat, or raising both hands if they believe the string is in tune.

Here are some tuning exercises that can work effectively with your elementary students:

1. As the students enter the room, they are instructed to take out their instruments and bows and bring them to the teacher for tuning. The teacher may tune all of the strings, return the instruments to the students, and instruct the students to sit quietly in their assigned seats until further directives are given.

2. Students enter the room and once again take out their instruments and bows. The teacher tunes all of the strings on all of the instruments, with the exception of perhaps five A strings on five students' instruments from one section or from different sections. The teacher then plays the correct A and has the class quietly hum the A pitch. One of the five students is then instructed to play his A. The teacher asks the student if the pitch is sharp, flat, or in tune. Adjustments are made as necessary until the string is tuned. The teacher then continues the procedure with the second of the five students with out-of-tune A strings. As students become more adept at tuning, the teacher may wish to leave more A strings untuned or may wish to leave both the A and D strings untuned until the students can quickly and accurately tune their instruments with reference pitches.

3. Once again, the teacher leaves the A string untuned, but instead of providing a reference pitch, the student is asked to play the D and A strings together. The student is asked to eliminate the beats from the sound while adjusting the A string. (Students need to be able to play double stops efficiently, and to play and turn the peg or tuner while tuning, to have this tuning system work effectively.)

4. The teacher leaves the A string untuned on one of the instruments of a student sharing a stand. While the teacher plays a reference pitch or the student plays a double stop, the stand partner is asked to tune the A string by turning the fine tuner. Double bass players using harmonics can also be tuned by their stand partners.

5. Many mechanical tuners on the market provide visual feedback. A small group of students individually can be instructed to use a mechanical

tuner to tune one string. The class can also observe the procedure and raise their right hands if the string is sharp, raise their left hands if the string is flat, or raise both hands if they believe the string is in tune.

Middle and Junior High Groups

If tuning has been included at the elementary instructional level, your middle and junior high students should now be able to tune their own instruments. If this is not the case, you should consider using some of the procedures suggested for elementary groups. While your middle and junior high students may be able to tune in the relative solitude of a practice room, tuning in an orchestra situation is more challenging.

If your students can tune their instruments, you have more flexibility to use student leaders to lead the tuning activity. This allows you the freedom to take roll or perform some other administrative duty that might otherwise take away from your rehearsal procedure. By using students, you encourage and further develop leadership skills among your players. You can use your concertmaster to provide reference pitches or principals from each section to provide respective reference pitches, or you can randomly select an individual from the group to act as the tuning leader. Here are some suggestions that may help your students accurately tune in the orchestra setting:

1. Tune each string individually. Give a reference pitch for each string. Have all students quietly hum the pitch for at least five seconds before they tune. Students should tune no louder than they were humming.

2. Tune by sections. Give a reference pitch for the first violins, and have them tune while the other sections are quietly humming the pitch. Again, make sure the section that is tuning plays no louder than the students are humming.

3. Tune using double stops. Once the A string is tuned, the upper strings and cellos can tune by sections, using double stops.

4. Use harmonics to tune. Encourage the cellos to use harmonics to tune. Touch the harmonic at the octave on the A string and tune it. Touch the D string with the first finger, where the note A on the D string would sound if it were fingered (fourth position). This will produce an A harmonic. Tune the D string using the A string harmonic (A) as the reference. Continue this procedure with the other strings. Your double bass players have already been tuning using harmonics. Your cellists will find it easier to hear when using harmonics to tune.

High School Groups

At the high school level, your students should be able to tune easily by sections and may be able to tune as a group when given a reference pitch, especially in a string orchestra setting. You may also be encouraging students to use mechanical tuning devices to tune prior to rehearsals. You may find that instruction in the use of tuning forks and other such devices will also help your students tune.

Tuning in a full orchestra situation may present greater challenges to the less-experienced high school player. While the concertmaster can still take the A from the principal oboe, especially when the oboe player is experienced, some directors encourage the concertmaster to tune using a tuning fork or mechanical tuner. The concertmaster then gives the A to the woodwinds. When they complete their tuning, the A is given to the brass, and once they have tuned, the A can be given to the combined brass and woodwinds. The procedure is then continued by section for the strings. Careful, meticulous, and accurate tuning is essential for effective performances. You will find that your orchestra will perform at a higher level when you insist that careful attention be paid to tuning—one of the first, if not the first, musical endeavors of each rehearsal.

WARM-UPS

The warm-up consists of two parts: the individual student warm-up and the planned warm-up you have devised for the group. As students enter the room before the bell rings, you need to let your students know what they can and cannot do as a warm-up. The student warm-up may change depending on the age and developmental level of your group. For example, in a beginning group, many teachers instruct their students to take out their instruments and bows, without playing them, and bring them to the teacher for tuning. Once they are tuned, students may be allowed to sit quietly in their seats and finger scales or musical selections, but not play them with the bow or pizzicato, until all students have been tuned and the instructor gives them permission to do so. A more advanced group may be allowed to play scales or musical works at their leisure until the bell rings, at which point a different type of tuning procedure may be introduced.

The personal warm-up procedure should be clearly articulated to each student in your group. If you want students to practice a particular rhythm or scale to warm up, then you need to let them know what scale or rhythm is to be used for the personal warm-up. This can be done verbally or, more appropriately, it may be written and displayed in front of the classroom for all students to see.

The next portion of your warm-ups is the group procedure. Group warm-up procedures often involve the performance of scales and arpeggios. Often scales and arpeggios chosen for warm-up procedures are based on the keys of the musical works to be performed during the rehearsal. You may also wish to select particular rhythms or bowing patterns from musical selections that students are to play while performing the scales and arpeggios. Many instrumental groups, especially bands, use chorales for warm-ups. The theory is that chorales can be used to promote blend and balance and encourage players to be more aware of individual as well as group intonation and balance requirements. In addition to, or perhaps in place of, scales, arpeggios, or chorales, some orchestra directors choose to use published warm-up exercises including materials that foster an extension of students' technical, rhythmic, dynamic, and articulation capabilities.

Whatever warm-up procedure you use, be sure to do the following:

1. Let the students know what procedures you want them to use for their warm-up.
2. Inform all students in your group of the warm-up procedure as they enter the rehearsal room. Materials can be selected from the folders at this time in anticipation of the group warm-up.
3. Choose your warm-up materials with an eye toward your overall rehearsal goals and objectives.
4. Use your warm-ups to prepare the students both mentally and physically for your rehearsal.
5. Plan the exact amount of time you will use on each specific warm-up procedure.

Your warm-up procedures set the tone for each rehearsal. Warm-up procedures that lack purpose and focus may produce a similar rehearsal. Your procedures should not only warm up your students physically for the rehearsal, but should also prepare them mentally.

REVIEW OF OLD AND INTRODUCTION OF NEW MATERIALS

Once you have completed your warm-up procedures, you are now ready for the second phrase of your rehearsal: the review of old materials and the introduction of new materials. Review of old literature refers to those musical selections that you have worked on in previous rehearsals. The introduction of new materials refers to those musical works that may have been handed out and read through but not yet rehearsed.

During this phase of your rehearsal, a run-through of each work is, generally, not recommended. A run-through of works is, often, not an efficient use of time. In a run-through, difficult sections do not improve significantly, if at all. When such sections are not improved, the overall quality of the piece, as well as student growth, suffers. Thus, your rehearsal strategy should include the selection and rehearsal of challenging passages within works.

Based on your score study as well as on notes and observations taken and made in previous rehearsals, you will have an increasingly better idea of what sections need additional attention to improve the overall quality of each piece. Your first task, isolating problem areas, soon is complete. Next, you need to determine what is causing difficulty for the group. Ask yourself the following questions:

1. Is there a difficult rhythm that needs to be isolated?
2. Are there awkward or unfamiliar bowings or fingerings?
3. Is there a problem with blend or balance that is preventing the section from working (melody line being covering by the accompanying line)?
4. Are there intonation problems caused by improper or poor fingering (strings), lack of breath support (winds), range problems (winds), shifting problems (strings), improper vibrato, poor posture, and so on?

5. Are there technical problems that require isolated practice or technical problems that have resulted because new techniques are required that students have not yet learned, such as triple tonguing, sautillé, and so on?

6. Are there phrasing problems or dynamic concerns, or is there a lack of articulation precision or cutoff awareness among the members of the group?

These and other questions must be asked in order to determine what problem or problems exist. Once you isolate the problems, solutions need to be developed to help remove them. Your solutions become the working material for your rehearsals. Your solutions and suggestions for improvement need to be identified, thought through, and written down in your lesson plans. As you use each of your solutions and determine the level of success they bring, you will begin to develop new solutions and identify additional problems that need new solutions.

This portion of your rehearsal, the review of old and the introduction of new materials, involves your ability to creatively offer solutions while keeping your students interested and motivated. Your teaching, musical, and creative skills all must be at their highest to achieve positive results. Effective rehearsals require you to be aware of the success, or lack thereof, of each solution as it is presented. Too much time spent with a solution that is not working will frustrate the group. Conversely, a solution that is stopped prematurely will also cause student frustration. In general, however, you should not spend any more than two or three minutes with any one section at the high school level. If a group is younger, even less time should be spent with any one section.

Your ability to read the group—to know when to try another solution, your sense of knowing when and how long to work with an individual or a section before engaging the whole group—is a skill that needs to be constantly honed. Just as you would avoid stopping the orchestra to correct obvious mistakes, the type of error that students have never done before but do make during one rehearsal, do not overlook mistakes that need corrective solutions. Playing through a work over and over will not correct an error.

Your ability to communicate effectively with your group is also important. Verbal responses are not always necessary, nor are they necessarily the most effective. A nonverbal gesture, a movement of the hand or body or a facial gesture, will often generate information more quickly and effectively than a verbal response, and you do not have to stop the group to give the information. At times, modeling for your group will be the best method of communicating your wishes. Having a member of your group model your wishes is even better, as it provides for individual praise through musical example.

Careful planning and problem identification, combined with your ability to present a variety of solutions to solve problems in a variety of ways, are needed to promote individual and group musical growth. Your ability to maintain a rehearsal setting that is stimulating and motivational is needed to promote individual and group interest. These elements are necessary if you are to produce effective results during this portion of your rehearsal.

SIGHT READING

One of the most effective ways of exposing students to a variety of musical styles and forms of music is through sight reading. A group's ability to sight-read is also an important part of many state contest festivals. The ability to sight-read requires individual and group psychomotor, cognitive, and affective skills, and encourages students to view the musical page in a different way.

Each rehearsal, with the exception of dress rehearsals, should contain some sight reading. The sight-reading portion of the rehearsal can be placed during the final third of the rehearsal. This portion of the rehearsal contains sight reading, announcements, the playing of a favorite work, and storage of instruments. The length of the sight-reading section depends on many factors, including closeness to performance dates, the progression of works for concerts, and other considerations. However, well-chosen sight-reading pieces can help reinforce such musical concepts as phrasing, dynamics, particular articulations and bowings, and rhythmic ideas found in works you are preparing for concert.

Each time you have your group sight-read, establish a goal for that session. Do not simply run through a work. Select one or more musical tasks upon which your group should focus, such as key signature, meter signature, style, phrasing, and the like.

Stress the positive during each sight-reading session. You already know that your students will miss certain things. Students are all too often aware of the problems they have in sight-reading tasks; therefore, stress the positive aspects of each performance.

END OF THE REHEARSAL

Announcements, while important, can distract from the flow of any rehearsal. Sometimes, you will not have any control as to when announcements are given, but if you do, announcements should be made at the end of the rehearsal, right before the final work is performed. Announcements presented at this time are more likely to be remembered.

Announcements should be informative but brief. If a student seeks specific or additional information about any announcement item, that information should be provided after the rehearsal. Avoid lengthy explanations that use precious rehearsal time. Prepare and edit your announcements in advance. If members of your group have announcements, they should inform you, and you can then present the information.

This is also a good time to summarize the overall effectiveness of your rehearsal—its strengths and its weaknesses. You can also tell your students what is planned for next time or future rehearsals.

Your announcements should be upbeat, informative, and delivered with impact. Your goal is to present information in a manner that your students will remember. Announcements presented with impact, in as concise a manner as possible while maintaining the integrity of the information being presented, will help ensure that students remember the facts presented.

Many orchestra directors choose to end their rehearsals with the performance of a work that has been played previously, or one that is being prepared for an upcoming concert and is nearing performance readiness. Making music as a group is an important motivational need. Allowing for the performance of a work, straight through, without stopping can help satisfy this need. It ends the rehearsal on a positive note and provides a reward and musical outlet for each rehearsal.

REHEARSAL FORMAT

You will need to establish a general format for your rehearsals. Decide how much time you will spend on your warm-up and your extension of technique materials. How much time will you need to review old materials and introduce new materials? What portion of your rehearsal will be devoted to sight reading? How much time will you need for announcements and for the performance of a familiar work before instruments need to be put away and stored? For example, you may wish to structure your time as follows:

- one-fourth of the rehearsal time for warm-ups and technical development exercises
- one-half of the rehearsal time for working on various sections of pieces
- one-fourth of the rehearsal time for sight reading, announcements, performance of a final work, and storage of instruments

Thus, in a forty-minute rehearsal you could spend three minutes on tuning, three minutes on warm-ups, and four minutes on technical exercises for a total of ten minutes. Twenty minutes could be devoted to perfecting passages from one or more selections (six to seven minutes could be spent on passages from three selections, or ten minutes on passages from two selections). The final ten minutes could be used sight reading (three to four minutes), a playthrough of a favorite piece (four to five minutes), and for announcements and instrument storage (one to two minutes).

Each of your groups' rehearsal plans may vary based on the age of your students and their stage of development. An elementary group may need more time for tuning, warm-up, and technical development portion of the rehearsal and less time for sight reading than would a middle school or junior high group. The effective rehearsal involves planning. The important point to remember is that you must plan every minute of your rehearsal and, once you plan, avoid straying from your timetable. Stay on task so you can accomplish the goals you set. Your goals for each of your rehearsals should include the following:

- students' awareness of the group's sound and their sound within the group
- the creation of music experiences that challenge students and enhance their technique
- development of students' musicianship via excellent repertoire

- enhancement of students' sight-reading abilities
- planning to create a peak musical experience in every rehearsal

Joseph Labuta (2000) and Jacquelyn Dillon and Casimer Kriechbaum (1978) offer several specific suggestions for rehearsing:

1. Speak up—Make sure you are heard by everyone in your orchestra.
2. Communicate—Give succinct directives or corrections. Avoid talking too much.
3. Explain repetitions—Stop only for specific purposes and tell your group why you stopped.
4. Don't stop the group if the students are aware of a problem and know how to correct it.
5. Be positive—Do not criticize individuals or dwell on mistakes. Emphasize the positive when possible. Let the students know that a criticism of playing is not a criticism of them personally.
6. Be demanding—Expect the best from each student in your group, insist on high standards, but set attainable goals for each rehearsal.
7. Be punctual—Start and end rehearsal on time and expect the same from your students.
8. Waste no time—Do not dwell on any one problem. Be prepared. Do not simply read through pieces. Work on sections and offer suggestions for improvement.
9. Use your ears—Listen and analyze constantly, offering suggestions for improvement and noting excellence when it occurs.
10. Evaluate—Determine what problems should be saved for later and what problems can be solved now.
11. Tape the rehearsal—Errors missed in rehearsal will be heard on the tape.
12. End each rehearsal on a positive note.

Use a systematic approach in your rehearsals. Listen to sections you plan to rehearse. Evaluate and correct errors through demonstration, explanation, and drill. Listen to the section again and evaluate the effectiveness of your suggestions. Offer further suggestions if needed and repeat the process.

OTHER CONSIDERATIONS

Sometimes your rehearsals may not involve working with the group as a whole. You may wish to use some or all of your rehearsal for sectionals. If you work daily with a full orchestra, you may wish to work with strings only during part of some rehearsals, or work with just brass or woodwinds. If you have an assistant, part of the group can be turned over to her. If you don't have an assistant, you may need to rely on your section leaders or some student conductor from the group to work with the members of the orchestra with whom you are not working. Whichever is the case, you need to plan the rehearsal for your assistant, your section leaders, or your student conductor. You are responsible for all of the activities of your group even if you are not working with them directly.

If you are holding sectionals with your string orchestra and you are working with the violin I section, then you must plan not only your rehearsal procedures for the violin I group but also the rehearsal procedures for the other sections. Furthermore, you must make sure that you clearly articulate your rehearsal procedure directives to each of the other section leaders. The section leaders must know what pieces or portions of works you want them to work on with the section. They must know how much time they should spend working on each selection, and they must be informed of the ultimate goal you wish them to achieve on each selection during the rehearsal. Unplanned rehearsal activity will result in wasted rehearsal time.

The effectiveness of special rehearsals will be only as good as your planning for those rehearsals. You will be required to do the following:

1. Select the most appropriate times to schedule special rehearsals.
2. Select appropriate personnel to conduct those members of your orchestra who will not be working with you.
3. Plan all rehearsal activities.
4. Communicate your rehearsal plans to all individuals in charge of instructional duties.
5. Be sure that all additional instructors know exactly how to conduct an appropriate rehearsal.

Your responsibilities as orchestra director increase as you ask others to take on roles of leadership in rehearsal situations. Not only are you responsible for the planning of all rehearsal groups, you are additionally responsible to ensure that the individuals you have selected are instructed in the art of effective teaching.

THE FIRST REHEARSAL

You have planned and scheduled and are now ready for your first rehearsal. Your first rehearsal is one of the most important ones you will hold, for through it, the tenor and discipline of your group will be established for the year. You establish your expectations for your students, and your students establish their expectations for the group. Classroom management procedures, discipline, and rehearsal procedures are all initiated during your first rehearsal. It is extremely important that you carefully think through, rehearse, and be ready for your first rehearsal.

Preparation for your first rehearsal includes materials setup. An appropriate number of chairs and stands must be set up, folders must be marked with music, and pencils should be inserted in the folders. Any bowings, measure numbers, and other such markings should be placed on the music prior to being put in the folders. Seat assignments, if not already made, should be completed at this time. You should clearly display any information you want students to note. Rehearsal procedures, musical selections, and so on should all be prominently displayed.

Consider what rules you want to enforce; they should be few and simple. Many teachers have only two or three rules they enforce immediately. Two rules that are commonly quoted are, "Do not play unless you are directed to do so," and "Do not talk unless you raise your hand and are directed to do so."

In most situations, you will need to develop a procedure to take roll. If you have a seating chart, you may consider assigning a student helper to assist you in taking roll. If you feel that you must take roll yourself, consider assigning student helpers to lead the group in warm-up procedures.

In an elementary or middle school setting, some teachers create name cards with the students' names on them. These name cards (a piece of paper folded in half with the name written on one side) are placed over the stand. The teacher can easily see which students are not present. This not only helps the orchestra director take attendance but also helps the teacher call each student by name on the first day and helps him learn the students' names more quickly.

You also need to think carefully about the placement and storage of instrument cases during the rehearsal. Are the cases to be placed to the right side of the chair, or are the cases to be left in the back of the room or in the storage lockers? Whatever the procedure, students should be informed of it at the first rehearsal. The same applies to putting instruments away. If there are no storage lockers, where should the instruments be stored? What is the procedure for getting instruments out of storage lockers to be taken home for practice? What is the policy on taking instruments home for practice?

To ensure that your first rehearsal is successful, consider the following for a younger group:

1. Greet or welcome the students as they enter the room. Point out any rule you want to enforce immediately, such as, "Please find your assigned seat quickly and quietly and do not talk." Enforce any given rule immediately.

2. Once students have entered the room, you must establish yourself as the teacher. With confidence and poise, introduce yourself and give a brief but sincere welcome speech. State your rules at this time. Have the students introduce themselves.

3. Tell the students what they will learn or do during the rehearsal.

4. Establish the procedures for attendance, case storage, tuning or warm-up procedures, and so on.

5. Point out to the group that rehearsal activities are displayed at the front of the room. Have the students play. Regardless of the length of the rehearsal, make sure that you allow enough time for the students to play their instruments. You may only have them pluck one or two open

strings, but remember that the students join orchestra to play orchestral instruments. Make sure that their expectations are satisfied during the first rehearsal.

6. Provide enough time for announcements and review of the learned activities for the day, plus a critique of their participation during the rehearsal. Assignments should be given at this time.

7. The procedure for instrument storage should be completed. For younger students, this may require you to review procedures for loosening the bow hair, cleaning the rosin off the strings, and so on.

First rehearsal procedures for established groups should follow the structure previously outlined once the greeting, welcome speech, and introductions have been completed. In addition, you need to think about your basic rehearsal approach. The use of a directive feedback loop has been found to be very effective in rehearsal situations. The approach is as follows:

1. Give a specific directive to your group. When needed, a model can follow a directive. A model can be provided through demonstration and verbal or nonverbal instruction. For a rhythmic problem you could sing, clap, or count the rhythm. You could have a student model the correct rhythm. Whatever the approach, you want to provide a specific directive. Avoid general, nonspecific directives such as, "Play measures 6 and 7." A specific directive such as, "Play measures 6 and 7 with attention to the dotted eighth-sixteenth rhythm" is more specific and helps the students focus on the objective.

2. Follow through on the directive. Have the students play the section or measures you want performed. Allow for a practice of the passage.

3. Evaluate and provide feedback to the students after the performance of the passage. Provide another directive with another model when necessary (see Step 1). Continue the process until maximum success has been attained, given your time allotment.

4. Continue the process (i.e., Steps 1, 2, and 3) with another passage or section of music.

The key to successful rehearsals is planning and preparation, along with effective rehearsal techniques. Just as you know when students have not prepared, students know when you are not prepared. It is impossible to have effective rehearsal techniques without appropriate planning.

TROUBLESHOOTING DURING REHEARSALS

Much of your success during a rehearsal will depend on your ability to identify problems and offer corrective solutions. This is a skill that will continue to develop with continued focus and training. The following table is not meant to be exhaustive, but rather to provide a point of departure from which you can begin and enhance your ability to troubleshoot in your rehearsals.

Problem	Possible Cause	Possible Solution
Pitch/note intonation problems	Wrong key	Point out correct key signature and notes.
	Tuning	Not tuned properly. Adjust and tune. Not listening to chord. Work with chord structures and point out individual lines and tuning within this structure. Change the dynamics of the section, especially in loud sections, to encourage listening and adjustment among sections. Have sections play alone or with one other section and adjust. Have one individual from each section play the parts while fellow section players offer suggestions.
	Poor posture	Correct posture among players.
	Poor left-hand position	Correct left-hand positions as needed.
	Poor instrument positioning	Correct instrument positioning as needed.
	Missed accidentals	Point out accidentals and have students mark them.
	Poor rhythmic alignment.	Individual sections are not on the proper part of the beat, causing incorrect chord/pitch alignment within the measure/section.
	Poor/inappropriate/ incorrect fingerings	Inappropriate finger pattern solutions or incorrect fingerings are being used. Appropriate solutions should be offered.
	Incorrect transposition (winds)	Improper transposition in one of the wind sections, such as trumpets in F. Appropriate transposition should be suggested.
	Written mistakes in parts	Find and correct the mistakes in the parts.
	Technically difficult parts	Reduce the tempo; drill and practice; suggest individual practice procedures.
Poor tone quality	Improper right arm level (strings)	Right arm level is too high or low to contact string at optimum point. Adjust arm level as needed.
	Improper bow placement (strings)	Bow is too near the bridge or fingerboard. Adjust as necessary.
	Bow not parallel to bridge (strings)	Right elbow (opening and closing) are not correct. Adjust as necessary.

Problem	Possible Cause	Possible Solution
	Improper speed to bow weight relationship (strings)	The bow is either moving too slowly or too quickly for the amount of bow weight. Adjust either the bow speed or the bow weight.
	Improper left-hand finger position (strings)	Left-hand fingers are not centered on nor holding down the string properly. Center the finger weight into the string.
	Immature vibrato	Vibrato is too fast, too slow, or not adequately controlled. Offer suggestions for improvement and model appropriate vibrato control.
	Poor posture	Raised shoulders; shoulder, arm, or hand tension exists; student(s) slumping, etc. Correct and adjust as necessary.
	Improper breath support (winds)	Adjust posture and/or breathe from diaphragm.
	Poor embouchure (winds)	Check embouchure for appropriateness and offer suggestions for improvement or offer model.
	Fatigue (winds)	Embouchure is tired. Work with other sections or work with strings to provide rest, as needed.
	Overblowing (winds)	Too much air for proper embouchure to be maintained. Correct as necessary
Poor articulation	Improper bow hold (strings)	Gripping the bow; tension in right-hand thumb or fingers; etc. Correct bow hold as necessary.
	Incorrect bowing or bow changes (strings)	Correct the bowing or refine the bow changes as necessary.
	On- or off-string bowing required (strings)	Student(s) not using proper on- or off-string bowing technique. Make suggestions and corrections.
	Tone not centered	Fuzzy tone center impairs clarity of articulation. Focus tone center.
	String crossings (strings)	Rapid string crossing or string crossings not appropriately completed, causing poor articulation. Review procedure for string crossing and arm levels.
	Tonguing (winds)	Improper tonguing. Tongue hitting the reed or between the lips. Correct and adjust as required.
	Tonguing—improper syllables (winds)	Appropriate syllable not being used for desired articulation. Offer suggestions for another syllable.

(continued)

Problem	Possible Cause	Possible Solution
Incorrect rhythm	Complex or unfamiliar rhythms	Model and demonstrate the correct rhythm. Review the procedure for working out such rhythms for outside practice.
	Dotted rhythms	Subdivide the rhythm into the smallest component and have students say the subdivision while clapping the printed rhythm. Technical problem may exist with a bowing. Offer practice suggestions for improvement.
	Rests	Improper counting of rests. Demonstrate and review counting procedures.
Tempo not steady	Technically difficult passages	Slow the tempo. Practice with a metronome. Offer suggestions for different fingers, bowing, etc., to help the tempo. Change the rhythmic pattern of the section for practice and then try the passage with the written rhythm.
	Pizzicato	Tends to rush. Practice with metronome. Have students subdivide rhythm (count and play). Play with bow, then pizzicato.
	Beat not solid	Provide suggestions to internalize the beat. Have some clap and some students play. Use a metronome. Tap big toe inside of the shoe. Make sure you are providing a clear beat pattern.
	Not watching conductor	Sensitize students to your beat pattern and have them observe while various other sections play. Have students finger while watching or blow air through horn or bow above the string while observing you.
Poor balance or blend	Melody covered	Sustained chords cover the melody. Adjust as necessary. Increase dynamic level of melody or decrease dynamic level of nonmelodic lines. Play melody line alone and make sure accompanying players can always hear the melody when playing. Have students sing their parts and balance the lines.

Problem	Possible Cause	Possible Solution
Wrong style	Lack of awareness or inattentiveness	Students may not know the appropriate style (notes played on the string or off the string, etc.). Inform students and provide a model. Point out accents, dynamics, and articulations. Have students mark parts. Have students sing the parts with appropriate dynamics, articulations, accents. Check parts against score. Provide appropriate bowings or articulations if not in parts. Show students your conducting approach for various styles. Have them follow changing conducting style patterns as they play or sing a scale or familiar musical passage.
Poor phrasing	Technical problems	Not enough breath to support or bow to carry the line. Breathe from diaphragm, move bow closer to the bridge (slower bow with more bow weight). Use staggered breathing. Offer alternate bowing suggestions. Mark breathing or phrasing places.
	Lack of interpretive skill or knowledge	Model for students. Show them how to shape a line by demonstration, through visual models (having students add crescendos or diminuendos), or by listening to a recording. Use the group as its own model when you hear an excellent phrase.
Lack of ensemble precision	Technical difficulties or inattentiveness	Have students sing their parts. Have one player from each section play his or her part while others sing or listen. Move chairs and stands so players can face each other. Have group play without you conducting. Have concertmaster lead the group.

REFERENCES

Dillon, Jacquelyn A., and Casimer Kriechbaum. 1978. *How to design and teach a successful school string and orchestra program.* San Diego: Kjos West.

Garofalo, Robert. 1976. *Blueprint for band*. Portland, Maine: J. Weston Walch.

Gattiker, Irvin. 1977. *Complete book of rehearsal techniques for the high school orchestra*. West Nyack, N.Y.: Parker Publishing.

Green, Elizabeth A. 1999. *Teaching stringed instruments in classes*. Bloomington, Ind.: American String Teachers Association with National School Orchestra Association c/o Tichenor Publishing.

Hovey, Nilo. 1976. *Efficient rehearsal procedures for school bands*. Elkhart, Ind.: Selmer Company.

Kohut, Daniel L. 1973. *Instrumental music pedagogy*. Englewood Cliffs, N.J.: Prentice-Hall.

Labuta, Joseph A. 2000. *Basic conducting techniques*. Upper Saddle River, N.J.: Prentice-Hall.

Lisk, Edward S. 1987. *The creative director: Alternative rehearsal techniques*. 3d ed. Ft. Lauderdale, Fla.: Meredith Music Publications.

Music Educators National Conference (MENC). 1991. *Teaching stringed instruments: A course of study*. Reston, Va.: Music Educators National Conference.

Rabin, Marvin, and Priscilla Smith. 1991. *Guide to orchestral bowings through musical styles*. video 1991, manual 1990. 2d ed. Madison, Wis.: University of Wisconsin–Madison, Liberal Studies and the Arts.

Righter, Charles B. 1959. *Success in teaching school orchestras and bands*. Minneapolis: Schmitt, Hall, and McCreary.

Walker, Darwin E. 1989. *Teaching music: Managing the successful music program*. New York: Schirmer Books.

Weerts, Richard. 1976. *Handbook of rehearsal techniques for the high school band*. West Nyack, N.Y.: Parker Publishing.

PRACTICAL APPROACHES TO TEACHING IMPROVISATION IN THE SCHOOL ORCHESTRA

Why should I teach my students to improvise? This is an excellent question to ask when instrumental teachers already have so much to do in their jobs. However, improvising is valuable in many ways. It encourages both students and teachers to be creative and provides a practical means for doing so. Also, it motivates students, sometimes those who are not the most gifted players but who still want to excel. In addition, improvising also gives students an opportunity to focus more on aural and ear-to-hand skills.

Through improvising, students improve their basic musicianship skills, including listening skills, pitch discrimination, intonation, and memorization. Teaching improvisation helps incorporate the national teaching standards established by MENC into the orchestra rehearsal: National standard number 3 encourages teachers to instruct students how to improvise melodies, variations, and accompaniments as a part of students' music education experience (MENC 1994).

Including improvisation in the school orchestra also gives teachers the opportunity to reinforce the playing techniques students are learning in class. For example, if students are working on vibrato, specify that students' improvisation examples must include vibrato; if students are working on spiccato bowing, then the students' examples must include spiccato bowing.

Improvising is also exciting, and all students—and teachers—like to have some excitement and fun in their lives. The enjoyment that both teachers and students feel while improvising can enliven their string playing experience. As students' improvisation skill develops, give them opportunities to improvise on concerts. They will like it, and their parents will have fun seeing and hearing their children create their own music right on the spot!

A teacher whose primary background is classical music can be successful when teaching students to improvise in the school orchestra. The following are five different ways to help you get started: a creative drone approach, a riff approach, a call-and-response or question-and-answer approach, a chordal approach, and a rhythmic ostinato approach.

A CREATIVE DRONE APPROACH

A drone is a sound that is continuously sustained. Have the class begin by sustaining an open string drone while single or small groups of students vary the pitch. The pitch may be varied by the following methods:

- adding rhythms
- adding dynamics
- adding articulations
- adding pizzicato
- adding different sound effects like glissandos, instrument knocks, and so on
- adding a different octave of the pitch

This is improvisation in its simplest form. Lead students first through each of the previous variations and then introduce combinations (e.g., varying rhythms and dynamics). Any pitch can also be used for the drone. A new note that students are learning to play makes a great drone.

An added hint: Be sure the drone is always sounded so that all students are involved by either playing the drone or using one of the previous techniques to vary it. The more students are actively involved and the more continuous the drone is sounded, the safer students will feel to participate. An effective teaching sequence is to first demonstrate how to vary the drone and then ask students to volunteer. Once a few of the students have attempted and been successful, others will want to try.

A RIFF APPROACH

A riff is any musical fragment that is repeated. The fragment alternates with an improvised example. The form follows: riff–improvisation–riff–improvisation–riff, and so on. Hint: It is easier for students to learn to improvise using a riff approach if the riff and the improvisation are the same length.

Begin with an open-string, four-quarter-note riff, played by the orchestra, while one student alternates with a riff by improvising on that note for four beats. The student can use any of the improvising techniques suggested in the drone approach. Figure 8.1 gives an example.

Once students feel comfortable using one note as material for the improvisation, add other notes one at a time. For example, the riff could remain four-quarter-note open Ds, while the improvisation could contain four quarter notes made up of Ds and Es. Adding only one note at a time for the improvisation

Figure 8.1 Open-string riff and improvisation.

makes it easier, and the students will feel more comfortable. Eventually an entire scale, such as the D-major scale, could be used as material for the improvisation. Students will discover that any notes in the scale will work.

Other material for other riffs can also be used, such as major or minor scales, a pentatonic scale, tetrachords, or arpeggios. It is great when the riff incorporates a new playing technique or scale that is being studied in class. Because the playing technique is a riff, it will be reinforced as it is repeated.

Many other variations using a riff approach may be used to teach students to improvise. For example, the orchestra plays a melody as a riff, and the alternating improvisations must be variations of the melody. Of course, the improvisation also can be a freely composed melody created by a student that is completely different from the riff.

A CALL-AND-RESPONSE OR QUESTION-AND-ANSWER APPROACH

A call-and-response approach involves a melodic fragment that is played by one student and then answered by another student. It is also sometimes referred to as a question-and-answer approach. The call/question can be any short phrase in one key that does not end on the tonic; the response/answer is any phrase in the same key that ends on the tonic.

Hint: One of the easiest ways to get started using this approach is the following. Ask the class to sustain an open-string tonic pitch (open D is a good one to start with). While the open-string pitch is being sustained, one student can make up a fragment in the key of the drone pitch that does not end on the tonic. Students will discover that ending on the third, fourth, or fifth scale degree sounds the best. Then another student may respond/answer by playing a fragment in the same key that ends on the tonic. The calls and responses can be any length. Begin by having students volunteer or carefully select students who will be successful. Then others will want to try. Figure 8.2 is an example.

Variations of this approach include having two students call and respond back and forth many times, creating something like a conversation. The first student calls, the second student responds ending on the tonic. Then she creates a call and the first student responds. Another method is to require that the response/answer be a variation of the call/question, though ending on the tonic. Changing the rhythms, range, dynamics, articulations, and so on of the original melody can produce the variation. Another fun method is to select a key (perhaps one the orchestra is first learning or one that is used in some of the repertoire the orchestra is learning) and then designate instrument sections of the orchestra to be callers or responders. Then challenge each section to cre-

Figure 8.2 Call and response.

ate together their own unison call or response. Give each calling section an opportunity to play their fragment, and select one of the responding sections to reply with their response.

A CHORDAL APPROACH

Students learn to improvise above chords played by the orchestra in a chordal approach to teaching improvisation. Begin by assigning the pitches in a tonic chord. It is easiest to begin by assigning the root of the chord to be played by the cellos and basses, the third to the violas and second violins, and the fifth to the first violins. Have students play the pitches in first position, later in different octaves. Once students can play the tonic chord divided among the orchestra, assign them to play corresponding pitches in the dominant (V) chord. Practice alternating the tonic and dominant chords. Add the pitches to the subdominant (IV) chord when students are ready. You may need to write the pitches on the board first for younger students to help them remember the notes they are supposed to play.

Now the orchestra is ready to play a chord progression, with each section of the orchestra playing one pitch in each of the chords. Practice simple chord progressions like I–IV–V–IV–V–I. You may want to add other chords, such as ii or VI chords, as students' ability to change from one chord to the next increases.

Various strategies can be used to help students play the chord progressions. For example, the orchestra can play chord progressions that are written on the board. Also, a student can stand in front of the orchestra and hold up fingers to indicate the number of the chord the orchestra is supposed to play (e.g., holding up five fingers to show that the orchestra should play a dominant chord). Eventually give students the opportunity to create their own chord progressions and to lead the orchestra in performing the progressions that they created.

Now, improvisations can be added above the chords that are performed by the orchestra. First have students improvise on one of the pitches in a primary chord by adding rhythm or dynamics, or by changing the articulation of the note. Then add the other pitches of the chord so that students can use any of them while improvising. As students' skills increase, have them improvise a short melody in the key of the chord while accompanied by chords in the orchestra playing the chord (e.g., a student improvises a short melody using the pitches in the D-major scale while the orchestra plays a D-major chord). The opportunity to create an improvised melody may be continuously passed among students while the orchestra sustains the chord. When students are comfortable, add other chords so that they may improvise from one chord to another. Students will be most successful if their improvised melodies are always created in the same key that is based on the chord the orchestra is sustaining (e.g., if the orchestra is playing a G-major chord, then the improvised melody would be in G major).

Figure 8.3   Rhythmic ostinato.

Figure 8.4   D-major tonic chord ostinato.

A RHYTHMIC OSTINATO APPROACH

In the rhythmic ostinato approach, one or more students may improvise above a rhythmic ostinato. Use the following steps:

1. Select an ostinato rhythm for students to pizzicato, such as Figure 8.3.
2. Assign chord pitches to the rhythm. An example, using the D-major tonic chord, is shown in Figure 8.4.
3. Select one or more students to improvise short melodies based on the chord while accompanied by the orchestra playing the ostinato pizzicato.

Continue by changing the rhythm of the ostinato or by adding chords to form a chord progression (or do both). Percussion instruments such as sand blocks, wood blocks, tambourines, and claves can be used to enhance the timbre of the ostinato.

SUMMARY

Incorporating improvisation in the school orchestra is practical at all levels of student achievement, from first-year players to advanced high school students. If you are a string teacher without any prior experience in improvisation, you can be successful if you and your students move forward one step at a time. Try some of the strategies suggested in this chapter, as well as others. You will open a new door to creativity and music making for yourselves and your students.

REFERENCES

Music Educators National Conference. 1994. *National standards for arts education: What every young American should know and be able to do in the arts.* Reston, Va.: Music Educators National Conference.

Many printed improvisation texts, websites, and workshops are available. Some of the best are by Julie Lieberman (www.members.aol.com/julielyonn), Matt Turner (TurnMatt@aol.com), Randy Sabien (www.RandySabien.com), Daryl Silberman (darylds2@aol.com), and Jamey Abersold (www.jazzbooks.com).

9

STRING STUDENT RECRUITMENT AND RETENTION

One of the most important activities that you perform as an orchestra director is to introduce students to the study of stringed instruments. You will enhance the lives of every child through the study of music. Additionally, you will enhance your string program. When you share your enjoyment and enthusiasm for playing string instruments, your students will share that joy with others. If this is your goal for recruitment, then the development of your orchestra program will follow. Students who are excited about playing music soon recognize that your orchestra program is an excellent place to share their enthusiasm.

PHILOSOPHY

The purpose of your recruitment efforts is to find out which students are interested in string study and to contact them. Your goal is to get as much information as you need to contact students and tell parents about your program. Generally, the names of the students and their parents/guardians, home addresses and sometimes work addresses, telephone numbers (home and work), and e-mail addresses are gathered.

PREPARATION FOR RECRUITMENT

Preparation is needed to successfully recruit students for string study. First, find out if your school has a tradition of recruitment activity. If your school does have a traditional recruitment plan, learn as much as you can about the plan. Use the plan as it was designed and determine the merits of it. After you have seen how the plan works for you, you may then wish to modify the plan once you have discussed your ideas with other music educators in your school. Whether or not you have an established recruitment plan in your district, it is vitally important that you communicate your recruitment plans and activities with other music educators and your principals. Your colleagues can help you with your recruitment plans and help you avoid conflicts and various pitfalls. Your principals can also help you arrange and plan or find appropriate recruitment dates and venues. Since principals are ultimately responsible for the activities in their schools, it is imperative that you seek and get their permission to conduct recruitment activities in their school before you begin such activities.

If you find that your school does not have an established recruitment procedure, one of your first decisions will be when to hold your recruitment activities—in the fall or in the spring? Your school system may already have an agreed-upon recruitment schedule; if not, you should determine when it is best to recruit students. If you recruit in the spring, beginning instruction may be delayed until the fall. Some school districts do have summer programs at which beginning instrumentalists can begin instruction. If your school district does have such a program, the spring term may be an excellent time to recruit. If you need to wait until fall to begin instruction, you may find that some of your potential string students will have moved or changed their minds over the course of the summer.

If you recruit in the fall, you will have little delay in the beginning of instruction; however, your instructional time may be diminished. If you are not able to begin recruitment until a week or two after the start of school, and if your recruitment takes three to four weeks to complete, with another week for meetings and so on, this may delay the start of string instruction up to two months.

Whether you recruit in the fall or the spring, you will find advantages or disadvantages for you and your program. Thus either approach should be weighed and considered carefully.

Once you have decided when to recruit, you will need to contact the schools at which you will be recruiting. Arrange the dates and times you will be conducting your recruitment sessions. Determine whether you are going from one classroom to another, or whether you want to plan presenting at a large assembly. The length of the presentation needs to be determined. If you have any special equipment needs such as playback equipment, VCRs, music stands, and so on, you need to make sure you can have access to these materials.

If you are using performing groups made up of students, you will need to arrange for class release time. Permission slips will be required, in most instances, for the students to leave campus. Permission slips should be secured long in advance of the actual recruitment demonstrations. Arrangements for student and equipment transport will also require advance planning. You need to plan the music that will be used in the recruitment demonstrations, and that music must be rehearsed and polished.

You must prepare a handout, letter, or brochure to be distributed to all students attending your recruitment demonstrations. The handout or announcement should explain that students have seen a demonstration of the various bowed string instruments and that sign-up for study on these instruments is now available. Contact and additional information concerning further meetings or sign-up procedures must be provided in your handout. The handout can also contain a statement concerning the value of string study, whether it is for college scholarships later on, for performance opportunities in the near future, or for educational enhancement. Your program goals can be outlined, as well as the importance of parental involvement in helping students achieve these goals. Information concerning the possibility of instrument rental or other types of instrument procurement should be included in your handout.

The handout should be printed on brightly colored or fluorescent paper so it will stand out among the papers that are brought home. In most cases, it is best if the classroom teacher can distribute the handouts to eligible students at the end of the day. Students should then be encouraged to take the handout home to their parents/guardians.

Another consideration that you need to address is instrumentation balance. Many orchestra directors feel that students should be able to select the instrument of their choice, given that they have appropriate physical stature to play that instrument. Some orchestra directors feel that an attempt should be made to balance the instrumentation of the beginning group, placing emphasis on instruments that are needed to produce a balanced ensemble. You will need to determine your approach to instrument selection. Your recruitment approach will be affected by this decision.

One of your final preparations is the actual sign-up meeting with students and parents. You will need to be prepared to discuss specifics of the orchestra program during this meeting. Instrument selection and instrument rental or purchase is often completed at this meeting. Many school districts permit you to invite local instrument dealers to participate in the parents' meeting. They can provide information concerning instrument rental or purchase, instrument insurance, equipment needs such as strings, rosin, endpin holders, and so on, and method book purchase. Instrument dealers can also help with instrument sizing and selection information. Make sure you communicate your exact needs to the dealers. Provide all dealers with copies of information you will be distributing. Make sure your dealers know the date, time, and location of your parents' meeting. Provide ample time (two to three months if possible) for the dealers to get the products you want for the meeting. Let the dealers know what type and quality of instrument you want for your students. Instrument recommendations should be as specific as possible to ensure quality instrument purchase or rental (or both). Inform the dealers to prepare information packets concerning things such as repair services and so on for distribution to parents and students.

A handbook should be assembled for distribution at your parents' meeting. This handbook should contain information concerning policies about class attendance, behavior and conduct, practice, grading, concert performance and attire, concert attendance requirements, care of music and equipment, instrument insurance, a calendar of events, and other pertinent information. The handbook should be distributed and reviewed during this meeting.

You will need to reserve a space to hold your parents' meeting. The time and date need to be confirmed with appropriate school officials. Speak to the custodial staff to make sure the school is open and to arrange setup needs (tables, chairs, etc.). You may also wish to enlist the aid of other music teachers or older students to help you with the various tasks that will need to be completed.

RECRUITMENT PROCEDURES

Now that you have planned your parents' meeting, the dates and times for your recruitment presentations, handouts, and equipment needs, you need to plan your recruitment procedure. You can consider several different recruitment procedures. Those include the announcement and test approach, the lecture method, the demonstration routine, the performance procedure, and the hands-on technique. The least effective recruitment procedures tend to be those in which little or no contact is made by orchestra teachers, and those that do not involve potential students in the recruitment presentation.

Announcement and Test Approach

The use of announcements in classes, assemblies, or newsletters, along with contact by mail, telephone, and e-mail, is perhaps the least effective method of creating interest in strings and recruiting students to your program. With this approach, students are either given an announcement to take home to their parents or guardian or are contacted by telephone, mail, or e-mail concerning string study. Initial contact is made by you or by classroom teachers in individual classrooms or in assemblies, but is not accompanied by any form of presentation of instruments or performance.

Music tests can be used to gather information that can be used to contact students and inform them of the opportunity to study strings. A musical aptitude, musical interest, or similar test can be administered to students. It is important that any administered test have strong reliability and validity. The test should be designed so students can include all forms of contact information on the answer sheet. After the tests have been gathered, follow-up letters, e-mails, or telephone calls can be made to parents/guardians inviting them to a conference, demonstration concert, or meeting. Information about your program and the benefits of string study should also be shared at this time. The purpose of testing should not be to eliminate students from program participation, but rather to gather information that will help you introduce them to the benefits of string participation. Thus, while individual students' scores can be shared with parents/guardians, this is not the main focus of the testing approach.

Lecture Method

Often, classroom or general music teachers teach music at the schools from which you wish to recruit. With prior discussion and planning, you can request that these teachers include a unit on strings. Recordings, pictures, and in some cases actual instruments can be included in this unit. One of the drawbacks of this approach is that you, the orchestra director, do not make contact with your potential students. Thus, it is a good idea for you to at least arrange to attend a class or present one of the lectures if possible so students can associate you with the string program.

Films, slide shows, computer-generated productions, and similar such presentations can be used for recruitment purposes. Prepared recruitment films and so on, available from national organizations such as ASTA with NSOA and MENC, as well as from locally or state-produced sources, generally include a discussion about the importance of music in students' lives and education. Some have demonstrations of the various instruments of the orchestra. You can also make your own recruitment films, slide shows, or computer-generated presentations. Your recruitment materials can use clips of your students playing in recitals or concerts, traveling to concert sites out-of-state or in different countries, or enjoying social functions or "free times" at away concerts or trips.

Advantages of using films and similar presentational approaches are the ease with which they can be presented and their availability from year to year. Films and similar presentations, however, are not the most effective means of getting students interested in string study. They can, however, produce modest student interest.

The Demonstration Routine

In the demonstration routine, the orchestra director visits individual classrooms or arranges assemblies at which he discusses and demonstrates the various bowed string instruments. Each instrument is shown and discussed. The teacher then plays a representative musical example on each instrument or plays a recording in which the instrument is featured.

A variation on this approach is often referred to as the story approach. The orchestra teacher creates a fictional and interesting story. As the story is told, the various stringed instruments are introduced. Musical selections or unique instrumental sounds are used within the presentation to highlight the story line.

In both approaches, the purpose of the presentation is to discuss the various bowed string performance options available to the students and to present the characteristic sounds of each instrument. In this type of format, it is an excellent idea to get students from the audience, such as class leaders, to play the instruments. Student selection can be arranged with classroom teachers prior to your presentation. The student performance task should be simple enough to ensure that success is quickly and easily achieved. A simple duet can then be played by you and the student, or a prerecorded accompaniment can be played while you assist the student performer.

The Performance Procedure

Many orchestra directors use orchestra concert performances as a tool to interest potential students in string study. If you use this type of system, you should print invitations that can be distributed to potential string students. Parents of students are also invited. You may elect to use an RSVP system. This enables you to welcome students from the various elementary schools during the concert. Students and parents can then be acknowledged by having them stand up. The RSVP system also enables you to construct a list of potentially interested students. These students can then be contacted individually with additional information concerning string study.

You should consider inviting students to all of your concerts, whether they are given by your high school, middle/junior high school, or elementary groups. Chamber music concerts, strolling strings performances, and so on are all excellent events to which you should consider offering invitations.

In larger school districts, the possibility exists of combining recruitment efforts with other string teachers. You and your colleagues can form a small chamber ensemble or string trio, quartet, or quintet and perform at various schools. Not only does this give students a chance to see you and your colleagues playing stringed instruments and talking about them, it also allows them to realize the scope of the orchestral program in the district.

Individual performances by guest artists are another recruitment tool that can be used to interest students in string study. Generally, the guest performer presents an abbreviated program of various works. Selections should be short, ideally one to two minutes, and should be works that are familiar to the students. Such performances are generally entertaining and can generate limited interest among students; however, other recruitment approaches are usually more effective.

Using student performance groups to interest students in string study is a commonly used and effective recruitment procedure. In this approach, student groups are brought to school recruitment sites. While it is always a good idea to use peer performance groups, it is not necessary. If you are recruiting from the third or fourth grade, a group of middle school students could be used as the performance group. Ideally, both a peer group (string students from the previous year) and an older group (middle school or even high school students) could perform for the third or fourth graders. Potential students can then envision their own progress on a stringed instrument in a year and beyond.

Groups chosen for performance presentations can vary from a select chamber music or chamber ensemble to a complete string class or orchestra. The groups can be from the same school at which you are presenting or from one of your other schools. No matter who you select for the performance presentations, it is extremely important that you ensure quality performances. Performances must be polished. If your group sounds polished and is exciting, students will want to become members of the string program. You may have heard the phrase "excellence attracts excellence." Students want to be part of excellent groups. Excellence attracts excellence and interest.

During the performance presentation, time should be allotted for discussion of the various instruments. Each of the instruments should be featured in a performed work with a brief discussion of that instrument before the selection is played. A student from each section of your group can demonstrate the instrument and can assist you with your discussion.

Here again, it is an excellent idea to choose individuals from the audience to play along with your group or conduct your group. A simple open-string pizzicato part can be quickly taught and played with the group, or a conducting pattern can be taught. With your assistance and guidance, a student playing with or conducting your group can be successful. The thrill of seeing a fellow classmate conduct, or hearing a classmate play with your group, can immediately spark students' interest in string study.

The Hands-On Technique

One technique that has met with resounding success in many areas involves students recruiting students. In this approach, each of your string students recruits other students to play a stringed instrument. Once recruited, the new string students are given lessons by the string students who recruited them. The recruiters show them the basics, which may include the instrument and bow hold, left-hand position, note reading, and so on. Not only do new students receive lessons from their peers, veteran students have the opportunity to teach their instrument to others, thus reinforcing the concepts that have been presented to them. Of course, you will need to carefully supervise students to prevent inaccurate information being shared. In some string programs that use this approach, the orchestra teacher schedules "concerts," where "student teachers" showcase their students displaying skills they have learned through their instruction, such as holding the bow or instrument, playing open strings with the bow or by plucking them, or playing a short selection from a method book. At some point during this recruitment process, parents/guardians must be contacted to inform them that their child is interested in string study. Enrollment and other pertinent information are shared at this time as well.

While individual peer lessons can be a very effective method of getting students interested in string study, introductory lessons provided by the orchestra teacher can also be effective. By working with small groups of students during, before, or after school hours, you can expose prospective string students to the joys of string study. The goal of your compact mini-lessons is to expose as many students as possible to a hands-on trial of the strings. Thus, success in a brief time frame is essential. A rote approach, using pizzicato, is often used to teach a simple song over which an accompaniment is played. The success of this approach is that students are participants and not observers.

Some schools offer exploratory instrumental study programs in the year prior to enrollment in orchestra, band, or choir. In such programs, students can explore various instruments, including strings, brass, woodwinds, and percussion, for periods of four to six weeks. Once one group of instruments has been studied and played, another group is introduced, exposing students to a variety of instruments. This approach enables each child to try a variety of instruments before making a choice to continue study on any of the instruments. As the orchestra teacher, you may be part of a team that provides instruction to the class. If you are not an instructor, you should visit the class and the students frequently so you can become acquainted with the students and they with you.

Summary

Your goal in recruitment is to offer students an opportunity to play a bowed string instrument. The approach you use to accomplish this task will vary depending on your time and availability, access to schools and students, and school policies and procedures. Given these constraints, it is important to remember that the more active and involved your potential students are in your recruitment approach, the more success you are likely to experience.

When recruiting, keep the following ideas in mind as you plan your strategies:

1. Create the idea of a real concert.
2. When music is played, perform music that students will recognize, such as music from films, commercials, musicals, or shows on television.
3. Limit the length of the performed selections to one or two minutes.
4. Include brief descriptions about the music and the instruments.
5. Highlight each instrument (emphasis can be given to instruments as needed to produce a well-balanced beginning instrumental ensemble).
6. Ask questions of students.
7. Get students involved. Plan for individual/group participation. You may wish to arrange to preselect students from the audience. With the help of classroom teachers, student audience participants can meet with success and will ensure a smooth presentational flow.
8. Select audience members as special assistants, performers, or conductors when possible.
9. Set aside time for students' questions.
10. Talk to the students about the joys and benefits of music study.
11. Prepare performed music thoroughly. Take time to have a dress rehearsal.
12. Students must have something to take home telling their parents/guardians about the program and the event. Use brightly colored paper if possible. Include your telephone number, e-mail address, and like information so students and parents/guardians can contact you.

Once parents/guardians have contacted you about string study, you should provide follow-up information and reminders concerning the parents' meeting. This can be done through telephone calls, e-mails, or mailings. To facilitate your follow-up procedures, consider using responsible students or parent groups, such as a music booster club, to help you. Telephone calls, mailings, or e-mail contacts can be completed quickly when students or parents help distribute the information.

If you send out a printed sheet of information about the parents' meeting as part of your follow-up procedure, the sheet should provide the date, time, and location of the meeting (with directions or a map if necessary), as well as a reminder of what to bring (e.g., checkbooks, credit cards, and so on). The sheet should also indicate what music dealers will be present, the expected length of the meeting, and what exactly will take place. All arrangements for the meeting must be cleared through the school office and appropriate administrative offices prior to the event.

The parent's meeting is the capstone to your recruitment process. The purpose of this meeting is to disseminate concert schedule information, outline rules and program policies, discuss expectations concerning participation in the program, and explain the responsibilities of both students and parents. It is at this time that instruments are obtained, accessories are purchased, and method books are bought. Keep in mind that the music companies attending the meeting must be equipped to handle all forms of payment, supply appropriate instruments, have required accessories and method books, and provide such services as insurance and rental possibilities.

At the meeting, you must allow yourself to be in a position to greet parents and students on an individual basis as they arrive. A formal welcome is given at the start of the meeting. This is followed by a brief explanation of the benefits of music study. In addition to covering the items discussed earlier, you should outline the procedures you want to use to help students and parents acquire instruments, accessories, and music. Remember, the success of your recruitment hinges on your ability to organize and to excite students and parents about the study of strings.

RETENTION

Once you have recruited students into your program, your next task is to train and retain them. According to Hamann, Gillespie, and Bergonzi (2002), the national orchestra student retention rate, from the first to second year of instruction, elementary to middle/junior high school, and middle/junior high to high school averages approximately 73 percent. Assuming you are retaining your students at the national average and you began with one hundred at the elementary level, you would have seventy-three students at the middle/junior high school level, and approximately fifty-three students at the high school level. Thus, most orchestra teachers are retaining about 53 percent of their students from the beginning of their study to the high school level.

With all of the challenges, choices, and decisions students are faced with, how do you keep them in your program? The key to retention is motivation. Motivation is also the key to musical learning. When motivation is high, learning potential is also high. When learning potential is high, retention is also high. The question is, then, how do you encourage and promote student motivation? Setting challenging standards for admittance into your program is one of many ways that will be discussed to enhance student motivation and hence help in the retention of students.

Retention through Valuing and Supporting Your Students

Student pride is developed when you sincerely value student opinions and ideas. Treat all students and their ideas with respect. Consider your students' opinions and ideas in as many venues as possible, remembering of course that the ultimate responsibility for your program rests with you. Give orchestra members positions of responsibility within your groups. Have section leaders conduct section rehearsals with guidance and assistance, as needed, from you. Create student organizational offices within your orchestra (president, vice president, secretary/treasurer, members at large, etc.) to enable student input, ideas, and suggestions to be shared and used effectively with the framework of your group.

Retention through Admittance Standards

One constant in life is that the more difficult it is to get something, the more that "something" is desired. It doesn't seem to matter what the something is; the desire to have or be part of something that is exclusive creates an internal desire and motivation for many people. To become a member of a select group also motivates students. Therefore, when you are establishing your entrance standards, consider fair yet demanding criteria. Setting high standards for entrance into your program can instill a desire in students to become part of that organization because it is exclusive.

Retention as a Result of a Tradition of Excellence

As mentioned previously, excellence begets excellence, and quality begets quality. A program that has been developed and built on a tradition of excellence will be attractive to those individuals not already in the program as well as to those students in the program. Developing positive and favorable attitudes toward your orchestra program and building esprit de corps is one component of several that will be needed to develop program excellence.

As part of your responsibilities as the orchestra director, you will need to create a plan that will encourage student development of pride in your organization. Orchestral performance excellence is perhaps the most important component in the development of student pride. Consistently successful orchestral performances help instill pride in the group and in individual students. If your orchestra sounds wonderful and performs quality music, students will want to become part of your group and, once in the group, will want to remain there.

Retention through Performance Venues and Public Relations

Student pride is enhanced not only through successful local public concerts and performances, but also through excellence at such performance venues as regional and state contests, exchange concerts between schools, and regional and state tours. Extensive publicity should accompany these events. When students see or read about themselves, their fellow orchestra members, or the group itself, whether it is on television, in newspapers, or on radio, a sense of group pride is achieved. Thus, success at contests, plans for tour travel, or like events should be shared with as many media outlets as possible.

Retention through Recognition of Achievement

Awards such as medals, plaques, uniform service stripes, chenille letters, certificates of merit, and scholarships can all be used to acknowledge students' achievements within your group. Individual and group awards can help establish pride within the program, for they represent the contributions individuals have made toward the group and the individuals in that group. Acknowledgments can be given for musical achievement, exemplary service in the organization, continuous participation with flawless attendance, and similar accomplishments.

Retention Due to the Learning Environment

Several aspects of the learning environment can positively or negatively contribute to student retention. The physical learning environment, the room in which your orchestra rehearsals are held, can often play a significant role in student perceptions. New, well-designed, well-lit rehearsal facilities with proper storage areas, acoustics, and recording and playback equipment can be perceived as positive indicators of a healthy and vital program. In the same vein, new instruments and uniforms also signal program vitality. Proper physical environments and support systems can enhance student attitudes and promote retention.

A healthy learning environment also involves well-articulated teacher goals and objectives. As the orchestra teacher, you must set achievable yet challenging goals for your orchestra. As you plan for each day, keep in mind your weekly and monthly goals. Share these goals and objectives with your students so that the process of learning is a shared activity.

As you create your daily rehearsals, plan to relate technical drill development to the music selected. Technical drill development can include the performance of scales and arpeggios in the keys that are included in your musical selections. Relative or parallel minor keys and arpeggios can also be played. Rhythmic and bowing patterns found in the music can be used as technical drill exercises using scales or arpeggios. Whatever technical drill development exercises you use, remember that you can and should consider relating your exercises to your music.

In addition to the development of technical skills, plan to develop student factual musical knowledge as well as musicianship skills. Inform students of the characteristics of each piece being performed including such items as the stylistic considerations of the period in which the music was written, information about the composer and his or her style of composition, and perhaps the form of the work.

Consider competitive seating plans, challenge systems, and tryouts for chairs or advancement to more advanced ensembles. Competitive and fair systems that allow students to benefit from their individual practice and studies encourage internal and external motivation among your players. Well-conceived and constructed seating plans, challenge systems, and tryouts for chairs or advancement provide students the forum in which they can excel in your groups.

Create rehearsals in which you demand nothing less than the best from each player. Use praise and criticism appropriately. Never use sarcasm or ridicule, and remind yourself and the student that you are not criticizing the student but are correcting a problem.

Effectively plan the use of tape recordings, CDs, and videotapes to enhance students' learning and understanding. When your students listen to other groups or themselves, whether it is through recordings or live performances, you need to present them with a structure for such listening sessions. Present them with a plan for critical evaluation of these performances. Be sure to stress that a critical evaluation includes noting both positive and negative aspects of a performance.

Encourage private lesson study, practice partners, and participation in small ensembles. Private lesson study has been found to enhance performance practice among students, whether in a solo or group situation. Practice partners help forge stronger relationships among your players, encourage critical evaluation, and provide another forum in which students can gain valuable feedback. Small ensemble performance, such as playing in quartets, allows students the opportunity to perform as soloists in a group situation, taking away some of the pressures of solo performance while adding the support of a group. In such settings, students often enhance many aspects of their musical development while providing another outlet for musical expression and learning, all of which can then be carried into the larger group setting.

Part of your motivational techniques and planning must also include assessment. Fair and informative assessment is important to promote student growth and maintain student interest. The use of grades, practice or progress charts, point systems, and other assessment systems must be reviewed and considered for your particular situation. Remember to keep parents informed of student progress as well as practice requirements and objectives.

As the orchestra director, your responsibility is to be the most inspiring teacher you can be. You must show that you care for the welfare of your students and want to be involved and interested in their learning and growth as musicians and as individuals. Your inspirational teaching, along with your well-planned and well-paced musical rehearsals, rehearsals with a shared agenda, planned around quality music from a wide musical repertoire, one in which supporting players can also be the stars of the group, will provide for a positive learning environment. This is the type of environment that provides a comfortable and secure yet stimulating learning environment for students, one in which students will want to remain.

Retention through Social Interaction

Part of the motivational excitement of belonging to any musical organization, besides the performance of the music itself, is the interaction and sense of group identity the organization provides for its members. Your orchestra may be a key element in the social lives of many of your students. This may be their only or one of the main sources for social interaction. Keeping this in mind, plan social activities with your students. Going to concerts, attending and performing at conferences, going on tours, and conducting fund-raising activities for the orchestra (car washes, etc.) can all be very stimulating and rewarding for your orchestra students. Interaction with guest artists and clinicians is a form of social interaction that can hold and promote student interest and motivation. Creating interest in student attendance at summer music camps or weekend workshops can also provide social outlets for your orchestra members.

Summary

Recruiting students into your program is one of the first goals that you will realize as an orchestra director. Effective recruitment strategies and procedures will bring students into your orchestra. Once you have your students, your next and ongoing task is to keep them in your orchestra. Just as you had to plan and develop goals and objectives for your recruitment procedures, so too will you need to develop effective strategies for student retention. There are no better means of getting and keeping students in your orchestra than maintaining program quality and excellence. An attitude that values student learning and worth, that recognizes student achievement, and that creates positive learning environments and experiences will help you achieve your recruitment and retention objectives.

REFERENCES

Colwell, Richard J., and Thomas Goolsby. 1992. *The teaching of instrumental music*. 2d ed. Englewood Cliffs, N.J.: Prentice-Hall.

Dillon, Jacquelyn A., and Casimer Kriechbaum. 1978. *How to design and teach a successful school string and orchestra program*. San Diego: Kjos West.

Hamann, Donald L., Robert Gillespie, and Louis Bergonzi. 2002. Status of orchestra programs in the public schools. *Journal of String Research* 2:9–35.

Klotman, Robert H. 1996. *Teaching strings: Learning through playing*. 2d ed. New York: Schirmer Books.

Music Educators National Conference (MENC). 1988. *The complete string guide: Standards, programs, purchase, and maintenance*. Reston, Va.: Music Educators National Conference.

———. 1991. *Teaching stringed instruments: A course of study*. Reston, Va.: Music Educators National Conference.

———. 1994. *Strategies for success in the band and orchestra*. Reston, Va.: Music Educators National Conference.

Schleuter, Stanley L. 1997. *A sound approach to teaching instrumentalists*. 2d ed. New York: Schirmer Books.

Witt, Anne C. 1984. *Recruiting for the school orchestra: A comprehensive manual*. Elkhart, Ind.: Selmer Company.

10

METHOD BOOKS AND MUSIC FOR THE SCHOOL ORCHESTRA PROGRAM

One of the more challenging and important tasks you will perform as the orchestra director is to select music. Music selection is central to the success of the group with which you work. In Chapter 6, the process of selecting music based on the goals and objectives of your groups, selecting music by style and period, and selecting music based on the ability level of your group was discussed. An excellent summary of the various aspects to be considered in the music selection process can also be found in the book *Teaching Music through Performance in Orchestra* (Littrell and Racin 2001). Here, Dillon, Kjelland, Gillespie, Bergonzi, and Straub discuss the various considerations that must be made to successfully choose music for your groups.

Why do we perform? There are numerous reasons, including the development of physical skills, music appreciation awareness, concept comprehension, aesthetic appreciation, and so on. As teachers and performers we are also aware that personal satisfaction, self-esteem, and internal motivation play a major role in our drive to perform. We recognize that quality is the key to performance satisfaction. Thus as orchestra directors, we must make sure that our primary performance goal is to produce a quality performance. In order to ensure quality performance, selecting the most appropriate music for our groups is imperative.

Imagine a high school orchestra concert at which master works from the standard orchestral literature, including Beethoven and Brahms symphonies, were programmed. When the concert ended, students, parents, and the conductor all seemed pleased that a high school group performed an impressive program, and yet the quality of the performance was lacking. The group was well rehearsed, and the students had diligently practiced their parts. The orchestra was well supported and had the best equipment and facilities, and the parents and administration enthusiastically supported the group. So, what was the problem, why was the performance lacking quality? The answer: overprogramming.

Overprogramming refers to the practice of selecting a repertoire that completely surpasses the technical and musical capabilities of the students. If the majority of students are able to play the notes, and they are actively engaged in the issues of balance, blend, style, and phrasing, the conductor has not overprogrammed. If the majority of students are absorbed in a frantic approximation of the notes with little or no regard as to how the notes should be played, the conductor has overprogrammed. Poor tone quality, intonation, articulation, clarity, expression, or phrasing may have all contributed to the lack of quality, but the problem lies in overprogramming.

To avoid overprogramming, the first key in music selection is to know the ability level of your group. A simple rule of thumb to use when selecting works for your group is that your group should be able to read through the works with few major breakdowns. If your group can do this, then the work is most likely appropriate for more in-depth study. Another rule of thumb often cited is that you should select music that is at or one level below the average ability level of your group. Some educators advocate that within a certain level, and given that three works are selected, one of those pieces should be easy to reach a quality performance level, one should be attainable with moderate rehearsal, and one should stretch the abilities of the group. Part independence is also a critical criterion in music selection, especially if an orchestra has sections that are not as strong as they should be. Whatever rule of thumb you use, it is imperative that a quality performance is your outcome goal when selecting music for your group.

PRINTED METHOD BOOKS

Several excellent group string methods books are available for use in homogeneous and heterogeneous settings. Every day new method books are being developed and printed. While it is wonderful that we have such a wealth of materials, deciding which is best for you and your program is sometimes difficult. In order to make an appropriate method book selection, you must review the goals and objectives for your groups. Next, determine the sequence of learning activities you feel is best for rapid yet careful development of students' playing skills. Now you can review each method book to determine which one best fits the learning sequence you feel is most appropriate and which method book will help you reach your goals in the most efficient manner.

The following list of method books is not meant to be exhaustive but rather represents some of the more popular and widely used texts in heterogeneous and homogeneous group string instructional settings.

Author	Text
Allen, Gillespie, and Hayes	*Essential Elements for Strings* (Hal Leonard)
Anderson and Frost	*All For Strings* (Neil A. Kjos Music)
Applebaum	*Belwin String Builder* (CPP-Belwin)
Bornoff	*Finger Patterns* (Foundation for the Advancement of String Education)

Author	Text
Dillon, Kjelland, and O'Reilley	*Strictly Strings* (Highland/Etling [Alfred])
Dabczynski, Meyer, and Phillips	*String Explorer* (Highland/Etling [Alfred])
Etling	*Etling String Class Method* (Highland-Etling [Alfred])
Frost and Fischbach with Barden	*Artistry in Strings* (Neil A. Kjos Music)
Gazda and Stoutamire	*Spotlight on Strings* (Neil A. Kjos Music)
Herfurth	*A Tune a Day* (Boston Music)
Johnson	*Young Strings in Action* (Boosey and Hawkes)
Klotman	*Action with Strings* (Southern Music)
Matesky and Womack	*Learn to Play a Stringed Instrument* (Alfred Music)
Muller-Rusch	*Muller-Rusch String Method* (Neil A. Kjos Music)
Wisniewski and Higgins	*Learning Unlimited String Method* (Hal Leonard)

RECOMMENDED PUBLISHERS

With the advent of music notation programs and desktop publishing, an increasing number of musical compositions for strings is being published by private or small companies. Even with this trend, there are still a number of publishers who publish a large portion of the works available for string groups. The following is a list of some of the major publishers for group string literature:

- Alfred Music
- Belwin Mills (CCP/BM)
- Boosey and Hawkes
- Boston Music
- Bourne
- Broude Brothers
- Carlin
- Elkan-Vogel
- Carl Fischer
- Galaxy Music
- Heilmann Music
- Highland/Etling
- Kalmus Music
- Kendor Music
- Neil A. Kjos Music
- Hal Leonard
- Luck's Music Library
- Ludwig Music
- Oxford University Press
- C. F. Peters

- Theodore Presser
- G. Schirmer
- Southern Music
- Summy-Birchard
- Warner Brothers
- Wingert-Jones Music
- Wynn Music
- Young World

Specific contact information and addresses or imprint information for most of these companies can be obtained by going to the Music Publishers' Association website: www.mpa.org.

STRING ORCHESTRA LITERATURE

There is perhaps no more beautiful sound than that of a string orchestra. The rich sonorities and melodic capabilities of the string orchestra have and continue to capture the attention of major composers. Thus, there is and continues to be a wealth of outstanding educational and professional works for the string orchestra. The following presentation of string orchestra works includes a listing of representative works for various string ability levels. A brief discussion of the technical demands and musical considerations at each level is also presented.

Music for First- and Second-Year String Classes

Some works are more popular or more frequently performed by students in their first and second year of string class. Works for the first-year student tend to be in the keys of D, A, and G, have the meter signature of either 4/4 or 3/4, and are generally playable in first position by all instruments, with the possible exception of string bass. At times, the bass part may involve playing notes in second position. The rhythmic patterns involve combinations with whole, dotted half, half, dotted quarter, quarter, and eighth notes. The détaché, legato, marcato, slurs, and staccato bow strokes are used at this level along with pizzicato.

The following works (with composer and publisher) are representative of the first-year literature:

- *Apollo Suite*, Merle Isaac, Highland/Etling
- *Cross Country*, Bruce Chase, Lake State Music
- *Fiddling A-Round*, John Caponegro, Kendor Music
- *March of the Metro Gnome*, Fred M. Hubbell, Kendor Music
- *Star Valley Suite*, Robert Frost, Southern Music
- *Suite for Strings*, Edmund Siennicki, Highland/Etling
- *Ukranian Folk Songs*, arr. Dackow, Southern Music

The following collections are also representative of the first-year literature:

- *Concert Tunes for Beginning Strings*, Dale Brubaker, Jlj Music
- *Fiddlers Philharmonic*, Dabczynski and Phillips, Alfred Music
- *Learn to Play in the Orchestra* (Book I), Ralph Matesky, Alfred Music
- *Performing Strings*, Fran Feese, Young World
- *Young World of Strings*, Fran Feese, Young World

Second-year works begin to introduce the key signatures of F, C, and some minor keys. While the upper string parts can still be performed in first position, the cello parts sometimes require second position work and extensions. Double bass parts can require third position work. Rhythmic patterns are similar to first-year patterns but may now require syncopations and more slurred combinations. The brush stroke, repeated down bow strokes, and martelé patterns are often used.

The following works are representative of the second-year literature:

- *Appalachian Sunrise*, Doris Gazda, Neil A. Kjos Music
- *Baroque Fugue*, Ed Siennicki, Highland/Etling
- *Brandenburg Concerto No. 5*, Bach arr. Isaac, Highland/Etling
- "Dance of the Tumblers" from *Snow Maiden*, Rimsky-Korsakov arr. Dackow, Ludwig Music
- *El Toro*, Brubaker, Highland/Etling
- *Little Bit of . . . Space . . . Time*, Samuel Adler, Ludwig Music
- *Petite Overture*, Del Borgo, Kendor Music
- *Quinto Quarto Suite*, Isaac, Neil A. Kjos Music
- *Star Valley Suite*, Robert Frost, Southern Music

Representative Music for Third- and Fourth-Year String Classes

As students play literature composed for the third and fourth year of string classes, they will find compositions written in more flat keys, such as B-flat and F, and more minor keys. Time signature requirements include simple and compound meter.

Position work from first to fourth or fifth position is evident in the first violin parts, while second violin and viola parts include half to second or third position work. Cellos will find passages that require half to fourth position work, and basses may go up to sixth position. Rhythmic complexities increase and include triplet patterns and dotted eighth and sixteenth note patterns. Slurred patterns, runs, arpeggios, scale passages, and leaping patterns are much more common at these levels.

Bowings now include spiccato, louré, and hooked bowings, with two to three articulations required in one bow direction. Shifting, use of all finger patterns, frequent finger pattern changes, double stops, chromatic passages, grace notes, mordents, appoggiaturas, and long trills are some of the technical demands now required.

The following works are representative of the third-year literature:

- *Air for Strings*, Dello Joio, E. B. Marks
- *Brandenburg Concerto No. 3*, Bach arr. Isaac, Highland/Etling
- *Brook Green Suite*, Holst, G. Schirmer
- *Contrasts in E Minor*, Feese, Young World
- *Danza*, Nelhýbel, E. C. Kerby
- "Farandole" from *L'arlésienne Suite No. 2*, Bizet arr. Isaac, Alfred Music
- *Lullaby*, Hofeldt, Neil A. Kjos Music
- *M to the Third Power*, Nunez, Shawnee Press
- *Serenade for Strings*, Leyden, Sam Fox
- *Suite for Strings*, Washburn, Oxford University Press

The following works are representative of the fourth-year literature:

- *Andante Festivo*, Sibelius, Southern Music
- "Ase's Death" from *Peer Gynt Suite No. 1*, Grieg, Carl Fischer
- *Capriol Suite*, Warlock, Curwin
- *Concertino for String Orchestra*, Adler, G. Schirmer
- *Dance of Iscariot*, Mosier, Neil A. Kjos Music
- *Drawings, No. 8*, Hodkinson, Theodore Presser
- "Serenade" from *Eine kleine Nachtmusik*, Mozart, C. F. Peters
- *Folk Tune and Fiddle Dance*, Fletcher, Boosey and Hawkes
- *Preludio for String Orchestra*, Whear, Ludwig Music
- *Romanian Folk Dances*, Bartok, Boosey and Hawkes
- *Sanseneon*, Frost, Neil A. Kjos Music

Representative High School String Literature

Demands for the high school literature include performance of works in virtually all keys, but most generally in keys with no more than four sharps or flats. Mixed meter is now much more common. Violin I parts often require position work up to ninth position, and similar demands are also found in the other parts.

The full range of dynamics is now used, and students are required to be able to control their sound at these various dynamic levels while producing beautiful, seamless tones. Complex bowings are often necessary to perform various passages that may contain elaborate articulation requirements or intricate rhythmic patterns.

The following works are representative of the fifth- and sixth-year literature:

- *Choreography for String Orchestra*, Dello Joio, Hal Leonard
- *Concerto Grosso*, Bloch, Broude Brothers
- *Don Quixote Suite*, Telemann, Kalmus Music
- *Fantasia on Greensleeves*, Vaughan Williams, Oxford University Press
- *Fantasia on a Theme by Thomas Tallis*, Vaughan Williams, Oxford University Press
- "Hoe Down" from *Rodeo*, Copland, Boosey and Hawkes
- *Holberg Suite*, Grieg, Kalmus Music
- *Irish Tune from Country Derry*, Grainger, Oxford University Press
- *Molly on the Shore*, Grainger , Luck's Music Library
- *Psalm and Fugue*, op. 40a, Hovhaness, C. F. Peters
- *Rakastava*, Sibelius, Southern Music
- *Simple Symphony*, Britten, Oxford University Press
- *St. Paul's Suite*, Holst, G. Schirmer

FULL ORCHESTRA LITERATURE

The thrill of playing full orchestra music can be as exciting as playing string orchestra music. With the addition of the winds, brass, and percussion, a new and vibrant palate of sound becomes available for each group to explore. Even the easiest full orchestra literature places demands on string players that surpass the ability of first- and second-year players. Thus, many composers concentrate on writing full orchestra literature for students at the intermediate or advanced level.

The following pieces are representative of the literature available for students at intermediate and advanced levels. Your students will find these works, whether arrangements or original compositions, to be exciting and rewarding to perform.

The following works are representative of the intermediate full orchestra literature:

- *Ballet Parisien*, Offenbach, Carl Fischer
- "Berceuse and Finale" from the *Firebird Suite*, Stravinsky arr. Isaac, Warner Brothers
- *Celebration*, Meyer, Highland/Etling
- *Essay for Orchestra*, Del Borgo, Neil A. Kjos Music
- *Fantasy on America*, Nelhýbel, Great Works
- *Great Gate of Kiev*, Mussorgsky arr. Reibold, Fitzsimmons
- "Grand March" from *Aida*, Verdi arr. Isaac, Warner Brothers
- "March to the Scaffold" from *Symphonie fantastique*, Berlioz arr. Carter, Oxford University Press

- *Marche militaire francais*, Saint-Saëns arr. Isaac, Carl Fischer
- *March Slav*, Tchaikovsky arr. Herfurth, Carl Fischer
- *Montagues and Capulets*, Prokofiev arr. Siennicki, Highland/Etling

The following works are representative of the high school full orchestra literature:

- *A Mighty Fortress*, Nelhýbel, E. C. Kerby
- *Carmen Suite No. 2*, Bizet, Kalmus Music
- *Danse macabre*, Sains-Saëns, Kalmus Music
- *Finlandia*, Sibelius, Kalmus Music
- *Hungarian March*, Berlioz, Kalmus Music
- *Night on Bald Mountain*, Mussorgsky, Kalmus Music
- *Outdoor Overture*, Copland, Boosey and Hawkes
- *Peer Gynt Suite No. 1*, Grieg, Kalmus Music
- Prelude to *Die Meistersinger*, Wagner, Kalmus Music
- "Procession of the Nobles" from *Mlada*, Rimsky-Korsakov arr. Isaac, Highland/Etling
- *Russian Easter Overture*, Rimsky-Korsakov, Kalmus Music
- *Variations on a Shaker Melody*, Copland, Boosey and Hawkes

REFERENCES

Daniels, David. 1996. *Orchestral music: A handbook*. Lanham, Md.: Scarecrow Press.
Littrell, David, and Laura Reed Racin, eds. 2001. *Teaching music through performance in orchestra*. Chicago: GIA Publications.
Mayer, Frederick R., ed. 1993. *The string orchestra super list*. Reston, Va.: Music Educators National Conference.

ADDITIONAL RESOURCES

Numerous sources may be consulted to obtain information pertaining to string and full orchestra literature. String teachers are a valuable source of information. Publications such as the *American String Teacher* and the *NSOA Bulletin* periodically did and still do reviews of orchestral literature. *The String Orchestra Super List*, edited by Frederick R. Mayer, is an excellent publication that lists major string orchestra works. It was published by MENC but is currently out of print. A new book, *Teaching Music through Performance in Orchestra*, by GIA Publications, has reviews of one hundred select full and string orchestra works for all levels. Edited by David Littrell and Laura Reed Racin, this book contains useful information for every orchestra teacher. A second volume of this book is currently in progress and will soon be released. A standard for many years, David Daniels's book *Orchestral Music: A Handbook* lists works for the orchestra.

Various states have published festival contest lists. These lists usually contain some of the popular and educationally worthy works available for string and full orchestra performance. The Pepper Music Company's website (www.peppermusic.com) has each state's contest list available for review online. The Internet has become an ever-expanding source of information. Practically every major music company has a website from which a listing of publications can be found. Sheet music dealers also have websites from which music can be found and ordered. The following is a listing of some sites that carry string and full orchestra music for educational settings.

The Pepper Music Company's website (www.peppermusic.com) offers several different string and full orchestra music lists including the State/Festival lists and the Best Sellers in Full and String Orchestra list. This is a comprehensive site with a helpful staff and a large selection of orchestral works for your orchestra.

Luck's Music Library (www.lucksmusic.net) is a well-known dealer that handles orchestral publications for the educational setting. Luck's is also a publisher of full and string orchestra materials.

Stanton's Music Company (www.stantons.com) and The Music Mart, Inc. (www.musicmart.com) also deal in orchestral literature for the educational setting. Both companies have extensive holdings of literature.

The resources already mentioned will help you select music appropriate for your orchestra for several years. However, orchestra reading sessions, generally held at string conferences or state MENC conferences, are a valuable source of information for new materials. Music publishers also send CDs of their current music, free upon request. These and other sources, such as articles and Internet chat room discussions, will help you in your search for orchestral music for your groups.

APPENDIX: ADDITIONAL PEDAGOGICAL RESOURCES

SPECIAL PEDAGOGICAL APPROACHES

Samuel Applebaum

Samuel Applebaum was one of the most prolific composers of string educational materials for the classroom. He edited and authored more than four hundred method books, chamber music collections, solo collections, and pedagogical materials for bowed string instruments.

Awarded the ASTA Teacher of the Year Award in 1967, Applebaum was an active string clinician and teacher trainer at ASTA workshops in the 1950s and 1960s. A student of Leopold Auer, Applebaum taught at the Manhattan School of Music for thirty-five years. One of his most popular publications was the *String Builder*, a method book still used in many string classrooms today.

George Bornoff

George Bornoff developed an approach that introduces all four strings of the instrument and five left-hand finger patterns at the beginning of string study. The Bornoff approach also uses the fundamental bowing techniques (détaché, legato, spiccato, staccato, and slurred bowings) early in the course of study. By introducing his broad approach to the left hand through the use of his five finger patterns, which encompass the entire fingerboard, and by encouraging right-hand technique through a comprehensive approach using various bowings, students are capable of performing music in any key early in their study.

Bornoff's approach is intended to produce facility on the instrument as well as develop a beautiful, expansive tone quality. He published several technical method books, which are now available through the Foundation for the Advancement of String Education (www.fase.org/index.html). Several other books are also available through the foundation and include songbooks, literature, technical studies, and orchestral materials, as well as a comprehensive study of Bornoff's life and work, traced from his growth from a concert artist to teacher.

Kato Havas

One of Kato Havas's more well-known books is *Stage Fright*; however, her book *New Approach* outlines her approach to string performance. *New Approach* stresses tension-free playing, physical free-flowing movement, and mental balance. Players experience freedom made possible through active rhythmic pulse and the sensation of having no violin or bow hold. Two right-arm motions or swings encompass all bow strokes, and balanced left-hand movements are responsible for tone, intonation, and vibrato.

The system is an organized approach that is designed to prevent or eliminate the tensions and anxieties normally associated with string performance. Havas highlights the combination of the physical, mental, and social aspects of performance and encourages the unification of the mind, body, and spirit in her approach.

François Rabbath

François Rabbath began his study of the double bass as a self-taught student aided by a tutorial written by Edouard Nanny. Rabbath is known for his unique pedagogical approach and techniques to double bass playing.

Rabbath divides the fingerboard into six sections or positions, which simplifies the fingering of notes. The natural harmonics of the instrument form the basis of this method of division. In each position, it is possible to play an entire octave on three strings without moving the thumb on the neck or shifting the hand. This is accomplished with the use of a technique called a pivot. In traditional systems, the middle finger remains over the thumb (the thumb remains under the second finger). In the pivot system, the thumb remains in one position, but the hand is allowed to move forward of the traditional position, thus allowing the middle finger to move forward of the thumb, enabling the double bass player to play more notes without shifting. In the crab technique, a technique also coined by Rabbath, a finger is never lifted from the string until the next finger is placed. These techniques, along with others, have captured the attention of bass players and teachers around the world.

Paul Rolland

Paul Rolland was born in Budapest, Hungary, and was trained in Europe. Before becoming a professor of music at the University of Illinois, he spent many years as a concert artist. While at the University of Illinois, Rolland founded the Illinois String Project (1964–1976) and along with Dr. Marla Mutschler produced the book *The Teaching of Action in String Playing*, which was accompanied by fourteen color films. Rolland made significant contributions in the development of his pedagogy based on movement and balance in string playing. The method book *Prelude to String Playing* reflects the culmination of his action studies. His action study ideas for teaching shifting and vibrato are still very popular to this day.

Paul Rolland served in leadership positions in many national education associations, including the American String Teachers Association. In 1973, he was awarded the ASTA Distinguished Service Award.

Shinichi Suzuki

Shinichi Suzuki is credited as being one of the most influential string pedagogues of the twentieth century. Influenced by Jean Piaget's learning theory and Friedrich Froebel's kindergarten movement, Suzuki's talent education method is based on the premise that children can learn to play the violin just as they learn to speak the native language. In this method, there are four general steps to development. First, the student must be ready and willing to play the violin. The child is surrounded by music, specifically the Suzuki repertoire, from birth. Since a parent is present at all lessons and must learn to play before the child begins study, the child observes the parent (traditionally the mother) learning to play the violin. Second, once the child does show interest, the focus of each lesson is on the performance of organized, sequential music based upon technical and musical levels of ability, centering on tone production and intonation. Third, each of the learning objectives prescribed for each selection is learned before the student progresses to the next piece. The parent reinforces the learning of each skill, and the student reinforces concepts by listening to recordings of the work by leading artists. Fourth, a rote approach is used to learn each musical selection, and note reading is delayed.

While the Suzuki method is not designed as a class technique, the Suzuki method has met with tremendous success in Japan, the United States, and many other countries. Interest in the method began when Suzuki first presented his ideas at a Music Educators National Conference in 1964. Suzuki's pedagogy was originally developed only for violin, but his methods have been adapted for other string instruments, as well as for piano and flute.

Phyllis Young

The author of two widely distributed pedagogy books, *Playing the String Game* and *The String Play*, Phyllis Young has served as national president of the American String Teachers Association and was the recipient of its 1984 Distinguished Service Award. In addition to teaching cello performance majors, for thirty-five years she directed the University of Texas String Project, a large teacher-training program that has been a model for many of the string programs throughout the United States and abroad.

Phyllis Young's unique teaching approach is captured in her two books. Both *The String Play* and *Playing the String Game* are designed to aid string teachers, students, interested parents, and student teachers. Each book contains practical material that relates to all stringed instruments, all ages, and all levels beyond the first year of study. Using a distinctively late-twentieth-century outlook, her approach makes the techniques of playing a bowed string instrument logical and natural. Phyllis Young's approach is designed for use in the studio, classroom, and home, and can be used with any repertoire or method, including the Suzuki method.

PROFESSIONAL STRING ASSOCIATIONS

American String Teachers Association with the National High School Orchestra Association

"ASTA with NSOA helps string and orchestra teachers and players develop and refine their skills at any point in their careers. ASTA with NSOA members receive a host of services that are tailored to their needs and are offered only through membership. Some of these include the *American String Teacher* journal, group insurance programs, job posting service, professional development and networking, publications and special programs, state chapters, and student chapters" (www.astaweb.com).

International Society of Bassists

"The International Society of Bassists was founded by the world-renowned virtuoso Gary Karr in 1967. With some three thousand members in over forty countries, the ISB is dedicated to inspiring public interest, raising performance standards, and providing an organization for those who teach, study, play, repair, build, research, and enjoy the double bass. The ISB is a forum for communication among bassists throughout the world and across a wide variety of musical styles. Members receive our triannual journal, *Bass World*, and, two times a year, the *Bass Line* newsletter. Every two years the ISB holds an international convention and double bass competition at a host university, as well as a composition contest. If you love the double bass, you'll enjoy being a member of the International Society of Bassists!" (www.isb-worldoffice.com).

Suzuki Association of the Americas

"The Suzuki Association of the Americas (SAA) is a coalition of teachers, parents, educators, and others who are interested in making music education available to all children. The SAA provides programs and services to members throughout North and South America. With the International Suzuki Association (ISA) and other regional associations, the SAA promotes and supports the spread of Dr. Suzuki's Talent Education" (www.suzukiassociation.org). The SAA offers teacher development programs and training, the *American Suzuki Journal*, teacher referral, conferences/retreats, summer student workshops, and resource materials.

American Viola Society

In 2001, the American Viola Society (AVS) marked its thirtieth anniversary. Founded in New York in 1971 as the Viola Research Society by Myron Rosenblum, the AVS continues to play a vital role in the shaping and development of the viola community worldwide. Mission statement of the AVS Constitution: "The American Viola Society promotes interest in the viola by encouraging performance and recording at the highest artistic level, by the continued study and research of our instrument and its repertoire, and by providing a vehicle for the ongoing development of the fraternal bond among violists" (www.americanviolasociety.org).

Viola da Gamba Society of America

"The Viola da Gamba Society of America is dedicated to the support of activities relating to the viola da gamba in the United States and abroad. It is a society of players, builders, publishers, distributors, restorers, and others sharing a serious interest in music for viols and other early bowed string instruments" (www.vdgsa.org).

Violin Society of America

"Dedicated to promoting the art and science of making, repairing, and preserving stringed musical instruments and their bows. The Violin Society of America reflects a broad range of interests and concerns of those interested in violins and the art of making instruments and bows of the violin family. Founded in 1974, the Violin Society of America is a nonprofit organization created for the purpose of promoting the art and science of making, repairing, and preserving stringed musical instruments and their bows. Membership in the VSA is open to all who share an interest in the violin, viola, cello, bass, and their bows, and thus reflects a broad and diverse range of interests and concerns, including the history of instruments and performers, technique, performance practice, repertory, and other matters pertaining to instruments of the violin family" (www.vsa.to).

INDEX

A

Accessories, 5–7, 208
  anchor, 6
  bass stool, 36, 37
  bridge, adjustable, 6
  bridge jack, 7
  chin rest, 6
  clean cloth, 5, 9
  cleaner fluid, 9
  endpin holder, 6, 202
  humidifier, 5
  metronome, 5, 91, 102, 145, 148, 176
  mute, 6
  peg compound, 5, 11
  powdered graphite, 5
  rosin, 6, 9, 202
  rubbing alcohol, 9
  shoulder rests, 6, 33–34, 35
  strings, 7
  tuning device, 5
  See also Instrument parts
Acoustics, 210
Add-a-Lift (strategy), 103
Add a Note (strategy), 82
Advanced Sliding between Strings
  (strategy), 122
Aesthetic sensibilities
  creativity, 153, 195, 199
  cultivation of, 154, 213
  expressivity, 17, 18, 132, 139, 148
  imagination, 152
  musicality, 150
  sensitivity, 143
  in smaller ensembles, 211
Air Vibrato (strategy), 91
All Finger Pinches (strategy), 66

All the Way Up, All the Way Down
  (strategy), 66
Altered Melodies (strategy), 93
Alternating Arm to Hand Tremolo,
  Accented, and *Fp* Tremolo (strategy),
  101
Alternating On to Off (strategy), 103–4
Alternating Vibrato Type (strategy), 124
Anchor and Slide (strategy), 82
Anchor and Tap (strategy), 82
Applebaum, Samuel, 222
Arco, 149
Articulation, 136–37, 178
Assessment systems, 202, 211
Attack Stroke Vibrato (strategy), 124
At the Bout (strategy), 86
Auditions, 172–78
  evaluation of, 172–76, 177
  length of, 173
  location of, 173–74
  materials for, 172
  procedure and policies of, 176–77
  use of information from, 177–78
Auer, Leopold, 222
Aural perception skills
  advanced, 97–98, 124–26
  audiation and, 135
  beginning, 29, 30, 31, 59–60
  critical evaluation of, 211
  imitation, 31
  improvisation, 195
  intermediate, 64, 92–94
  intonation and, 134–35
  playing by ear, 125
  See also Chords; Intonation; Pitch;
  Tuning
Autoharp, 26

B

Back Down the String (strategy), 89–90
Balance Point Bounce (strategy), 67
Balance Point Bows (strategy), 51
Balance Point Rub (strategy), 67
Balancing and Rubbing (strategy), 65
Banjo, 26
Base Hand Knuckle Checks (strategy), 44
Bassoon, 17
Block Fingering (strategy), 47
Blues, 59
Bornoff, George, 222
Bounces on the Board (strategy), 104
Bouncing All the Way (strategy), 67
Bow
    care and maintenance of, 9
    construction of, 4–5
    French, 5
    German, 5
    parts of, 4, 5, 9, 35, 52
    quality relative to sound, 4, 8
Bow hair, use of, 99, 100–101
Bow Hand Shapes on the Go (strategy),
    55
Bowing and fingerings
    advanced, 97, 98–104, 133
    balance point and, 47, 48, 56, 65, 102,
        103
    beginning, 29, 30, 47–59, 131–32
    bow hand shape and, 30, 47–52, 131
Bowing choices, 146–47
Bowing Parts (strategy), 65
Bowing skills
    coordination with left-hand skills, 29,
        47, 83, 85, 123, 149
    different sections of the bow and, 52,
        53, 65, 66, 147, 148
    direction changes and, 52, 63, 65
    equal sound throughout, 98
    intermediate, 63, 64–67, 132
    parallel bowing, 30, 63, 64–65, 131
    unity of sound and, 147
Bow Paths (strategy), 51
Bow Pivots (strategy), 58
Bow placement, 53, 134, 148
Bow speed
    changing speeds, 98
    in dynamics, 150
    lower strings and, 149

    miles per hour and, 148
    tonal color and, 149
    tone intensity and, 131
    tone quality and, 134
    up and down bow strokes and, 66
Bow strokes
    accented, 132, 147
    bound sounds and, 103, 104
    brush strokes, 103
    collé, 97, 102
    détaché, 30, 52–56, 97, 98, 131, 132, 133,
        143
    double stops and, 47, 64, 93, 94, 132,
        179, 180
    louré (portato), 97, 98–99
    marcato, 133
    martelé, 63, 66–67, 131, 132, 133
    off-the-string, 143
    ponticello, 97, 99–100, 133
    ricochet, 133
    sautillé, 97, 132, 133
    slurs and, 30, 59, 63, 66, 102–3, 131, 132
    spiccato, 63, 67, 97, 103–4, 132, 133,
        143, 149
    staccato and hooked bowings, 30, 58,
        99, 131, 132, 133, 143, 147
    sul tasto, 97, 99, 133
    timed bowing, 98
    tremolo, 97, 101, 123, 133
    up and down bow strokes, 65–66,
        147
Bow weight/pressure
    in dynamics, 65, 150
    in phrasing, 150
    in ponticello bowing, 99–100
    in shifting, 83, 123
    in sul tasto bowing, 99–100
    in tonal color, 149
    in tone quality, 134
Breathing and Playing (strategy), 68
Breath support, 33, 36
Bridge Rocking (strategy), 56
Brush Strokes (strategy), 103
Buddy Bowing (strategy), 54, 64

C

Calendar of events, 202
C Clamp (strategy), 44

Chamber music, 25, 129
Change Up Ensemble Primary Chords (strategy), 94
Changing Speeds with Clicks (strategy), 98
Checkpoints, Checkpoints (strategy), 122, 123
Chords
  to accompany melodies, 126
  to accompany scales, 98, 125
  ensemble secondary triads, 98, 125
  Geminiani, 43–44, 85
  in improvisation, 198–99
  in tuning, 150
Chords on the Boards (strategy), 94
Circle Bowing (strategy), 64
Clarinet, 136
Claves, 199
Climate, impact of, 6, 7
Compositions, 16
Conducting, 147–51
  communication and, 148, 183
  cueing and, 148
  following of, 132
  rehearsal of score and, 148
  transposition and, 137–39
Connect the Hooks (strategy), 58
Contact (sounding) point
  in dynamics, 65
  in sound production, 65
  in tonal color, 149
Counting the Oscillations—Counting the What? (strategy), 124
Crab technique, 223
Crunches (strategy), 68
Curriculum, 16, 22–27
  enhancement of, 24–27
  guides for, 151
  skills and concepts in, 23–24
  See also Repertoire selection; Teaching strategies

D

Defending orchestra programs, 18–21
Descending Melodies (strategy), 47
Descending Scales (strategy), 47
Détaché bowing, 30, 52–56, 97, 98, 131, 132, 133, 143

Direction changes, 63, 65
Doorknob (strategy), 58
Double Bass Dots (strategy), 123
Doublin' (strategy), 42
Doublin' Up (strategy), 82
Down Equals Up (strategy), 65–66
Downs and Up and Ups and Downs (strategy), 104
Dueling Strings (strategy), 125
Dulcimer, 1
Dynamics, 30, 63, 131, 150, 196
  beginning, 30, 131
  expressive, 98
  intermediate, 63, 65–66, 132
  subito changes and, 98
  in sul tasto, 99

E

Embouchure, 133, 136
Ensemble Primary Chords (strategy), 94
Equal Sound Throughout (strategy), 98
Exploratory instrumental study program, 206
Expressive Dynamics (strategy), 98
Extending Backward (strategy), 82–83
Extending Forward (strategy), 83
Extensions, 46, 77–79
Eyes Closed! (strategy), 50

F

Facility, 132
Farnsworth, Charles, 14
Festivals and contests, 15, 184, 209, 221
Fiddle groups, 26–27, 59
Finding Harmonics (strategy), 122
Finding Octaves (strategy), 92, 125
Finding Our Elbow (strategy), 44
Fingerboard Lanes (strategy), 99
Finger Bowing (strategy), 50
Fingered Martelés (strategy), 67
Finger Markers (strategy), 47
Finger patterns and placement
  advanced, 104–23, 133
  beginning, 31, 45–47, 131, 132
  block fingering, 47

Finger patterns and placement (*continued*)
  the crab technique and, 223
  extended finger patterns, 132
  intermediate, 63–64, 132
  role in sound, 134
  See also Extensions; Finger positions; Left-hand skills; Pivoting; Scales and arpeggios; Shifting
Finger positions
  for cello, 77, 79, 84, 132
  for double bass, 79, 84, 132
  for violin and viola, 75–76, 84, 112, 132, 133
  See also Extensions; Finger patterns and placement; Left-hand skills; Pivoting; Scales and arpeggios; Shifting
Finger Signals (strategy), 94
Finger Teeter-Totters (strategy), 66
Fingertip Fingering (strategy), 44
Fixin' the Nanny Goat (strategy), 124
Flop Hand (strategy), 51
Flute, 136
Foot and Metronome Bounces (strategy), 104
Foot Crossings (strategy), 102
Form, 210
Four-Note Echoes (strategy), 59, 92, 125
Frog Collé (strategy), 102
Frog to the Floor (strategy), 55
Front Half of the Chair (strategy), 40

G

Gambas, 1
Geminiani Chord (strategy), 43–44, 85
Giddings, Thaddeus, 15
Give Me an SWS! (strategy), 65
Glissando, 196
Goals and objectives, 210
  first-year, 30–31, 131
  high school, 97–98, 133
  second-year, 30–31, 131–32
  third- and fourth-year, 63–64, 132
Grow an Inch (strategy), 39, 68
Guitar, 16, 26
Guitarrón, 26

H

Hand Waving Tremolo (strategy), 101
Harmonics
  in fingerboard division, 223
  in shifting, 84, 122
  in tuning, 64, 94–95, 178–79, 180
  in vibrato, 91
Harp, 1
Harpsichord, 1
Havas, Kato, 223
Heard But Not Seen (strategy), 67, 103
Hook and Pull (strategy), 58
Hooked bowing. *See* Staccato and hooked bowings
Hooked Staccato vs. Louré (strategy), 99
Hooking for Slurs (strategy), 59
Horn, 33
How Many Harmonics Can You Find? (strategy), 84

I

Illinois String Project, 223
Improvisation, 98, 131, 132, 133, 195–99
  in audition, 173
  call-and-response and, 195, 197
  chordal, 195, 198–99
  creative drone and, 195, 196
  rhythmic ostinato and, 195, 198, 199
  riff and, 195, 196
  value of, 195
Index Finger Pinches (strategy), 66
Instrument
  care and maintenance of, 9–13, 202
  construction of, 1
  cracks in, 3
  insurance for, 202, 208
  purchasing/renting, 7–9, 202
  quality of, 7, 78, 134
  range of, 3
  repairs and, 3, 8, 9, 10–11, 202
  sizes of, 3–4, 31–33
  storage and, 184, 188, 210
Instrumentation, 142, 202
Instrument Buddies (strategy), 69
Instrument parts, 1–3
  adjusting screw, 1
  back, 3

bass bar, 2
bridge, 2, 7, 11, 35, 52, 131, 135
"C" bout (waist), 3, 35, 36, 37, 39
chin rest, 1, 3, 6, 35
end button, 1–2, 34, 35
endpin, 1, 3, 6, 35, 36, 37, 38, 39
F holes, 3
fine tuners, 2, 6, 7, 60
fingerboard, 1, 3, 6
neck block, 3
nut, 1, 3, 37, 38
peg box, 3, 12
purfling, 1, 3
saddle, 1
scroll, 3, 35, 37
side (ribs), 3
sound post, 2, 7, 11
strings, 1–2, 3, 6, 7, 9, 11–12, 202
tailpiece, 1, 2
varnish, 9
See also Accessories; Bow
Instrument position, 131
balance and, 39
for bass, sitting, 36–38
for bass, standing, 38–39
beginning, 29, 30, 33–40, 131
button positioning and, 34
for cello, 35–36
checkpoints and, 68
guitar position, 33, 34
independent from bowing, 47
intermediate, 63, 68–69
intonation and, 135
left-hand shape and, 40–44
platform/shelf, 34, 35
shoulder position and, 34
sound and, 134
for violin and viola, 33–35
See also Posture
Instrument Position Checkpoints
   (strategy), 68–69
Instrument Tubing, 53
Intonation, 29, 134–35, 150, 176
Invitational Matching (strategy), 125

J

Jack-in-the-Box (strategy), 40
Jazz, 59

Jazz strings, 173
Journals/newsletters, 220, 225

K

Keyboard, 17, 18, 26
Keys
advanced, 97, 104, 112, 133
first-year, 31, 45–46, 131
intermediate, 63, 64, 132
in repertoire selection, 142
second-year, 31, 45–46, 132
See also Scales and arpeggios
Kinesthetic memory, 135
Knuckle Knocks (strategy), 44
K shape (strategy), 44

L

Lane 5 (strategy), 100
Lanes (strategy), 64, 65
Learning
hands-on, 16
styles of, 29–30, 141, 151, 154
taxonomies of, 151, 153–54
Left-hand shape, 31, 47, 63, 70
for bass, 79
beginning, 40–44, 131
for cello, 77, 78–79
descending melodies and, 47
intermediate, 63, 82
in shifting, 122
Left-hand skills, 104, 149
advanced, 97
beginning, 29, 30–31, 40–44, 45–47
crab technique and, 223
facility and, 132
intermediate, 70–92
sound and, 134
See also Bowing skills; Finger patterns
   and placement; Finger positions;
   Scales and arpeggios; Shifting;
   Vibrato
Lend a Helping Hand (strategy), 89
Lesson planning, 151–54, 178
Letting the Air Out (strategy), 64
Lift, Set, Settle (strategy), 54
Listening. *See* Aural perception skills

Literature
  for full orchestra, 219–21
  for string orchestra, 216–19, 221
  See also Method books
Loud, Fz, and Fp Tremolos (strategy), 101
Loud Rests (strategy), 58
Louré (portato) bowing, 97, 98–99
Lower Collé (strategy), 102

M

Maddy, Joseph E., 15
Mandolin, 26
Marching band, 14,, 15, 17, 26
Mariachi bands, 26, 129, 173
Martelé bowing, 63, 66–67, 131, 132, 133
Matching Arpeggios (strategy), 92, 125
Matching Leaps (strategy), 92, 125
Matching Octave Doubles (strategy), 93
Matching Octaves (strategy), 93, 125
Melody, 145
  descending, 47
  playing by ear and, 64, 97, 125
  See also Score preparation
Method books, 202, 208, 213–15, 222,
    223. See also Literature
Metronome Crossings (strategy), 102
Miles per Hour (strategy), 65
Mitchell, Albert, 14
Modeling
  beginners and, 30
  internal student models, 139
  musicality and, 150
  as nonverbal tool, 139
  playing and, 148
  singing and, 148
  tone quality and, 134, 135
  in tuning, 60
  visual/aural, 29, 139
Motivation, 129, 154, 183
  challenge and reward as, 141, 144
  enjoyment as, 143, 195, 200
  external pressures as, 143
  improvisation and, 195
  in retention, 208
  run-throughs and, 185
  self-motivated practice, 144
Movin' Those Feet While Vibrating
    (strategy), 91

Multiple Bounces (strategy), 67
Multiple Flexes (strategy), 65
Musical independence, 132
Musicianship, 195, 210
Music reading
  in audition, 177
  beginning, 29, 31, 131, 132
  intermediate, 63, 64
  in music selection, 144
  rote to note and, 140
  sight reading and, 26, 31, 64, 132, 184
  time signatures and, 131, 132
  See also Keys

N

Nanny, Edouard, 223
National standards, 16–17
  ASTA, 160–62
  improvisation and, 95
  MENC, 162–64
  sample repertoire for, 164–68
Neighbor Bowing (strategy), 91

O

Oboe, 17
One-Finger Melodies (strategy), 85
One-Finger Scales (strategy), 85
One-Time Matching (strategy), 125
On the String (strategy), 87
On the String First (strategy), 104
Open strings
  in improvisation, 196, 197
  pitch and, 3
  in string crossings, 102–3
  in tempo control, 149
  in tuning, 60, 94
  in vibrato, 91
Ostinato, 195, 198, 199
Overprogramming, 213–14

P

Palms an' Knees (strategy), 40
Paper Slides (strategy), 85
Parallel bowing, 30, 63, 64–65, 131

Parallel Motion (strategy), 124
Pedagogues and their approaches, 222–24
Pencil Bowing (strategy), 50
Pencil Crossings (strategy), 56–57
Pentatonic scale, 197
Percussion, 15, 33, 133, 199
Phrasing, 132, 150
Piaget, Jean, 224
Piano, 1, 148
Pinch and Glide (strategy), 67
Pinched Bows (strategy), 58
Pinch, Pull, Release (strategy), 67
Pitch, 3, 7
Pitch-matching
    advanced, 97, 125
    beginning, 31, 59, 131
    intermediate, 64
Pit orchestra, 17
Pivot, The (strategy), 88
Pivot and Bow (strategy), 89
Pivoting, 88, 89, 92, 223
Pizzicato, 45, 47, 131, 196
    compared to collé, 102
    in recruitment, 206
    to reinforce rhythm, 149
    right-hand and left-hand, 133
Pizzicato Collé (strategy), 102
Pizzicato Martelés (strategy), 67
Ponticello, 97, 99–100, 133
Ponticello vs. Sul Tasto (strategy), 100
Positions. *See* Finger positions;
        Instrument position
Posture
    beginning, 30, 47, 131
    intermediate, 68
    See also Instrument position
Pounds (strategy), 65
Primary Chords by Ear (strategy), 94
Private lessons, 129–30, 211
Problem solving, 182–83, 189–93
    advanced, 127
    beginning, 60–62
    intermediate, 95–96
    rehearsals and, 189–94
Professional organizations, 225–26
    American String Teacher's Association (ASTA), 16, 25, 160, 204, 224, 225
    American Viola Society, 225
    Chamber Music America, 25

Foundation for the Advancement of String Education, 222
International Society of Bassists, 225
Music Educators National Conference (MENC), 15, 17, 162, 195, 204, 221, 224
Music Publishers' Association, 216
Music Supervisors National Conference (MSNC), 15
National Association for School Superintendents, 15
National School Orchestra Association, 16, 25, 204, 225
Suzuki Association of the Americas, 225
Viola da Gamba Society of America, 225
Violin Society of America, 225
Publishers, 215–16, 221
Pull Aways (strategy), 43
Puppet Shoulders (strategy), 39
Purchasing guidelines, 7–8

R

Rabbath, Francois, 223
Range, 3, 136
Recipe, The (strategy), 101
Recording, 148, 154, 172, 176, 210
Recruitment, 15, 200–208
    audience participation and, 204
    communication and, 200–201
    contact with schools about, 201
    contact with students/parents about, 200, 201–2, 204
    enthusiasm and, 200
    handouts and, 201–2, 203
    instrumentation balance and, 202
    parents' meetings and, 202, 203, 208
    performing groups and, 201, 204–6
    philosophy of, 200
    preparation for, 200–202, 207
    presentation equipment and, 201, 203–4
    presentation length and, 201
    procedures for, 203–5
    purchasing/renting instruments and, 7–9, 202
    student involvement and, 207
    timing of, 201
    traditional plan for, 200

Recruitment (*continued*)
  transport and, 201
  See also Retention
Reeds, 133, 136
Rehearsal techniques, 128–94, 148–50
  announcements and, 178, 184
  articulation and, 178
  balance and, 150
  chorales and, 178
  communication and, 148, 183
  dynamics and, 150, 178
  end of rehearsal, 178, 184, 185
  equipment and, 171–72
  first rehearsal and, 187–89
  folders and, 187
  format and, 185–86
  goals and objectives in, 128–33
  interpersonal skills and, 171
  intonation and, 150
  lesson plans and, 178
  motivational level and, 129
  musicality and, 150
  musicianship of director and, 171
  organizational abilities and, 171
  performing opportunities and, 129, 130
  planning and, 128–68, 171, 183
  preparation and, 128, 148
  prioritization and, 148
  private/small group training and,
    129–30, 211
  problem solving and, 189–93
  rehearsal room and, 171–72, 210
  repertoire rehearsal and, 29, 140, 178,
    182–83, 185
  review and, 29, 140,178
  rhythm and, 178
  roll and, 188
  scales and arpeggios and, 178
  school orchestra tradition and, 129
  school system and, 128–29
  seating and, 177, 210
  sectionals and, 186–87
  sight reading and, 178, 184
  special rehearsals and, 187
  storage and, 184, 188
  teaching the standards and, 164–68
  technique and, 150
  tuning and, 178–81
  warm-ups and, 140, 178, 181–82
  See also Aesthetic sensibilities;

Articulation; Auditions; Goals and
  objectives; Intonation; Motivation;
  Music reading; National standards;
  Problem solving; Repertoire
  selection; Scales and arpeggios;
  Score preparation; Sound
  production; Teaching strategies;
  Tuning
Relaxation, 54, 64, 131
Rental programs, 8–9
Repairing instruments, 9–12
Repertoire rehearsal
  of challenging passages, 182
  introducing new material and, 178,
    182–83
  reviewing old material and, 29, 140,
    178, 182–83
  run-throughs and, 182, 185
Repertoire selection, 141–44
  ability level and, 142, 144
  balance of challenge and, 144
  contest lists and, 221
  goal-based, 142–43, 144
  Grades 3 through 5 and, 104
  group strengths and numbers and,
    142
  importance of, 144
  instrumentation and, 142
  Internet and, 221
  keys and, 142
  length and, 142
  orchestra reading sessions and, 221
  overprogramming and, 213–14
  part independence and, 214
  period performance practice and, 144
  publishers and, 215–16, 221
  for quality performance, 213
  reassessment after audition and, 177
  student preferences and, 143
  style and period and, 142, 143–44
  technical and musical requirements
    and, 142–43, 144
  for technical development, 141, 144
  wide musical repertoire and, 211
  See also Keys; Literature; Method
    books; Style and period
Replacing strings guidelines, 11–12
Rest Crossings (strategy), 57
Retention, 208, 212
  admittance standards and, 209

assessment systems and, 211
challenging standards and, 208
competitive advancement and, 210
critical evaluation and, 211
equipment and, 211
inspirational teaching and, 211
knowledge and skills development and, 210
learning environment and, 210–11
motivation and, 208
performance and public relations and, 209
praise and criticism and, 210
private lessons and, 211
recognition and, 209–10
retention rate and, 208
small ensembles and, 211
social interaction and, 211–12
student pride and, 208
technical drill development and, 210
tradition of excellence and, 209
valuing students and, 208–9
See also Recruitment
Rhythm, 149, 178, 196
beginning, 30, 31, 131
intermediate, 64, 132
teaching sequence and, 149
Ridin' the Rails (strategy), 42, 55
Rockin' Bows (strategy), 64
Rolland, Paul, 223
Rolling Pitches (strategy), 59
Rosin Bowing (strategy), 54
Rounds, 131

S

Sand blocks, 199
Scales and arpeggios, 178
advanced, 104–22, 133
in audition, 177
beginning, 31, 45–47, 131–32
descending, 47
four-octave, 3
intermediate, 64, 70–75, 132
one-octave, 45, 70–75
styles and, 99
three-octave, 3, 97, 112–22
two-octave, 97, 104–11

See also Extensions; Finger patterns and placement; Finger positions; Keys; Left-hand skills; Pivoting; Shifting
Scales and Tonics (strategy), 125
Scales Are a Bouncin' (strategy), 104
Scales with Chords (strategy), 126
Scales with Roots (strategy), 125
Scaling Styles (strategy), 99
School orchestra programs
defense strategies of, 18–21
full orchestra, 33
history of, 14–16
string orchestra, 33
support of, 21–22, 129
value of, 16–18, 26
Score preparation, 144–51
bowings and fingerings and, 146–47, 148
musical and technical considerations for, 144–45, 147
score analysis and, 145, 146, 150
score review and, 145
See also Bowing skills; Conducting; Style and period
Section Matching (strategy), 93
Sequential teaching. *See* Teaching strategies
Shelving! (strategy), 51
Shifting
for cello, 77–79
for double bass, 46, 79
general principles of, 83–84
objectives of, 136
pedagogy for, 84–85
refining of, 97, 122–23
technique of, 149
tremolo and, 123
for violin/viola, 75
See also Extensions; Finger patterns and placement; Finger positions; Keys; Left-hand skills; Pivoting; Scales and arpeggios
Short Bows to Long Bows (strategy), 54
Shoulder, Arms, and Tubes! (strategy), 53
Show choir, 26
Shuttle Shifts (strategy), 85
Sight reading. *See* Music reading
Simple Double Stopping (strategy), 47
Singing/humming
chorales and, 178

Singing/humming (*continued*)
  choral students and, 17–18
  in modeling, 148, 150
  in score analysis, 145
  in tuning 179, 180
Six-Note Echoes (strategy), 93, 125
Slide, The (strategy), 86–87
Slides in One Bow (strategy), 122
Sliding between Strings (strategy), 84
Sliding Geminiani Chords (strategy), 85
Sliding Pitches (strategy), 59
Slurred String Crossings (strategy), 102–3
Slurs, 30, 59, 63, 66, 102–3, 131, 132
Sodas and Fruits! (strategy), 44
Sound lanes, 64, 149
  in beginning détaché, 52
  exploration of, 52
  fingerboard lanes, 99
  in phrasing, 150
  in ponticello, 100–101
  in sul tasto, 99, 101
Sound production, 134, 148–49
  adjustable bridge and, 6
  balance and, 132, 150
  bass bar and, 2
  in basses, 149
  blend and, 132
  bow quality and, 8
  compared to brass, woodwinds, and
    percussion, 134, 135
  at different dynamic levels, 63, 65–66
  equal sound throughout and, 98
  instrument quality and, 7, 8
  intensity of tone and, 131
  listening and, 149
  with mute, 6
  orchestra placement and, 149
  quality of, 131, 132, 133, 135
  sound post and, 2
  sound production principles and, 65
  string types and, 7
  in sul tasto and ponticello bowing,
    99–100
  unity of sound and, 147
  See also Bowing skills; Bow speed; Bow
    weight/pressure; Contact (sounding)
    point; Sound lanes; String crossings
Spiccato bowing, 63, 67, 97, 103–4, 132,
  133, 143, 149
Spyglasses and Telescopes (strategy), 50

Square First Finger (strategy), 43
Staccato and hooked bowings, 30, 58, 99,
  131, 132, 133, 143, 147
Stacked Melodies (strategy), 125
Statue of Liberty (strategy), 65
Storing music, 9
Straw Bowing (strategy), 50
Straws in the F Hole (strategy), 54
String crossings, 30, 56–57
  advanced, 97, 102–3
  balance point and, 56, 102
  beginning, 30, 36–37, 131
  with French vs. German bow, 5
  intermediate, 63, 66
  with metronome, 102
  pedagogy for, 56–57
  slurred, 102–3, 132
  in spiccato, 104
String Crossings Bounces (strategy), 104
String family, modern, 1
String Flying (strategy), 68
String teacher training, 15, 16
Strolling strings, 25, 129, 173
Strums (strategy), 43
Student-Led Accompanied Melodies
  (strategy), 126
Student-Led Chord Progression
  (strategy), 94
Style and period, 142, 143–44, 145, 210
  intermediate goals and, 132
  performance practice considerations
    and, 144
  in score preparation, 146
  sight reading and, 184
Subito Dynamic Changes (strategy), 98
Sul tasto bowing, 97, 99, 100, 101, 133
Sul Tasto Dynamics (strategy), 99
Suzuki, Shinichi, 224
Suzuki instruments, 4
Suzuki method, 224
Suzuki students, 16
Swingin' Out (strategy), 54
Swingin' to the Floor (strategy), 55

T

Tambourines, 199
Tanglewood, 16
Tap and Slide (strategy), 85

Tappin' (strategy), 82
Taps (strategy), 42
Tap, Tap, Tap (strategy), 51
Teacher-Led Accompanied Melodies
  (strategy), 126
Teaching strategies, 30, 139–41
  appropriate touch and, 140
  atmosphere and environment and, 154,
    176, 210–11
  for balance, 150
  behavior recognition and, 141
  careful skill building and, 141
  classroom management and, 141
  dissect and combine, 140, 149
  flexibility and, 141
  goal-setting and, 210
  group level and, 139
  humor and, 140
  inspirational teaching and, 211
  leadership and, 140
  learning style and, 30, 141, 151, 154
  lesson planning and, 151–54
  memorization and, 148
  modeling and, 139
  movement and, 140
  multiple strategies and, 140
  for musicality, 150
  national standards and, 160–64
  nonverbal, 139, 154, 183
  pacing and, 140, 211
  planning and, 211
  practice partners and, 211
  prioritizing and, 148
  private/small ensemble participation
    and, 129–30, 211
  proximity to students and, 140
  reading student feedback and, 154, 183
  repertoire selection and, 141
  review and, 29, 140, 178
  for rhythm, 149
  rote teaching strategies and, 39, 140,
    206, 224
  routine and, 140
  self-evaluation and, 141, 154–59
  sequential, 22–24, 29, 47, 140, 141, 149,
    214
  shared agenda and, 211
  sound production and, 148–49
  student leadership and, 141, 180
  students as teachers, 141

taping and, 148
teaching teams and, 141
technical drill development and, 149,
  210
technical vision and, 139
for tempo, 149
vocal delivery and, 154
See also Goals and objectives; Learning;
  Lesson planning; Modeling; National
  standards; Repertoire selection;
  Scales and arpeggios; Sound
  production
Tempo, 149
Theme from Beethoven's Symphony
  No. 7 (strategy), 99
Thumb Bends (strategy), 51
Thumb Slides (strategy), 43
Thumbs Up (strategy), 51
Thumb Taps (strategy), 43
Timbre, 132, 136, 147
Timed Bowing (strategy), 98
Time signatures, 131, 132
Timing (strategy), 69
Tissue Vibrato (strategy), 91
Tone production. *See* Sound production
Tonguing, 133, 137, 139
Top of the Hand Down (strategy), 42
To the Frog We Go (strategy), 67
Trampoline Bounces (strategy), 103
Transposition, 46, 137–38
Travelin' Down the Road (strategy), 55
Tremolo bowing, 97, 101, 123, 133
Tremolo Shifts (strategy), 123
Trilling Slurs (strategy), 66
Trill Slurs (strategy), 59
Trumpet, 26, 126
Tuning, 178
  advanced, 126, 180–81
  in auditions, 176
  bass machine head pegs and, 60
  beginning, 31, 60, 131, 178–80
  devices for, 60, 179–80, 181
  double stops and, 64, 94, 179, 180
  exercises and, 179–80
  in full orchestra, 181
  high standard for, 60
  intermediate, 64, 94–95
  metal core strings and, 6
  meticulous, 181
  new strings and, 12

Tuning (*continued*)
 open strings and, 60, 94
 plucking and, 60
 reference pitch and, 179, 180
 as routine, 140
 routines for, 95, 126
 without vibrato, 150
 See also Harmonics
Tuning fork, 180, 181
Tuning routines, 95, 126
Tuning Section Doubles (strategy), 93
Tunneling (strategy), 42, 84
Two-Handed Pulls (strategy), 65

U

Uniforms, 172, 210
University of Texas String Project, 224
Up and Light (strategy), 40

V

Variable Place Crossings (strategy), 66
Variable Speed Crossings (strategy), 66
Varying the Speed (strategy), 124
Varying the Width (strategy), 124
Vibrating to the Click (strategy), 91

Vibration, 2, 3
Vibrato
 advanced, 97, 123–24, 133
 arm, 85
 hand, 85
 intermediate, 64, 75, 85–91, 132
 The Pivot and, 88, 89
 The Slide and, 86–87
 in tuning, 150
Vibrato Feelings (strategy), 124
Vibrato Harmonics (strategy), 91
Vihuela, 26
Viols, 1
Vocal sacred music, 14

W

Wavy Bows (strategy), 99, 123
We Get to Play Out of Tune! (strategy),
 59–60
Wood blocks, 199
Woodwinds and brass, 15, 17, 133–39

Y

Young, Phyllis, 224
You've Made It! (strategy), 91